IN BETWEEN DAYS

AN ARMCHAIR GUIDE TO

First edition published in 2005 by
Helter Skelter Publishing
South Bank House, Black Prince Road,
London SE1 7SJ

Copyright 2005 © Dave Thompson

All rights reserved
Cover design by Chris Wilson
Typesetting by Caroline Walker
Printed in Great Britain by CPI, Bath

All lyrics quoted in this book are for the purposes of review, study or criticism.

A CIP record for this book is available from the British Library

ISBN 1-905139-00-4

IN BETWEEN DAYS

AN ARMCHAIR GUIDE TO The Cure

BY DAVE THOMPSON

Helter Skelter Publishing

AUTHOR NOTE

IN BETWEEN DAYS: AN ARMCHAIR GUIDE TO THE CURE represents the largest and most complete discography ever published around the life and times of Robert Smith and the Cure, reviewing and documenting the historical and musical background to the band's entire catalogue of singles, albums, remixes, compilations and more.

Based upon years of avid collecting and listening, the book also utilises material from a series of interviews conducted with individual members between 1995 and 2004, together with further first-hand material dating back to the late 1970s. Other sources, including quotes and excerpts from press encounters elsewhere, are acknowledged in the text and in the bibliography at the end of the book.

HOW TO USE THIS BOOK

For hopefully obvious reasons, *IN BETWEEN DAYS: AN ARMCHAIR GUIDE TO THE CURE* is laid out chronologically by year, with all entries then following, again, in chronological order. Although the emphasis is on material considered to have been released officially, a small number of bootlegs are also noted. Within these parameters, the following headings should be similarly self-explanatory. But, just in case…

SINGLES: includes 45rpm, 10-inch, 12-inch, EP and CD single releases, including collaborations with other artists. The Glove, Siouxsie and the Banshees, And Also The Trees and all similarly associated spin-offs and outside projects are, for the most part, noted in Appendix Two. Exceptions include those recordings and appearances where the Cure were either integral to the recording (the Cult Heroes, Tim Pope etc), or where a band member was unquestionably 'representing' the band as a whole – Robert Smith's appearance at the 1980 Stranglers Rainbow gig, for example.

In general, only basic UK catalogue numbers are given – any given single might well appear in a dozen different permutations, with some tracks (usually remixes) exclusive to one pressing, but others common to all of them. Rather than double the size of the book with repetitive lists and largely similar numbers, all versions of each single are rounded up into one entry, identified by the most simple of the many catalogue numbers.

ALBUMS: includes LP, cassette and CD full length releases, and Various Artist compilations featuring newly recorded material.

LIVE: Officially-released concert recordings are listed by date of original show, where known. Performances by associated spin-offs are not included.

STUDIO: Unreleased studio material, or recordings subsequently released on compilations and anthologies (detailed in Appendix One), listed by date of original recording where known. Undated material is listed either following the main chronological sequence, or where it would seem to fit in regard to the band's repertoire of the time. When in doubt, performances are dated to the year in which the song was first recorded. Material by associated spin-offs is not included.

RADIO/TV: Specially recorded material out for radio/TV broadcast.

For ease of reference/cross-reference, every Cure song is individually numbered according to the year in which it was recorded (the first two digits – 77, 78, 79 etc) and by the release's position within the above sequence. Unreleased songs known to have been recorded at listed events are noted UNR (UNRELEASED). Subsequent (live, radio or rerecorded) appearances of the same song receive a new number. However, alternate recordings/mixes from the original session, or commercial remixes of a previously released recording, when issued under the original title, retain the original number, suffixed a, b, c etc.

Releases by associated groups are unnumbered.

Further material is included in the appendices: (I) Compilations and Anthologies; (II) Related Releases; (III) Tribute albums; and (IV) A Brief Directory of Cure-men Past and Present.

INTRODUCTION

Ask your Average Joe In The Street... 'hey, Average Joe In The Street, what can you tell me about the Cure?' And his brow will furrow and his teeth will show, and he'll go, 'oh yeah'. And then he'll slash his wrists.

See, the Cure have done lots of interesting things, and are full of interesting people. But what they've done most of all, is create a heap of records that has established them as an almost generic brand-name, dial 1-800-MISERYGUTS, and purge your sins with this fabulous television offer... plus, if you order now, you'll also receive a shapeless item of baggy black clothing to put on your head while you listen. After all, there's image and there's Image, and the Cure have so much Image they make the rest of the world look faceless.

More than a quarter century after the slow-burning 'Killing An Arab' was ignited by an unknown band from deepest southern England, Robert Smith and the Cure have established themselves as the grand-dames of alternative rock, quick enough to keep ahead of the baying pack, but in tune enough with their audience's expectations to ensure that almost every album they have released can be deemed, in some way, 'definitive'.

Their reputation, of course, paints them as gloom-mongers supreme, the soundtrack to so many suicides that rock comedians can still get a laugh out of suggesting they give out free nooses at each concert. And, it is true, there are not many laughs to be found in 'The Funeral Party'; nor, as one journeys through the manifold convolutions that paint the Cure's musical make-up, can one deny the sombre undercurrents that swirl beneath all; the taste for musical grandiosity that, even at its breeziest, conjures images of echoing cathedrals and long, moonlit miles. Play *Carnage Visors* when you're driving in the dark. The night will never look the same again.

But there is also a vivacity, a joy, even a glee to be gleaned from the Cure's back catalogue, together with a sense that, even if the group tried to stand still, it would be creeping forward all the same. From the sharp, shocking pop of their debut *Boys Don't Cry*, to the raging ultra-volatility of *The Cure*; from the mythic psychedelia of *The Top* to the impassioned intensity of *Bloodflowers*... indeed, from the stylistic poles of any pair of albums you can name... the Cure have rarely remained in one spot for two songs, let alone too long.

Medieval minstrels would have been burned at the stake for dashing from 'The Lovecats' to 'Lullaby', from 'Faith' to 'Friday, I'm In Love'. The Cure not only made those same mad manoeuvres, they accomplished them without losing sight of their own selves for a second.

The journey has not been without its casualties. Robert Smith aside, no member of the Cure has lasted the entire course (bassist Simon Gallup comes closest). It is only over the last decade that a single Cure line-up has even recorded more than two new albums together. But, whereas other bands would find that such flux leads to inconsistent confusion, for the Cure it offers a continuity which their peers and contemporaries would kill to possess, as Smith sheds ideas that no longer fit, then tailors their replacements to his own requirements precisely.

That such spectacular development can be cast as the miraculously evolving vision of one man is not, however, to decry the contributions of those bandmates. Smith has rarely proclaimed the Cure a democracy (and usually expresses regret when he does). But the colours that flavour each of the Cure's best records are those of the unit as a whole. Smith is the Cure's guiding light. But the Cure is the flame that keeps him blazing.

THE EARLY UNIMAGINARY YEARS

Robert Smith put it best. "Trust in me through closing years," he sang, midway through the title track of the Cure's third album, *Faith*; and, more than two decades later, trust remains the bond that cements the Cure to one of the most loyal audiences in rock'n'roll history, just as it is trust that has sustained the Cure throughout its existence. That, and a healthy dose of what even Smith acknowledges to be sheer bloody-mindedness. *His* Bloody-mindedness.

This was the quality that transformed the Cure from a likeable pop group – the 'southern Buzzcocks' of late Seventies British press clippings – into the dark, depressed monolith whose shadow overhangs so much of even the most modern interpretation of the music scene. And bloody mindedness forced the band to keep going after it had all but split up; and it has seen the Cure swing from some wild highs to some mighty lows, album by album – sometimes track by track. Smith says it himself; he works to please himself and, if anybody else happens to like it as well, 'that's their tough luck'.

Born in the northern seaside resort of Blackpool on 21 April 1959, Robert Smith was brought up in the London commuter belt overflow of Crawley. He turned to music early. 'People are always surprised when I say this but I swear it's true. I started listening to rock music when I was 6,' Smith told the French magazine *Les Inrockuptibles*. 'Of course, at that time, the two unavoidable bands were the Beatles and the Stones, and I dived straight into [that]'. His older siblings, sister Janet and brother Richard, 'had all their records and, instead of listening to childish little songs, I was listening to some rock. My brother was also crazy about Captain Beefheart, Cream, Jimi Hendrix – so much so that, when I was 7 or 8, to the despair of my parents, I became some kinda little devil fed on psychedelic rock.'

By 1972, the devil was making his own musical choices – the first album he ever bought was David Bowie's *Ziggy Stardust*; his first concerts, the following year, starred Rory Gallagher, Thin Lizzy and the Rolling Stones. 'I wasn't really a big Rory Gallagher fan, but I thought his guitar playing was fabulous. But Thin Lizzy, they were fabulous. I saw them probably ten times in two years. The actual sound of them live was just so overpowering, it was better than drinking.' The Sensational Alex Harvey Band were another icon. Future Cure bassist Simon Gallup recalled, 'even before Robert and I met each other, we were both Alex Harvey fans. God knows how old Harvey was [pushing 40, if you must ask], but he was brilliant.'

Talking to *The Guardian* in 2003, Smith continued, 'Alex Harvey was the physical manifestation of what I thought I could be. I was 14 when I first went to see him, and then I followed him around to all the shows. He never really got anywhere, even though he had something so magical when he performed he had the persona of a victim, and you just sided with him against all that was going wrong. I would have died to have had Alex Harvey as an uncle.' Well into the Cure's third decade as a touring band, the stash of tapes that accompanied Smith on the road inevitably included at least one home-made Harvey compilation… together with Bowie, Thin Lizzy and (perhaps surprisingly) Evelyn 'Champagne' King.

Another childhood friend (and future bandmate), Laurence 'Lol' Tolhurst, continued, 'at the very beginning, another of the things that started the band off was… from the age of about 10 onwards, I slept under a huge poster of Jimi Hendrix. Robert and I both liked Hendrix – we were the only two guys, I remember, in our school who joined the Jimi Hendrix Appreciation Society; we sent our pound off and got some Photostatted little leaflet back and that was it.'

Smith agreed. 'Hendrix was the first person I had come across who seemed completely free and, when you're nine or 10, your life is entirely dominated by adults. So he represented this thing that I wanted to be. Hendrix was the first person who made me think it might be good to be a singer and a guitarist – before that I wanted to be a footballer.'

Smith was 14 when he formed his first band, the Crawley Goat Band with his brother, sister Janet and some like-minded friends. Another group, The Group, followed, before he put together the Obelisks with Tolhurst and yet another future Cure member, Michael Dempsey.

'The first songs we tackled, ever,' laughs Tolhurst, 'at school, we'd go in at weekends, or lunchtime, and rehearse, and we bought three sets of sheet music. We bought "Heart Of Gold" – Neil Young; "Whiter Shade Of Pale," and a Paul Simon Song, "Me And Julio Down By The Schoolyard". "Whiter Shade Of Pale" without keyboards, just guitar, bass and drums. The optimism of youth.'

The band was, Smith has since shuddered, 'horrible.' It took the Obelisks two years to even stage their first proper rehearsal, and even longer to play a gig, at their school, St. Woolfords. 'We didn't go out much after it,' Smith lamented. 'They hated us.'

By early 1976, bassist Alan Hill, guitarist Marc Ceccagno and the singularly-named drummer Graham had all quit, other members were passing in and out, and the band itself had changed its name to Malice. But, armed with a repertoire of old David Bowie, Alice Cooper and Alex Harvey songs, the trio of Smith, Tolhurst and Dempsey was completed by the arrival of guitarist Porl Thompson (he was going out with Janet Smith at the time) in late 1976 – around the same time as the first undercurrents of Punk Rock began swirling through nearby London. John Peel was playing the Ramones and the Damned, the Vibrators were in session on his show, the music press was filled with the Sex Pistols. 'Suddenly,' Smith recalled, 'we started rehearsing properly,' and pursuing Thompson's instincts into a 'straight new wave' phase.

The new group's first gig took place at nearby Worth Abbey on 18 December, 1976, underwhelming audiences with a performance that owed far more to enthusiasm than to any kind of ability. Few venues would invite them back; in fact, precious few were interested in them to begin with, an apathy that summed up the provincial British scene in the mid-1970s... even after Punk arrived to liberate us all from the beers and skittles crew. According to Tolhurst, 'the only way [clubs would] book us was if we were a folk band, so that's what we said we were. We even rearranged our set for acoustic instruments.' They did not, however, alter their repertoire.

'I was enamoured by the melody of the Buzzcocks and Elvis Costello, not the anarchy of the Sex Pistols,' Smith reflected. 'Living in Crawley, you really didn't have to go out of your way to get beaten up, so I couldn't see the point in putting a safety pin through my nose. But Costello always seemed that bit cleverer. I bought my first guitar, a Jazz Master, just because he looked so cool with his.'

For much of the band's first year as a live act, performing at the Rocket, in nearby Croydon, their set was largely comprised of cover versions: Jethro Tull's 'Locomotive Breath', the Doobie Brothers' 'Long Train Running', the Troggs' 'Wild Thing', Bowie's *Ziggy Stardust* anthem 'Suffragette City', Thin Lizzy's 'Jailbreak' and Jimi Hendrix's 'Foxy Lady'... while the first glimmerings of the band's own writing potential was also inching into place.

Smith's 'A Night Like This' and Tolhurst's 'Easy Cure' filtered into the group's set, with Tolhurst laughing, 'at one point, we had a virtual monopoly on writing trilogies in songs. We decided we were going to do songs that had three parts, the concept album kind of idea... very prog rock! They were down to what we could actually play – anything we could play, we'd adapt a few things and put some words that either Robert or I would do on top.'

A succession of vocalists filed through the ranks, while the band was also constantly considering a name change. By January 1977, however, the group had rechristened itself Easy Cure (after the song, of course); and, by the spring, had recruited a vocalist with the superbly resonant name of Peter O'Toole. And they had the dashing teenaged looks that the German label Ariola-Hansa was convinced might well conquer the universe.

Punk was in full swing by now, but the market for 'Boy Bands' (as a modern age so brutally terms them) was as powerful as it had ever been. The Bay City Rollers were still selling records in Germany, Japan and the United States, the likes of Flintlock and Racey were chart-bound across Europe... Ariola-Hansa itself was just gearing up for some remarkable success with Child, an almost cripplingly handsome combo whose hits... 'When You Walk In The Room', 'It's Only Make Believe' and 'Only You'... would swiftly be curdling the dreams of a continent full of impressionable weenyboppers.

In April 1977, the label dropped an ad into the British music press... 'Wanna be a recording star?'... calling for young, unsigned bands to enter a special talent contest – first prize, of course, being a Hansa record contract. Easy Cure entered, recording a haphazard demo at Smith's parents' house and, out of

some 1,400 entrants, were one of just 60 who were invited up to London for inspection. On May 13, the group found itself at Morgan Studios, there to record a couple of songs. And, five days later, they signed a £1,000 contract.

1977

LINE-UP #1 (to summer 1977): Peter O'Toole (vocals), Porl Thompson (guitar, keyboards), Robert Smith (guitar), Michael Dempsey (bass), Lol Tolhurst (drums)
LINE-UP #2: Robert Smith (vocals, guitar), Porl Thompson (guitar, keyboards), Michael Dempsey (bass), Lol Tolhurst (drums)

(LIVE) Queen's Square, Crawley, 3 June 1977
   7701 untitled
ORIGINAL RELEASE:
COMMENTS: It's not much to look at, and you wouldn't believe anybody envisioned this as the next Child (or even Flintlock). But the earliest available glimpse of the Cure comprises one minute, 50 seconds, of fuzzy hand-held footage, shot over the Queen's Jubilee Weekend in the local shopping precinct by Smith's dad. A tiny audience is countered by an awful lot of long hair, and the ensuing muffled drone of guitar and drums is a delightful surprise within the band's first videos collection, *Staring At The Sea*.

(DEMO) Sound And Vision Studios, London, October 1977
   7702 I Want To Be Old
   UNR Meathook
   UNR See The Children
   UNR I Just Need Myself
   UNR Pillbox Tales

(DEMO) Sound And Vision Studios, London, November 1977
   7703 I'm Cold
   UNR Killing An Arab
   UNR I Saw Her Standing There
   UNR Little Girl
   UNR Rebel Rebel
ORIGINAL RELEASE: 7702-03 on *Three Imaginary Boys* expanded edition
COMMENTS: November-December 1977 saw Easy Cure work towards what they dreamed would be their first album. Even the summertime departure of O'Toole (bound for a kibbutz in Israel, apparently) could not knock the stars from their eyes; rather, they simply promoted Smith to lead vocals, reasoning that, as he wrote most of the words, he ought to be able to sing them as well. Neither were Ariola-Hansa at all put out by the shift... Proof, Smith later mused,

that the label was more interested in what the band looked like, than how they actually sounded. He told *Sounds*. 'We did a video for them of us playing and I don't think they were listening. I remember my guitar strap broke in the middle of a song and the guitar fell on the floor. I was standing there looking at the control room and the bloke didn't take any notice, so I just picked it up and carried on playing. I later saw a run back of the video and it was like Monty Python, just a complete shambles. In fact, we counted one-two-three-four in one number... there were five of us at the time and two of us started on a completely different number and we sort of reconciled it about five minutes into the song. They just said, "It's a great act you've got there, boys, throwing the guitars around. That's the spirit".'

He continued, in conversation with the *New Musical Express*. 'They wanted us to be another Child. We were even offered a song that Child eventually put out as a single! They were giving us all these really old songs to cover. We couldn't believe it. This was summer 1977 and we thought we'd be able to do all these outrageous songs we'd written and all they wanted from us were versions of really banal old rock 'n' roll songs. Then they gave us the money to do our own demos. And of course they didn't like them. So they tried putting us into the studio with one of their soul producers, and that didn't work out either. It got to the stage where we would have become the Barron Knights of Punk...' The lie behind the label's convictions was revealed when the band unveiled the ten songs they'd cut for the label's approval. The label rejected them all.

The sessions themselves were a curious experience. 'We'd recorded little things at home but we'd never done anything in a quote-unquote professional studio,' says Tolhurst. 'And I remember they tucked me away in this little booth to play, apart from everybody else, so all the little cues that we'd worked out with one another, I couldn't have any of them because I couldn't see anybody. I remember thinking "this is kind of strange, I wonder if it's going to come out okay?"'

Indeed. 'See The Children' boasts a mocking Alex Harvey-'Vambo'-esque hookline, but is oddly reminiscent of a cross between ex-Roller Ian Mitchell's then embryonic Ian Mitchell Band, and a very early Japan (who emerged out of a similar talent contest competition to the Cure, and remained with Ariola for the next three years).

'I Want To Be Old' – an ironic comment on the 'hope I get die before...' refrain that was part of Punk's manifesto – is less intriguing, a guitar-led chunking that picks up a scratchy guitar solo amidships; while 'I Just Need Myself' and 'I'm Cold' are similarly snotty barrages that go a long way to justifying the Buzzcocks comparisons that would soon begin to flow. A compulsively rhythmic 'Meathook', on the other hand, is stronger in demo form than its eventual LP counterpart would prove, with Smith's echo-drenched vocal an effective portent of Things To Come; Hansa's disapproval of the band's efforts might well have reached their crest with this one.

(LIVE) Rocket, Croydon, 4 December 1977
  7704 Heroin Face
ORIGINAL RELEASE: *Curiosity – Live 1977-1984*, Fiction FIX 10, October 1984
COMMENTS: Recorded live at Easy Cure's most regular haunt, the fuzzy punk bass clatter of 'Heroin Face' only amplified Hansa's misgivings about Easy Cure, at the same time as giving the assembled masses of Croydon a furiously pogo-worthy time. (And Smith sounds more like Pete Shelley than ever).

1978

LINE-UP #2 (to May 1978)**:** Robert Smith (vocals, guitar), Porl Thompson (guitar, keyboards), Michael Dempsey (bass), Lol Tolhurst (drums)
LINE-UP #3 (from May 1978) Robert Smith (vocals, guitar), Michael Dempsey (bass), Lol Tolhurst (drums)

(DEMO) PSL Studio, January 1978
   7801 I Just Need Myself (version 2)
   UNR Plastic Passion
   UNR Rebel Rebel (version 2)
   UNR Smashed Up
ORIGINAL RELEASE: 7801 on Three Imaginary Boys expanded edition
COMMENTS: 'They sent us away to record some rock 'n' roll covers,' Tolhurst recollected. 'We handed them these.'

But, if Hansa thought that things were bad now, they were only going to get worse, as the time came for the band to record its first single, and Easy Cure informed their paymasters what it was to be: Smith's 'Killing An Arab', a captivating few minutes spent in the company of Albert Camus' novel, *L'Etranger*.

Hansa were horrified… by the suggestion, by the title, by the song itself. 'They said, even if "Arab" was a good song, they couldn't put it out because we had to keep in with the Arabs,' Smith snorted. 'It was ridiculous.' The group stood firm and deadlock naturally ensued – until, a year after winning the talent contest, Easy Cure were dropped from the label's roster. They celebrated by writing a new song about the label, 'Do The Hansa', and by changing their name to the Cure. 'Killing An Arab', however, remained their first choice for a single.

(DEMO) Home recordings, February-April 1978
   7802 10.15 Saturday Night
   7803 The Cocktail Party
   7804 Grinding Halt
ORIGINAL RELEASE: *Three Imaginary Boys* expanded edition
COMMENTS: '10.15 Saturday Night,' Smith said, 'was written at the table in our kitchen, watching this tap dripping, feeling utterly morose, drinking my dad's home-made lager. I'd fallen out with someone I was supposed to be going out with, so the evening fell apart and I decided to stay home and feel sorry for himself.' The murky solo home demo that features on the *Three*

Imaginary Boys expanded edition was recorded with a Hammond organ playing its programmed bossa-nova drumbeat, a guitar gently teasing out the signature riff, and the whole thing drifts along slow and melancholic. But already the rudiments of the future classic are in place.

The group's demos were recorded at Smith's parents' house. 'They'd remodelled the house,' Tolhurst recalls. 'They stuck this room on the side of the house, I think they intended it as some kind of family den or something, but we just moved in, moved all the gear in and didn't leave for three years. And we'd record things there, and we were quite serious. Apart from going down the pub, three nights a week, we'd all troop round to Robert's house and just rehearse.'

Two full band demos from this period appear on the expanded *Three Imaginary Boys*, although the still-murky sound makes it difficult to pick out either of the songs' distinguishing features. 'Grinding Halt', in particular, is a punky rumble with just a suggestion of an XTC quirk around the rhythm – Smith later revealed that Michael Dempsey was very keen to see the Cure pursue Swindon's finest into those convoluted waters, but Tolhurst's refusal to learn the required weird time signatures scuppered that notion, and the band returned to the areas they were best at – and 'The Cocktail Party' has a guitar sound lifted straight out of early Pink Floyd (via the Rolling Stones' *Let It Bleed*)

(DEMO) Chestnut Studios, Frensham, May 27 1978
    7805 Boys Don't Cry
    7806 It's Not You
    7807 10.15 Saturday Night
    7808 Fire In Cairo
ORIGINAL RELEASE: 7805 on *Curiosity – Live 1977-1984*, Fiction FIX 10, October 1984; all on *Three Imaginary Boys* expanded edition
COMMENTS: 'Killing An Arab' was surprisingly absent from the Cure's next demo, a four-song tape which instead highlighted the power-pop purity of the newly-composed, but already pristine 'Boys Don't Cry' ('a 70s attempt at a 60s pop song,' as Smith called it) and it was this clutch that brought the band to the attention of Polydor A&R man Chris Parry – the man who'd already brought the label the Jam, and who would have wrapped up the Pistols and the Clash as well, had the timing only been better. (Intriguingly, the 'new' vocal grafted onto 'Boys Don't Cry' for the 1986 *Standing On A Beach* compilation returns to the spirit of this original demo.)

There is a deceptive tinniness to the guitar cutting through the four songs, but the melodies are tight and compulsive, with 'Fire In Cairo' a danceably dramatic lope (with a subsequently abandoned lyrical section), and 'It's Not You' another beat-the-Buzzcocks race to the end. But it was '10.15 Saturday Night' that was to hold the key to the Cure's future, as Parry explained.

He first heard the Cure over the weekend of July 14, after he scooped up a pile of demos from his office that Friday afternoon, and spent the weekend playing through them. It was Sunday afternoon before he got to the Cure's offering... 'I just heard "drip drip drip" and I thought "that's rather nice," so I played the tape again,' and this time, glanced at the letter that accompanied it. The band was the Cure, the song was '10.15 Saturday Night' and, Parry recalled, 'the idea of a three piece excited me. The fact that they were a little bit spacey, and this cassette had come from the backwoods, and no-one else had touched it, excited me too.'

Back in the office, Parry wrote to Smith; days later, the band met their future at a pub just round the corner from the Polydor offices and, over the next few months, he made it apparent to all that he was not going to let the Cure get away. In August 1978, Parry announced he was forming his own subsidiary, Fiction, and the following month, the Cure became the company's first signing. Work began on the band's debut album a week later.

Lol Tolhurst still describes Parry as invaluable to the band, both in these earliest days and, later, as their cult (if not their success) developed. 'He knew where to take things, when to do them.... He was definitely the person. You might not always agree with what he said, or the direction he saw things going, but he gave us an overview that was very helpful.'

This entire demo was featured on the 2004 expanded edition of *Three Imaginary Boys*.

(STUDIO) Album out-takes: Morgan Studios, London, October 1978 – January 1979
  7809 Winter
  7810 Faded Smiles
  7811 Play With Me
  7812 World War
  7813 Pillbox Tales
  7814 Do The Hansa

ORIGINAL RELEASE: 7812 on *Boys Don't Cry* US LP; and alongside 7809-11 on *Three Imaginary Boys* expanded edition; 7813-14 'Boys Don't Cry' b-sides 1986.

COMMENTS: The first sessions for the band's debut album produced a number of tracks that would not, in fact, make it onto the LP, although several have since seen an official release. Much of the band's recording, incidentally, was undertaken on the quiet, creeping into Morgan Studios once the resident Jam had finished their sessions, and borrowing their gear through the night. 'We did it in three nights,' Smith later boasted – including 16 songs on the first night, all first takes.

'Pillbox Tales' is chunkier than its Sound & Vision counterpart of 14 months previous, but is still a song struggling to escape a punky racket; 'Do The Hansa', meanwhile, approaches the mutant funk territory that the Cure seemed only to reserve for piss-takes, and is a defiant thumbed nose at the band's former label. Cod-German lyrics, cool record exec speak and gibberish backing vocals all wrap around a compulsive quirk, to reveal a song that could, with more considered lyrics, have pushed the Cure firmly into Gang Of Four territory.

First available on the vinyl (and early CD) pressings of the *Boys Don't Cry* compilation, Tolhurst's 'World War' is a foreboding, bass-led grumble that might not have the best Cure lyrics, but nevertheless insinuates itself deep into the mind; while 'Winter' is a beautifully echoey ballad that would certainly remain on Smith's mind later in the band's career – rudimentary though it sounds, you could imagine it turning up as a b-side during the *Head On The Door* period. 'Faded Smiles' revised an older song called 'I Don't Know', and essentially offers up a punkier version of 'Fire In Cairo'. But the undisputed gem is 'Play With Me', a medium-paced punker that really is the equal of almost any track on the finished album.

(RADIO) BBC Radio/John Peel, 11 December 1978 (rec 4 Dec)
   7815 Killing An Arab
   7816 10:15 Saturday Night
   7817 Fire in Cairo
   7818 Boys Don't Cry
ORIGINAL RELEASE: *Peel Session* EP Killing Strange Fruit SFPS 050
COMMENTS: The Cure's first BBC session found the band laying down relatively straightforward versions of what, in many observers' eyes, were their best songs – with an emphasis, of course, on 'Killing An Arab'.

Bassist Dempsey recalled being disappointed that Peel himself was not present at the session. But the remainder of the experience 'lived up to expectations. The four songs we recorded captured the spirit far more than the [subsequent] album versions. I found that the producers had exactly the right approach; if you looked like you knew what you were doing, they let you get on with it. It was this lack of meddling that made the results more like the original demos, that had secured our recording contract in the first place, just better quality.'

(SINGLE) Killing An Arab
   7819 Killing An Arab
   7820 10:15 Saturday Night
ORIGINAL RELEASE: Small Wonder SMALL 11, December 1978; reissue

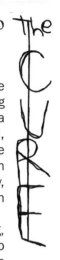

Fiction FICS 001, February 1979

COMMENTS: Gigging regularly through the remainder of 1978, the Cure were dedicated to releasing their first single immediately before Christmas. Having recorded it at Morgan Studios on 20 September, Parry and Fiction scheduled a December 22 release date; the label's distributor, Polydor, however, baulked, insisting that it would be impossible to make things happen that close to the holiday. They were, however, willing to listen when Parry put forward an alternative arrangement, whereby the first 15,000 copies were sold via the tiny, Walthamstow-based Small Wonder independent, with the regular Fiction release following through in the New Year.

'Killing An Arab' was an immediate critical success. Moody and mystifying, but powered by a fascinating Arabic guitar motif, and a lyric that fed directly into the New Wave penchant for cult literature, the record effortlessly sold out its original pressing, and even hung tantalisingly unavailable for a few weeks in January, before the Fiction version finally came to the rescue.

The record's makers, however, left many observers scratching their heads as they tried to pigeonhole this apparently image-less and rootless band. Then, when they failed, they coined the term 'anti-image', and let that serve the same purpose. Smith still remembers his mother reading some of the band's early reviews, then turning round and asking, 'what *is* an anti-image anyway?' He had to confess that he didn't have a clue.

In the meantime, Ariola-Hansa's misgivings over possible misconceptions of the song ('we have to keep in with the Arabs') showed some justification when the National Front attempted to hijack the Cure as one of their own: an act of crass political opportunism that has, sadly, been repeated – though only sporadically.

In 1986, the *Standing On A Beach* compilation was released in the United States with a sticker insisting 'The song KILLING AN ARAB has absolutely no racist overtones whatsoever. It is a song which decries the existence of all prejudice and consequent violence. The Cure condemn its use in further anti-Arab feeling.' Nevertheless, fifteen years later, it was among the songs placed on a No Play list in the United States, following the 11 September 2001 terrorist attacks.

The single's b-side, meanwhile, attracted its own share of attention as *Sounds* enthused, 'it hits upon the value of sparseness in rock 'n'roll like no other record has in oh, as far back as I can think. There's scarcely any playing in the song at all. Everything is left to your imagination.' Massive Attack later sampled the claustrophobia that ensues to extraordinary effect.

1979

LINE-UP #3 (to November 1979) Robert Smith (vocals, guitar), Michael Dempsey (bass), Lol Tolhurst (drums)
LINE-UP #4 Robert Smith (vocals, guitar), Simon Gallup (bass), Matthieu Hartley (keyboards), Lol Tolhurst (drums)

(ALBUM) Various artists: *20 Of Another Kind*
  7819a Killing An Arab
ORIGINAL RELEASE: Polydor POLS 1006
COMMENTS: An alternate version of the single joins contributions from Plastic Bertrand, the Jam, the Stranglers, Sham 69, Patrick Fitzgerald and Otway-Barrett, among others, on one of the finest (and most fondly-recalled) punk compilations of the age.

(SINGLE) Grinding Halt
  7901 Grinding Halt
  7902 Meathook
ORIGINAL RELEASE: Fiction CUR 1 promo
COMMENTS: Two cuts from the forthcoming debut album, tentatively (if not assuredly) scheduled as a possible single. 1,500 copies were pressed on 12-inch vinyl, to be spread around UK press and radio. Collectors drool.

(RADIO) BBC Radio/John Peel, 16 May 1979 (rec 9 May)
  7903 Desperate Journalist In Ongoing Meaningful Review Situation
  7904 Grinding Halt
  7905 Subway Song
  7906 Plastic Passion
  7907 Accuracy
ORIGINAL RELEASE: unreleased
COMMENTS: According to Michael Dempsey, the songs recorded at the Cure's second BBC session should, in tandem with those cut at the first, be regarded as 'the definitive sound of the early Cure' – which simply makes it all the more frustrating that only the first session has, thus far, seen official release.

Of the five, the most legendary is, of course, 'Desperate Journalist...', which sets Smith's interpretation of, and quotes from, *NME* journalist Ian Penman's disparaging review of the Cure's debut album to the frenetic rhythm of 'Grinding Halt': 'he uses long words like "symbiotics" and "semolina," but I counter with "enigma" and "metropolis".' To dwell on that, however, is to overlook the crucial romps through 'Accuracy' and 'Grinding Halt' itself; a positively chilling 'Subway Song' that builds out of locomotive discordance and a stygian bass; and the Roxy Music pastiche 'Plastic Passion', taken a shade faster, and a few degrees angrier than the familiar studio rendition.

(ALBUM) *Three Imaginary Boys*
   7820 10.15 Saturday Night
   7908 Accuracy
   7901 Grinding Halt
   7909 Another Day
   7910 Object
   7911 Subway Song
   7912 Foxy Lady
   7902 Meat Hook
   7913 So What
   7914 Fire In Cairo
   7915 It's Not You
   7916 Three Imaginary Boys
   7917 The Weedy Burton
2004 CD bonus tracks
   7702 I Want To Be Old (SAV demo)
   7703 I'm Cold (SAV demo)
   7704 Heroin Face (live)
   7801 I Just Need Myself (PSL demo)
   7802 10:15 Saturday Night (home demo)
   7803 The Cocktail Party (home demo)
   7804 Grinding Halt (home demo)
   7805 Boys Don't Cry (Chestnut demo)
   7806 It's Not You (Chestnut demo)
   7807 10:15 Saturday Night (Chestnut demo)
   7808 Fire in Cairo (Chestnut demo)
   7809 Winter (studio outtake)
   7810 Faded Smiles (studio outtake)

7811 Play With Me (studio outtake)
7812 World War
7918 Boys Don't Cry
7925 Jumping Someone Else's Train
7920 Subway Song (live)
7921 Accuracy (live)
7922 10:15 Saturday Night (live)

ORIGINAL RELEASE: Fiction FIX 1, May 1979

COMMENTS: 'The Recipe: take three intelligent, sheepishly good-looking, nice middle-class boys who have a flair for original, stylish music and who don't mind leaving their souls in the hands of a fourth streamlined highly successful party. Take this latter party's financial genius, add a pinch of wry, good-natured self-studying humour and here in one lavish package you have... The Cure' – *Sounds*.

The Cure's debut album – victim, of course, of the vitriolic *NME* review that so preoccupied Smith during the Peel session – was actually rather well received, despite the media's continued preoccupation with the 'anti-image' nonsense. 'The Cure are trying to tell us something,' the NME review concluded. 'They are trying to tell us they don't exist'; and the sleeve portrait of three decidedly non-imaginary household items (a lampstand, a vacuum cleaner and a fridge) played straight into that kind of commentary. Smith later revealed that Polydor's art department designed, approved and printed the sleeve without even mentioning it to the band: 'the album just arrived in the post with that cover, and they'd done it all without consulting us.'

But if the artwork was obscure, the music within was everything but. Angular and edgy, short and tight, and verging at times on the same sense of arty minimalism that characterized early Talking Heads and Wire, *Three Imaginary Boys* has held up a lot better than either of those bands... better, in fact, than the vast majority of its other spring 1979 contemporaries.

We remember, after all, an age when 2-Tone was *just* beginning to poke its head above the parapet, when Mod was first flirting with the ouija board of fashion, and Punk had splintered into either the Clever Camp or the Boot Boys brigade. And, into this morass there marches the Cure, a band that tore itself between the sharp power pop stylings of 'Fire In Cairo' (whose killer chorus simply spells out the title – 'eff-eye-are-eee-eye-en-cee...') and the unstated, understated, menace of 'Another Day'... songs that hailed, for the most part, from the band's earliest demos.

It is only with the benefit of extraordinarily liberal hindsight, however, that the future direction(s) of the Cure can truly be measured from the album's contents. At the time, it was such sparkling jewels as 'Fire In Cairo,' 'Object' and 'It's Not You,' and the snot-punk-a-rama of 'Grinding Halt' and the shopping list set to a rhythm 'So What' that appeared the best judges of the band's potential... one that lay them firmly in the same realm of resourcefulness as, indeed, the Buzzcocks.

Smith himself was very conscious of that fact. 'The songs on *Three Imaginary Boys* were really embryonic,' he condemned. 'They were just put down.'

According to Tolhurst, 'when we came to record the first album, being as we had absolutely no idea what we were doing, we just followed Chris Parry's direction – go in, record every song we knew, and come out. We didn't even stay for the mixing, we just left'; and Smith continued, 'there were so many songs on that record only because they were drawn from two years before we recorded it.'

The songs that the Cure themselves preferred were those in which a darker edge became apparent – 'Another Day', the cloying claustrophobia of '10.15 Saturday Night', with its vision of the tap incessantly 'drip... drip... drip... dripping'; and most powerful of all, the fear-tinged nostalgia of 'Three Imaginary Boys' itself. In years to come, it was apparent that everything which the Cure were to become was hinted at in those earliest songs – and most of what they would discard was what brought the album its most lasting celebrations.

'I've always written things down, ever since I can remember,' Smith mused. 'I've got a really bad temper, but it's not physical. I don't throw tantrums or anything like that, so I go off somewhere and rather than smash the room, I write things down. It's a release. I worry that my words aren't going to interest people because they're mainly about me. They're not just about world situations or alternatives.'

With such a welter of songs at the band's disposal, and vinyl able to accept no more than a dozen or so, the final choice of tracks was left to Parry – a decision that backfired only in as much as he omitted both 'Killing An Arab' and 'Boys Don't Cry' (now scheduled as the group's next single), in favour of the brief instrumental 'The Weedy Burton', a tribute-of-sorts to famed guitar tutor Bert 'Play In A Day' Weedon. (Unlisted anywhere on the original record, it meanders into view as the closing echo of the title track fades away). Other omissions, 'Winter', 'Faded Smiles' and 'Play With Me', were finally appended to the bonus disc affixed to the album's 2004 remastering.

In their stead, of course, there appeared the controversial, ramshackle cover of Jimi Hendrix's 'Foxy Lady' – controversial, that is, in that the band themselves never dreamed it would be included. Yet it was not so out of place as many might believe, as Tolhurst admitted. 'When we first started, we played a couple of Hendrix songs, and when Parry told us to record everything we had, that's what we did.' Even Smith's reluctance to sing the song did not faze the producer; he simply passed it over to Michael Dempsey.

Tolhurst continues, 'in the final cut of it all, we had very little choice in what went on the album and what didn't. I think Parry, in some way, wasn't quite sure what was going to go on with the Cure anyway, so he put "Foxy Lady" on there, thinking maybe it'll draw some people in, maybe it won't. I know Robert hates that song, but that was the first and last time that something like that occurred.'

Smith, too, recalled the frenzied genesis of the album, and the surprise of its generally approving critical reception. 'We were playing about 50 songs at the time, mostly in pubs and to people who didn't care if we fell over and died. I wrote most of them by myself without thinking they'd ever be heard by more than 30 people at a time. Chris Parry picked what he thought were the best of the 30 we recorded. They turned out to be some critics' ideas of "classic pop," but they obviously weren't because they weren't *popular*.'

The 2004 remaster expanded the album to double its original length via the cuts subsequently included on the *Boys Don't Cry* compilation, the relevant tracks from the long out-of-print *Curiosity* rarities collection, and half a disc's worth of 1977-78 era demos.

(SINGLE) Boys Don't Cry
    7918 Boys Don't Cry
    7919 Plastic Passion
ORIGINAL RELEASE: Fiction FICS 002, June 1979
COMMENTS: It was Smith's decision to release the Cure's second-best known song as a single – much to both Polydor and Parry's dismay. 'We were advised not to bring it out because of the fact that it was a pop single and it would be much better if we brought out something that was less commercial but more "artistically viable." "Boys Don't Cry," "10.15" and "Accuracy" have always been my favourite songs out of all that initial lot. I'm glad it didn't make it in a way because then the people who'd been saying we shouldn't put it out would then have turned round and said you've gotta give us another one like that one."

Nevertheless, he was adamant, 'in a perfect world, "Boys Don't Cry" would have been a #1 hit.' But he was also profoundly grateful that it wasn't. 'Imagine having to rewrite that song again and again, just to maintain the success,' he shivered. Instead, he waited seven years, and then rerecorded the vocal for the song's inclusion on the *Standing On A Beach* compilation – and this time, scored a hit.

'Forget all that rubbish about Arabs on beaches and conceptualisation of the album cover, this is a POP song and a pretty damn good one. Slightly Buzzcocks in feel, it's the presentable side of wimpery. Long may they wimp' – *Sounds*.

(LIVE) Reading Festival, 24 August 1979
    7920 It's Not You
    UNR 10.15 Saturday Night
    UNR Accuracy
    UNR Grinding Halt
    UNR Another Day
    UNR Object
    UNR Subway Song
    UNR Foxy Lady
    UNR Plastic Passion
    UNR Three Imaginary Boys
    UNR Boys Don't Cry
    UNR Fire In Cairo
    UNR Killing An Arab
    UNR Do The Hansa
ORIGINAL RELEASE: excerpt included on VHS *Staring At The Sea*

COMMENTS: On a bill that also featured the Police, the pre-Eurythmics Tourists and Motorhead, the Cure played the opening night of the annual Festival. "Boys Don't Cry" was dedicated, peculiarly, to Motorhead, but the *New Musical Express* was not impressed. 'Three infuriating berks.' The full 40+ minute set list is noted above; the VHS release, however, includes a mere 56 seconds of 'It's Not You'.

(RADIO) BBC, David Jensen, 29 August 1979 (rec 13 Aug)
UNR Boys Don't Cry
UNR Do The Hansa
UNR Three Imaginary Boys
ORIGINAL RELEASE: unreleased
COMMENTS: An odd session, marred by a throwaway 'Boys Don't Cry', restored to glory by the surprise inclusion of a super-funky 'Do The Hansa' and crowned by a truly atmospheric 'Three Imaginary Boys'.

(LIVE) Nottingham, October 1979
7920 Subway Song
7921 Accuracy
7922 10.15 Saturday Night
ORIGINAL RELEASE: 7920 on *Curiosity – Live 1977-1984*, Fiction FIX 10, October 1984; all on *Three Imaginary Boys* expanded edition
COMMENTS: A painfully boomy, muffled and generally messy audience recording that gives away little regarding the actual sound or feel of the live Cure; whose significance, therefore, is drawn from the time-and-place... midway through the UK tour that saw Smith playing with both his own band, and the headlining Siouxsie and the Banshees.

Kicking off in Bournemouth on 29 August, the tour was just four shows old when guitarist John McKay and drummer Ian Morris walked out on the Banshees on 6 September. The band were hosting a meet-and-greet at an Aberdeen record shop at the time; the pair simply walked out of the door and out on the band, without a word of warning or a note of notice. Later, it transpired that tensions had been building for weeks beforehand, simply waiting for a spark to ignite them. Misunderstandings over the nature of the in-store appearance provided that spark – and, once lit, there was no extinguishing it.

Amazingly, the evening's performance was not cancelled outright, although it was clear that the headliners themselves would not be performing. Instead, apologies from the surviving Banshees, Siouxsie and Severin, were followed by a dramatically extended set from the Cure, culminating in a shared version of the Banshees' own showstopper, a pop-culture riven rendition of 'The Lord's Prayer'.

After the show, both bands got together to drink, as Siouxsie put it, 'as much alcohol as we could get inside us.' Shocked and shattered, Siouxsie and Severin initially considered abandoning the band altogether – the tour, of course, was out of the question. But calmness followed the calamity. Severin continued, 'Robert was more incensed than anyone, because this was his first major tour and... the headline band had split up. He was furious. Half-jokingly, he offered to play guitar for us, as he knew all the songs and he was a fan. The more we thought about it, the better the idea sounded. We got on really well with him, so he was the perfect person to help out.'

No more than four subsequent shows were canned. On 18 September, less than two weeks after the split, the Banshees were back to full strength and on the road again, with Smith on guitar and former Slits drummer Budgie at the back. The first gig was in Leicester, and Budgie recalls, 'Robert wore his mac for his set with the Cure, then took [it] off to play with the Banshees. I don't know if he thought that was going to fool anyone. We caught each other's eye halfway through one of the songs, when neither of us had any idea what was supposed to come next. He was staggering around the stage looking for one of his scribbled bits of paper and I was just mouthing "what the fuck comes next?" The audience... knew the song... better than Robert and me.'

'Smith has a task which would have daunted lesser players,' the *NME* sympathised. 'But he handles this enforced schizophrenia with the minimum of fuss and, armed with a new guitar and flanger (to get that swishing McKay tone), [he] comes out on top, cautious but convincing.'

(SINGLE) THE CULT HEROES: I'm A Cult Hero
   7923 I'm A Cult Hero
   7924 I Dig You
ORIGINAL RELEASE: Fiction FICS 006, November 1979
COMMENTS: Released to little fanfare and even less sales (except, for some reason, in Canada), the Cult Heroes' 'I'm A Cult Hero' was a vehicle for a postman friend of the band's. Tolhurst explains, 'it was our friend Frank Bell. He'd always come to all of our shows from the very beginning, and he'd always expressed a desire to sing. Chris Parry was wanting us to do another single, so we thought we'd have a bit of fun at his expense; "okay, we'll do another single".'

'So we did that and he was horrified. But he still put it out, because he figured maybe it'll make us do something else, which it did. But that was just one drunken evening in Morgan Studios in London... plus, it was with Michael Dempsey, who was a little bemused over the way we were going, and we said "come along Michael, we'll do this." And he never drank, but he got drunk that night and played the bass with a bottle.' Smith's sister Janet, and former guitarist Porl Thompson were also present.

More novelty than nuance, 'Cult Hero' and 'I Dig You' are worth more as collectibles than as slabs of the Cure's musical prowess; even harder to find is the seven minute extended version of 'I Dig You' that entranced Canadian club-hoppers early in 1980, paving the way for the record's eventual release (and success... 35,000 record buyers cannot be wrong) in that country.

Melody Maker reviewed the single alongside the latest from California's favourite comedy punk band: 'Both the Dickies and the anonymous Cult Hero... make no bones about cutting novelty records. The second of the two belongs to the modern school, complete with tongue-in-chic po-faced vocals. The Dickies follow the thrash and snotty voices gang. Neither is particularly funny or satirical.'

Although 'I'm A Cult Hero' would occasionally wander into the Cure's own live set, albeit as an encore, the Cult Heroes themselves would play just one live show, opening for the Passions at the Marquee on 23 March 1980. Their set comprised both sides of the single, plus a recounting of sundry British Top 10 hits from the same month in 1973: 'Cum On Feel The Noize' (Slade), '20th Century Boy' (T Rex), 'Feel The Need In Me' (Detroit Emeralds), 'Cindy Incidentally' (The Faces), 'Blockbuster' (The Sweet), 'Part Of The Union' (The Strawbs), 'Whiskey In The Jar' (Thin Lizzy), 'Hello Hooray' (Alice Cooper), 'Do You Wanna Touch Me' (Gary Glitter)...

(SINGLE) Jumping Someone Else's Train
  7925 Jumping Someone Else's Train
  7926 I'm Cold
ORIGINAL RELEASE: Fiction FICS 005, November 1979
COMMENTS: For the past 14 months, the Cure had been a trio of Smith, Tolhurst and Dempsey, but the latter was growing increasingly uncomfortable with both the darkening direction of Smith's songs, and the singer's apparent stranglehold on the Cure's public image. Early into the Banshees tour, Dempsey told *Sounds* 'I don't want people to think of the Fatman [Tolhurst] and I as the Bruce Foxton and Rick Buckler of the band...' but it was plain that they did. And equally plain that Dempsey had had enough. Days after the end of the Banshees

tour, in London on 15 October, he quit. Or not. 'I suppose you could call it a clash of personalities,' he told the *NME*. 'But I was definitely booted out.'

The songs selected for the group's latest single, the anti-bandwagoning 'Jumping Someone Else's Train', and the icicle shards of (the admittedly substandard) 'I'm Cold' were among the final straws, as the Cure's music twisted further away from the bassist's own vision of how it should sound... even as Smith described the song as the last 'old style Cure' song in the arsenal. '"Jumping Someone Else's Train' was the last song of that period. We could've gone on doing songs like that but it would've been like, er, a Vapors trail' (a punning reference to the 'Turning Japanese' power-pop hitmakers) and we had no intention of doing that.'

'I'm Cold', meanwhile, was one of the songs the band had been carrying around since the Hansa days, although time (and boredom) had seen it contract from what Smith described as 'a 150bpm kind of song,' to a sombre, half-speed monolith, a showcase for 'another heavier, darker side of the band.' Banshee Siouxsie was in the studio the evening 'I'm Cold' was recorded, and offered up some characteristic wails by way of backing vocals.

The outbound Dempsey was replaced by two former members of the Magspies, bassist Simon Gallup and keyboard player, Matthieu Hartley. Tolhurst recalls, 'Simon had been in this band that got a record out before us, we kinda liked that, we'd always hung around and seen him play and stuff, so we said "okay, we'll get him in and, to entice him in, we'll bring in his friend Mathieu, and maybe that'll be good".'

This line-up debuted just weeks later at Liverpool's Eric's on 16 November, the opening night of another tour, a Fiction label package designed to showcase all three of the label's principle signings: the Associates (to whom Dempsey himself later gravitated) and the Passions opened the bill.

(TV) *Chorus* TV (France) 8 December 1979
UNR A Forest
UNR Three Imaginary Boys
UNR Killing An Arab
ORIGINAL RELEASE: unreleased
COMMENTS: Filmed at the Theatre de l'Empire in Paris.

1980

LINE-UP #4 (to November 1980) Robert Smith (vocals, guitar), Simon Gallup (bass), Matthieu Hartley (keyboards), Lol Tolhurst (drums)
LINE-UP #5 Robert Smith (vocals, guitar), Simon Gallup (bass), Lol Tolhurst (drums)

(LIVE) Holland, 15 January 1980
8001 In Your Houoo
ORIGINAL RELEASE: *Curiosity – Live 1977-1984*
COMMENTS: No sooner was the Fiction package over, in early December, than the Cure were touring the Low Countries; back to the UK, they started work on their second album in the new year, only to return to Holland on 15 January for one more show. This, the earliest available recording of the Gallup/Hartley line-up, indicates already just how drastically the group's sound had shifted, although the song itself would undergo considerable revision before being recorded for the new LP.

(RADIO) BBC, John Peel 10 March 1980 (rec 3 Mar)
    UNR A Forest
    UNR Seventeen Seconds
    UNR Play For Today
    UNR M
ORIGINAL RELEASE: unreleased
COMMENTS: 'A Forest' had gone through several lyrical and titular permutations since it was first demoed (as 'Into The Trees') the previous autumn. By the time of this, its recorded debut, however, the familiar miasma was firmly in place – albeit taken at a slightly slower, darker pace. The intro is especially haunting, while the transition into the rhythm is preceded by a pregnant silence that in no way prepares the unsuspecting listener for what is to come.

There again, little of what the Cure had been brewing up in the studio owed much to their past sound, as the remainder of the session would painstakingly reveal. Smith later described 'M' and 'Play For Today' as 'quite… catchy, really,' and sandwiched between 'A Forest' and a positively leviathan 'Seventeen Seconds', they were. But still, anybody tuning into the Peel show in the hope of hearing the next 'Boys Don't Cry' would soon be reaching for a tissue of their own.

(LIVE) ROBERT SMITH – THE STRANGLERS, London Rainbow 4 April 1980
    8002 Grip

8003 Hanging Around
8004 Down In The Sewer

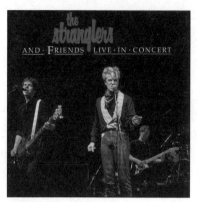

ORIGINAL RELEASE: *The Stranglers & Friends Live In Concert*, Castle 06076 81156-2, 2000

COMMENTS: Smith and Tolhurst had been Stranglers fans since they first encountered them, back in the very earliest days of both Easy Cure and the Punk explosion itself – indeed, looking back, Tolhurst pinpoints their mutual love of the band as one of the elements that eventually spelled the end of Michael Dempsey's stint with the group. 'I can remember going to see them in Croydon, we'd been sitting in rehearsal, it was early in the evening, and I said "let's go and see this band,' and Robert was "okay," so we all piled into his little Mini and off we drove. And Michael spent the whole evening at the bar, being a bit dismissive of the whole thing, and Robert and I were right in the midst of it all, in what now would be called the mosh-pit.'

Since that time, the Stranglers had established themselves among the most tenacious survivors of the first wave of punk, and the most controversial as well. Indeed, from the moment when Stranglers frontman Hugh Cornwell was busted for possession on 1 November 1979, it was widely assumed that the authorities would choose to 'make an example of him.' Drummer Jet Black reflected, 'he was a public figure from a successful band that everyone in the establishment seemed to hate, and it was their way of getting back at us.' He received an eight week jail sentence, wiping out the band's scheduled Far Eastern tour and, according to manager Ian Grant, pronouncing a death sentence upon the group. 'This decision will cost us £200,000 and, to be honest, I can see it being the demise of the group.'

Two shows at the London Rainbow in early April, however, would go ahead. 'Totally spontaneously, the phones in the office started ringing,' Black recalled, 'with people saying "we'll help you out".'

By the time of the gigs themselves, Cornwell's place in the band had been filled by more than close to 20 special guests, ranging from veterans Peter Hammill, Larry Wallis, Steve Hillage and Robert Fripp, to current stars Hazel O'Connor and Toyah Wilcox (the future Mrs Fripp), Ian Dury and his Blockheads, actor Phil Daniels and members of Steel Pulse, the Skids, the Members, Stiff Little Fingers and the Cure. Robert Smith appeared on two songs, playing rhythm guitar behind O'Connor's idiosyncratic vocals on the opening '(Get A) Grip (On Yourself)' and 'Hanging Around', two tracks from the Stranglers' debut album; then returning to the stage for the *tout ensemble* encore 'Down In The Sewer'.

(SINGLE) A Forest
　　8005a A Forest
　　8006 Another Journey By Train
ORIGINAL RELEASE: Fiction FICS 10, April 1980
COMMENTS: It's funny how tastes and opinions change. 'A Forest' might be seen as one of the classic 45s of the early Eighties, but, in April 1980, even an edited (3.56) version was widely regarded as among the most impenetrable records of the age – and certainly one of the daftest choices for a single that any band could make. Indeed, looking back from two decades hence, Smith gave a vengeful chuckle. '"A Forest" certainly wasn't considered to be a good single at the time. It was only after the event that everyone sat back and went "oh, what a fantastic single!" They don't remember how I had to convince them it would be.'

Nor do they recall the hostility with which the single was received, as the *NME*'s Julie Burchill complained about a band who were 'trying to stretch a sketchy living out of moaning more meaningfully than any man has ever moaned before... without a tune, too.'

Originally titled 'Horse Racing', the pulsing instrumental 'Another Journey By Train' b-side, meanwhile, finds a comfortable middle ground between 'Jumping Someone Else's Train' and 'A Forest', and remains one of the most propulsive numbers the band ever cut. A bootleg blending of both 'Train' songs, as a so-called 'full-length version,' may or may not be a genuine Cure cut – the band used to undertake that same segue on stage and, said Smith, 'I always felt really good when we did.'

'The Cure take a trip to the BBC Radiophonic Workshop in search of Dr. Who and find the ghost of Hawkwind' – *Sounds*.

(TV) *Top Of The Pops* (UK) 24 April 1980
　　UNR A Forest
ORIGINAL RELEASE:
COMMENTS: 'A Forest' pushed the Cure onto *Top Of The Pops* for the first time, as the single meandered up to the very edge of the Top 30. 'I just couldn't believe how boring it was to be on it,' Smith moaned afterwards. 'You know the [audience members] who go "whoop whoop"? I really hate them.'

His mood was not helped by an injured thumb he had picked up on the Cure's recent trip to the US – apparently Smith was in agony throughout the performance, and the physical pain was effortlessly translated into mental anguish. 'I just couldn't believe how painful it was being on [*Top Of The Pops*].'

(ALBUM) *Seventeen Seconds*
   8007 A Reflection
   8008 Play For Today
   8009 Secrets
   8010 In Your House
   8011 Three
   8012 The Final Sound
   8005 A Forest
   8013 M
   8014 At Night
   8015 Seventeen Seconds

ORIGINAL RELEASE: Fiction FIX 004, April 1980

COMMENTS: 'Oasis may be able to record an album in two weeks, but we did *Seventeen Seconds* in less than two weeks' – Simon Gallup, 1996.

The Cure's second album was released into a market that was still shell-shocked from 'A Forest', and proved there would be no relenting from the direction that record posited. Work on *Seventeen Seconds* began in mid-January, and always promised to deliver a very different proposition to its predecessor; excerpts had begun creeping into the band's live set as early as August 1979, while Michael Dempsey's departure, laden as it was with rumours of increasing darkness, likewise left many outsiders expecting the Cure (or rather, the increasingly dictatorial Smith) to deal a wild card. *Seventeen Seconds*, however, would shatter even those expectations.

'When we made *Seventeen Seconds*,' Tolhurst recalled, 'we said to Chris Parry, "well, can we do it ourselves now? Because we think we have a better idea of how to do it" – and that's one of the things I give him credit for, because he pushed his ego aside and said "Sure. Go and do it yourselves and, if it's rubbish, I'll just drop you." It was kind of intriguing to him, so he said go ahead.

'It was the first time we actually decided we had to move forward and play something different and, although you can look at [the record] now, and see some of it as being quite muted in its execution... that we could have gone a bit further with it, of course we couldn't, because that was the first time that we'd tried it. We were a little unsure anyway. And Mike Hedges was a fairly inexperienced young engineer. Things like that wouldn't happen nowadays, the head of the label saying "ok, you're an inexperienced band, you're an inexperienced engineer, go in and make a record".'

Still, Smith is adamant, 'we had to make *Seventeen Seconds* in ten days, because we couldn't afford to be in there for the eleventh. 'You don't have any choice when you're first making records. But marrying the two things together for me is redundant, how long something takes and what it's like; because what it's like is something more important. If you say you banged something out in two weeks, I'm not gonna go slack-jawed, "did it seriously take you two weeks to make it?" because it should have taken two hours.

'I'm glad I had that experience, going in, knocking out an album quickly, "the good old days." But I also remember the downside, the lack of time, the lack of money, the lack of belief. The intense frustration I used to feel. But it still seemed like forever.'

Which is just about how long the record lasted, according to many of the album's original critics. Smith himself insisted that the general mood of the record was more important than the songs, and that the generally damning reviews it received were the direct consequence of critics completely bypassing the album's obvious emotional content, while searching in vain for the next 'Boys Don't Cry'.

But an album that opens one side with the muted instrumental 'A Reflection', a recurring piano-led contemplation of ripples in a mill-pond (shades of the Banshees' 'Pure', if you seek such things); then kicks off the other with 'The Final Sound', 52 seconds of spooky discordance, and whose very title track insists that 17 Seconds 'is the measure of life,' was hardly going to register in the hot-house conveyor belt of the average record reviewer's attention span; while even witnesses to the Cure's most recent live shows could not have been prepared for the sheer intensity of an album which revelled in one wintry blast after another.

A dark, sombre, record, *Seventeen Seconds* developed from the songs which Smith himself had pinpointed as the most representative compositions on *Three Imaginary Boys*. 'I knew what I wanted [the record] to sound like, the general mood,' he explained. 'There's no point in trying to intellectualise about it because it's a genuine emotion that's on the LP.' It was an emotion that Smith was only able to verbalize as the product of what he described as 'a black period,' during which he sank into a depression so deep that even songwriting was suddenly an oppressive chore.

Smith undertook the majority of the writing on a Hammond organ, with the memory of the Banshees tour still fresh in his mind – a period when 'there were so many emotional wrecks walking around.' His own state of mind, he said, left him feeling as though 'I was looking down on myself. I was being two separate people... One day I'd wake up wanting to kill somebody, the next day I wouldn't even bother getting up. It was awful. I was letting myself slip in order to write songs. I wasn't fighting it, whereas in everyday life you have to control those feelings. All the things I went through, it was a really demented two weeks.' By the time the writer's block kicked in, his mood was unshakeable.

Yet the record needed to be finished, so he spun out in search of shortcuts... The instrumentals, of course, and the penultimate 'At Night', a song that he straightforwardly admitted 'was lifted from a Kafka story piecemeal, very Thin White Duke style, things that resonated in our lives. I just lifted a few phrases, put them together and it made sense. And that was because I couldn't be bothered to write a song.'

Reviews of this wholly unexpected, record were tentative. 'For anyone expecting *Seventeen Seconds* to be a collection of great pop music,' the *New Musical Express* warned its readership, 'the joke is definitely on them. Indeed, *Seventeen Seconds* is far more oblique in its arrangements and construction than *Three Imaginary Boys* could ever have been. The sleeve is littered with blurred, out-of-focus shots, while the record itself makes no concessions to alerting the listener to the Cure's current pitch.'

Even more damning, but in many ways accurate, was *Record Mirror*'s simple observation, 'This is a reclusive, disturbed, Cure, sitting in cold, dark, empty rooms, watching clocks.' The fact that the record prompted a lot of listeners to join them there remains one of the Cure's most remarkable achievements ever.

Of course, the band's workload did not lighten with the release of this new album: they continued on the longest – and darkest – period of gigging they have ever known; a time-span only interrupted by studio sojourns that produced their next two albums – which became, in themselves, milestones of the group's internal disarray and dismay.

STOP PRESS! 2005 BONUS DISC "Rarities 1979-1980"

Details of the 2005 Deluxe Edition were released as this book went to press. Contents are as follows:

PREVIOUSLY AVAILABLE MATERIAL
> 7923 I'm A Cult Hero
> 7924 I Dig You
> 8001 In Your House
> 8016 At Night

PREVIOUSLY UNRELEASED HOME INSTRUMENTAL DEMOS (January 1980)
> Another Journey By Train
> Secrets

PREVIOUSLY UNRELEASED ALTERNATE MIX
> Three

PREVIOUSLY UNRELEASED LIVE MATERIAL
> Seventeen Seconds (Amsterdam 1/80)
> I Dig You (Marquee Club, London 3/80)
> I'm A Cult Hero (Marquee Club, London 3/80)
> M (Arnhem 5/80)
> The Final Sound (France 6/80)
> A Reflection (France 6/80)
> Play For Today (France 6/80)

A Forest (live in France 6/80)

COMMENTS: The absence of any additional studio material testifies to just how swiftly the parent album was conceived and recorded. Even the home demos offer little more than a rougher version of the completed songs, and it is the live material that best indicates the Cure's development through 1980.

The two *Cult Hero* concert cuts, of course, are little more than completist curios. Elsewhere, however, comparing the Amsterdam recordings, with the French tapes six months later readily evidences the looming intensity of the shadows congregating around the Cure, and closes with a magnificent six minutes of 'A Forest.'

(LIVE) France 9 June 1980

8016 At Night

ORIGINAL RELEASE: *Curiosity   Live 1077 1081*, Fiction FIX 10, October 1984

COMMENTS: Midway through a French tour (which included a riot-torn festival alongside the Clash and UFO!), the Cure stopped by French radio to record what remains one of the key concert documents of the band's earliest years. One track was culled from the tape for *Curiosity*, but the entire show remains among the best-known of all the band's bootlegs, as much for its energy and atmosphere, as for its sparkling sound quality. The attack lines drawn up by Smith and Gallup are astonishing – 'At Night' itself sounds like an angry insect attack.

Yet this was not a one-off. Other shows from the tour – albeit preserved in less pristine quality – capture a Cure whose live energy was best summed up by Gallup, in conversation with *Sound International* magazine. 'Our aim on [*Seventeen Seconds*] was to create a mood. Not a series of moods, but different aspects of one mood.' In concert, that same mood was now being expanded across the band's entire repertoire, until the ghosts of the new record somehow infiltrated even the triumphant pop of the oldest favourites.

This particular recording is nevertheless significant, marking as it does Matthieu Hartley's final recording with the band. Complaining that the music was too dark, he quit immediately after the Australian tour in August. Never mind. 'It just means I have a lot more work to do,' Smith shrugged, adding that the band would not be replacing him. 'It would be impossible for someone else to fit into the Cure now, because [we're] so popular it's untrue. It would take 10 years to get accepted on the same level that we accept each other....'

(STUDIO) Morgan Studios, September 1980

ORIGINAL RELEASE: *Rarities 1980-81* Bonus Disc

COMMENTS: Coming off the road as a trio once again, Smith, Tolhurst and Gallup first rehearsed, then recorded demos for their third album, only to scrap the sessions at the end of the month and return to the road, with a month-long European tour. By the end of their next British excursion, in mid-November, the band would have visited 13 countries in six months, made their American debut and seen the album chart in Belgium, Holland and the UK.

According to Tolhurst, 'we went to Morgan and we didn't like what we were doing there. It was the first time we'd written a lot of the album in the studio, because for the first album, we had a whole pile of songs that we just went in and recorded; for *Seventeen Seconds*, we'd been at home rehearsing and writing. We went back to Morgan because, when we were first there, it was at its heyday. They had a restaurant on site, every day you'd go in and there'd be someone like Gary Moore in there, and it was kinda fun. By the point we were beginning *Faith*, though, it was getting a little run-down… I dunno, I think – for want of a better phrase – the whole vibe was wrong. Plus we'd done two albums there and we were getting a bit fed up.'

The sessions were relocated to Abbey Road, to a newly built studio wing called the Penthouse.

1981

LINE-UP #5 Robert Smith (vocals, guitar), Simon Gallup (bass), Lol Tolhurst (drums)

(RADIO) BBC, John Peel, 15 January 1981 (rec 7 Jan)
   UNR Holy Hour
   UNR Forever
   UNR Primary
   UNR All Cats Are Grey
ORIGINAL RELEASE: unreleased
COMMENTS: Although even a taster of the scrapped September sessions would remain unheard for the next 25 years, the Cure's next John Peel session offers up some clues as to both the songs attempted, and the state of those songs… and, perhaps, the reasons for their abandonment. Yet this also ranks among the Cure's greatest BBC performances, a worm's-eye view of the band as they stood poised at a peculiar juncture

Newly renamed from the demo 'Cold Colours', the version of 'Primary' is so radically different to its 'finished' counterpart that only the inclusion of the 'oh remember… please don't change' hook, and a sense of familial resemblance around the bass line truly ties the two together. 'Forever' itself is familiar only from the bootleg versions that stack up around the one officially released take (a 1984 live rendition included on *Curiosity*); this studio assault, all backward vocal effects, heavy phasing and a truly menacing bass line, hints at what might have come to pass had the band opted to take the song any further. '"Forever" really started out like this jam at the end of a show,' says Tolhurst. 'We never attempted to record it, it was just "okay, we'll start off in A and see where it goes." Every time. And it was usually just a reflection on what had happened that day.'

Although the lyrical construction remains tentative and cluttered, 'Holy Hour' places the material back on a familiar footing, both in terms of all that *Seventeen Seconds* portended, and the song's eventual appearance on *Faith*; while 'All Cats Are Grey' has an insistence that is almost metronomic in its unrelenting fury. In other words, *Faith* would have emerged a very different album, had the band not devoted the next month to revising its contents.
(RADIO) BBC, Richard Skinner, 2 March 1981 (rec 26 Feb)
   UNR Funeral Party
   UNR Drowning Man
   UNR Faith

ORIGINAL RELEASE: unreleased
COMMENTS: *Faith* was complete now; the first single ('Primary') was set for release in three weeks... and this session hangs in the memory as one of those monumental moments in music that you will never forget: 'Funeral Party' is a tragic overture, 'Faith' a mystical prayer, full of yearning, while a still-unformed 'Drowning Man' sits in the middle of a mesmerizing combination that somehow reaches the level of sacred music.

(SINGLE) Primary
   8101 Primary
   8102 Descent
ORIGINAL RELEASE: Fiction FICS 12, March 1981
COMMENTS: The head-on twin bass guitar assault of 'Primary' might not be the strongest song on Faith, but it was certainly the most single-like.

Loosely adapted from the main theme of the 'Carnage Visors' movie soundtrack (see below), the non-LP instrumental b-side 'Descent' returned the disc to the moods of the album itself, at the same time as retaining the two bass attack of 'Primary' itself. 'But where "Primary" was upbeat and thumping,' Smith chuckled, 'Descent' was hypnotic, atmospheric and gloomy in the extreme.

(TV) *Top Of The Pops* (UK) 16 April 1981
   UNR Primary
ORIGINAL RELEASE: unreleased
COMMENTS: The band's second appearance on *TOTP* was sufficient to push the single to #43, but that was it.

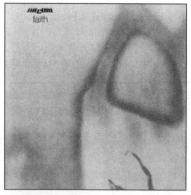

(ALBUM) *Faith*
   8103 The Holy Hour
   8101 Primary
   8104 Other Voices
   8105 All Cats Are Grey
   8106 The Funeral Party

8107 Doubt
8108 The Drowning Man
8109 Faith

ORIGINAL RELEASE: Fiction FIX 6, April 1981

COMMENTS: '*Faith* was going to be a very positive record,' Smith insisted of the Cure's third album as its release date approached. 'It turned out to be a very morbid one.'

Much had changed since the September demos: Tolhurst's mother had fallen terminally ill and Smith's grandmother had died; circumstantially, *Faith* was already taking control of the group, long before they realised that they needed to take control of it.

Tolhurst reflected, '[Robert and I] were very heavily immersed in religion up until our teens.' That, however, was when they understood that while 'organized religion tells you one thing... as life unfolds, you realise that there's an individual interpretation you can put on events. So there were a lot of personal things that went into that album.'

In hindsight, everything about Faith appeared pre-ordained: appeared, also, to hinge around the spectral sleeve photograph of Bolton Abbey, near Shipworth in Yorkshire, that only gradually resolves itself into any kind of coherent image. The sparse, skeletal, sound of the band echoes bleakly across just such a landscape, and the fading voice with which the record closes, the bleak assertion that 'there's nothing left but faith,' lingers long after the disc has finished playing. There is nothing but left faith, but what happens when you have none left to hang onto?

Yet, throughout the period during which this most intense album was being created (or was creating itself), Smith continued insisting, 'there was still some humour in what we did, but we never made anything of it. It was always kept well hidden. So we were seen to be very po-faced about everything. But it was quite good fun being like that because we could get away with an intensity which would otherwise have seemed manufactured.'

At the same time, however, 'there were personal reasons which affected everybody at the time,' personal crises which set everybody on edge, and which *Faith*, an album of unflinching unforgiving power, could not help but exacerbate. 'We then had to live with [*Faith*] for a year, in that we toured with it, and it was the one record we shouldn't have done that with, because for one year we lived with this doomy, semi-religious record. We sort of wore it everywhere we went, it was like sackcloth and ashes. It wasn't a very enjoyable year really.'

Neither was he entirely satisfied by the album itself. 'I have my own criticisms of the album. The production is really shit! We didn't allow ourselves enough time to develop the songs in the studio; then again if we'd taken longer *that* would've been self-indulgent. The last album took under 20 days, this one a bit more but even that was too much; we have self-imposed limits on how much time and money we should spend. It took so long because we kept getting thrown out of studios in favour of "more important" people and, once we lost the mood, we never quite got back the atmosphere we wanted. Also some of it could have been a little more cohesive.'

Taken track by track, *Faith* indeed remains a flawed masterpiece, inferior to both the preceding *Seventeen Seconds* and the subsequent *Pornography*. 'Other Voices' and 'Doubt' are both weak; 'Primary', filling the same kind of void in *Faith* as 'Changes Made' on John Cale's *Music For A New Society* (the only other emotional punch of the age that can be compared to *Faith*), is out-of-place. All three, however, serve their purpose as bridges between the album's key moments and, listened to as one solid body of work, *Faith* emerges, as perhaps the Cure's purest album, their masterpiece and the consummation not only of all that they had promised in the past, but also all that they have accomplished since then. Arguably, every subsequent Cure album has simply taken a different nuance from *Faith* and expanded upon it, drawn it out to its next most logical conclusion.

It is also, certainly, their darkest, and most atmospheric collection. Smith explained, 'I've always tried to make records that are of one piece, that explain a certain kind of atmosphere to the fullest. If you're going to fully explore something you need more than one song to do it. That's why I've always liked Nick Drake's albums, or Pink Floyd's *Ummagumma*. I like a lot of music which is built around repetition. Benedictine chants and Indian mantras. These musics are built around slow changes, they allow you to draw things out.'

And so, little about *Faith* adheres to even the loosest notions of commerciality; and, even at a time when groups like Bauhaus were already rallying around the latest convolutions within the Positive Punk axis, *Faith* loomed over them, a vast, dark cathedral of sound into which only the remotest glimmers of light could fall. 'At their best,' the *New Musical Express* agreed, 'their religious devotional care and slow stately pace takes over with a precision and a discipline that is breathtaking and, yes, religious.'

The title track itself remains one of the most affecting 'rock' songs ever recorded, and one whose power the Cure themselves were well aware of. Dropped from the live set in 1982, it remained in mothballs until April 1986 when, as he re-immersed himself in the emotions and moods that went into the song at the Royal Albert Hall, during Greenpeace's Soundwaves benefit, Smith found himself breaking down in uncontrollable tears. 'I was crying through it. It's like rereading a page from your diary, like Christmas Eve 1975, and all the hopes you had. When I hear it, I have to stop listening. I wish everything I did had such a strong effect on me.'

Even today, the Cure perform the song only when a show has gone particularly well, or when events around them seem especially deserving – the night the world learned of the Tianamen Square massacre, in 1989, the band unleashed a 15 minute version of the song on stage in Turin. 'I need to sing a song called "Faith",' Smith announced by way of introduction. 'Someone says you can't sing it, so what can you do? This is for everyone who died today in China.' The bootleg recordings of the song that circulate today are muddy and doom-laden, but the emotion is more than palpable. 'Someone walks up to you who is so much bigger than you and says "shut your fucking face..."' Many rock bands have drawn on real-life tragedy to illustrate fear, horror or despair, but few have extemporised it with such effectiveness.

'*Faith* wins. It swings like a warm summer night, it's warm breezes and rarefied beat transcend everyday dance music' – *Sounds*.

STOP PRESS! 2005 BONUS DISC "Rarities 1980-1981"

Details of the 2005 Deluxe Edition were released as this book went to press. Contents are as follows:

PREVIOUSLY AVAILABLE MATERIAL

8110 Carnage Visors
8111 The Drowning Man
8112 Faith
8113 Charlotte Sometimes
8115 Funeral Party
8115a Other Voices

PREVIOUSLY UNRELEASED ROBERT SMITH INSTRUMENTAL DEMOS (August 1980)

Faith
Doubt

PREVIOUSLY UNRELEASED HOME INSTRUMENTAL DEMOS (September 1980)

Drowning
The Holy Hour

PREVIOUSLY UNRELEASED MORGAN STUDIO OUT-TAKES (September 1980)

Primary
Going Home Time

PREVIOUSLY UNRELEASED GUIDE VOCAL OUT-TAKES (January 1981)

The Violin Song
A Normal Story

PREVIOUSLY UNRELEASED LIVE MATERIAL

All Cats Are Grey (summer/81)
Forever (summer/81)

COMMENTS: If the Deluxe Editions of *Three Imaginary Boys* and *Seventeen Seconds* were best distinguished by their oddities and live material, the repackaged *Faith* contrarily emerges one of the most significant upgrades of any album yet revised, by the Cure or anybody else. From Smith's earliest demos on, the story of the album's creation is laid bare; and, though the demos themselves add little to what we already know (beyond the sheer aggression of the instrumental 'Drowning'), by the time we reach the aborted Morgan Studios sessions, a very different *Faith* is beginning to emerge.

'Primary' is as radical as the Peel session version, but twice as atmospheric, while the previously unheard 'Going Home Time' could be described as a cross between 'Jumping Someone Else's Train' and a sober 'Love Cats.' Its omission from the finished album should come as no surprise to anyone.

Similarly, 'The Violin Song' has little more than the drum sound to tie it to the Faith sessions as we know them, although a more coherent vocal arrangement might well have remedied that. But 'A Normal Story' is the real surprise here, drifting and driving in a manner that could easily have seen it replace 'Primary' in the finished running order.

Of the live material, a previously unissued, nine minute version of 'Forever' is the most welcome inclusion, although it is certainly rewarding to have the 'Charlotte Sometimes' b-side version of 'Faith' available once again. And, finally, 'Carnage Visors' is on CD at last, and sounding better than your old cassette ever did.

(ALBUM) *Carnage Visors*
    8110 Carnage Visors
ORIGINAL RELEASE: Fiction FIXC 6, April 1981
COMMENTS: The state of isolation into which the Cure had crushed themselves was only intensified by their decision to discontinue the traditional rock 'n' roll practice of touring with a support band, and go out instead with a movie opening for them. *Carnage Visors* was a 30 minute animated film shot by Simon Gallup's brother Richard, accompanied by a lengthy (27 minutes, 29 seconds) instrumental recorded by the Cure themselves – a soundtrack whose sheer moody intensity set the stage for *Faith* even before the band came out on stage to deliver it.

Although elements of 'Carnage Visors' can certainly be detected in the b-aside 'Descent', the soundtrack was originally granted only one official release, as a bonus for purchasers of the cassette release of *Faith*.

(RADIO) Werchter Rock Festival, Belgium, 5 July 1981
    UNR The Holy Hour
    UNR In Your House
    UNR The Drowning Man
    UNR 10.15 Saturday Night
    UNR Accuracy
    UNR The Funeral Party

UNR M
UNR Primary
UNR Other Voices
UNR All Cats Are Grey
UNR Fire In Cairo
UNR Play For Today
UNR A Forest

ORIGINAL RELEASE: unreleased

COMMENTS: One of the best of the available early Cure performances, both in terms of performance and sound quality, the circulating tapes captured a near-complete *Faith*-era show. For all the tour's subsequent reputation for doom, this recording portrays a band of sparkling vibrancy and energy. True, Smith's vocal lacks something of the studio albums' practiced sobriety ('Funeral Party' sounds especially weary), but the pacing of the set allows every facet of the band to shine through, from the density of 'The Drowning Man', to the sparkplug energy of 'Fire In Cairo'.

'We'd only been on for about a half an hour and everything was running late so Robert Palmer's road crew started motioning to us to stop. This bloke ran on and said 'If you don't stop playing, we're gonna pull the plug'. Simon immediately walked to the mike and shouted "Fuck Robert Palmer! Fuck rock'n'roll!" and we started playing a really slow version of 'A Forest' that lasted about 15 minutes. It was fucking brilliant. Unfortunately, when we finished, they threw all our stuff off the back of the stage ...'

The festival was broadcast on Belgian radio, and subsequently bootlegged *ad nauseum*; unfortunately, neither the radio nor the boots include that version of 'A Forest', leaving it to live on only in the annals of Cure legend.

A number of other shows on these tours were recorded: the best known, perhaps, was that which took place in Sittard, the Netherlands, on 24 June. Shortly before the band took the stage, news came through that Tolhurst's mother had passed away. A tape of the entire concert was played at her funeral.

(LIVE) unspecified venue (Australia/New Zealand) August 1981
    8111 The Drowning Man
ORIGINAL RELEASE: *Curiosity – Live 1977-1984*, Fiction FIX 10, October 1984;

(LIVE) Capital Theatre, Sydney, 17 August 1981
    8112 Faith
ORIGINAL RELEASE: 12-inch b-side, FICS 14

COMMENTS: The Australian/New Zealand dates fell midway between visits to the US and Canada, which themselves were book-ended by tours of the UK and Europe. Taken from that outing, these beautifully clean recordings of two *Faith* mainstays offer a welcome glimpse into the ease with which the new material adapted to the live arena.

(SINGLE) Charlotte Sometimes
  8113 Charlotte Sometimes
  8114 Splintered in Her Head
  8112 Faith (live)
ORIGINAL RELEASE: Fiction FICS 14, October 1981
COMMENTS: A non-LP track, 'Charlotte Sometimes' was titled from the Penelope Farmer book, and boasted a Mike Mansfield-directed video to match. The song itself, however, only obliquely references the source, as the Cure continue driving through the fogs of *Faith*, but skew them with one of their most beguiling melodies, which itself is enhanced by the genuinely atmospheric harmonies.

On the 7-inch flip, 'Splintered In Her Head' (a line found, again, within Farmer's *Charlotte Sometimes*) is another in the long line of brittle Cure near-instrumentals, a tribal duet for bass and drums, over which the guitar echoes a belligerent elephant call; the 12-inch, meanwhile, appends ten minutes of the set-closing 'Faith', recorded live at Sydney's Capital Theatre on August 17 1981, and effective despite the apparently off-key bass that speeds through it.

'We played "Charlotte Sometimes" through for the first time when we went into the studio to record it,' Smith proudly informed the US magazine *Trouser Press*. 'The first take was perfect – although none of us told the others what to play at all. The B-side, though, "Splintered in Her Head," was pieced together: the drums were put down, then we sat and thought about what to put on top. Simon tried bass parts until bass and drums meshed, then I tried some guitar over that. So both sides were completely different processes. The only thing that runs through it all is that we are primarily concentrating on the atmosphere we want to create – and then, of course, Lol usually thinks of a title.'

An otherwise unreleased edit of 'Charlotte Sometimes' was featured on the Dutch compilation *Modern Dance* later in the year.

(LIVE) unspecified venue, November 1981
  8115 The Funeral Party
ORIGINAL RELEASE: Curiosity – Live 1977-1984, Fiction FIX 10, October 1984
COMMENTS: Of all the songs that made up *Faith*, few have the sheer emotive strength of 'Funeral Party', the one song (the title track included) that captures all the keening emotion, pleading heartache and ethereal beauty that otherwise takes an entire album to enunciate.

Live, too, it was an unimpeachable highlight – the sort of song that would, in later years, provoke entire audiences to start waving cigarette lighters (or, latterly, illuminated cell phones) in the air, while swaying, eyes closed, to an overture that is part-requiem, part-nursery rhyme, and partly responsible for a lot of what passed as Ultravox-shaped pomp rock as the year continued.

This particular rendition was recorded during the band's latest UK tour, an outing that saw them joined by And Also The Trees and Steve Severin and Lydia Lunch's 1313.

(TV) *Megahertz* (European TV) December 1981
UNR The Figurehead
ORIGINAL RELEASE: unreleased
COMMENTS: Counting down to their return to the studio, to begin work on the follow-up to *Faith*, an early indication that the new material was, if anything, even bleaker than that the band was currently touting.

(ALBUM) Various artists: *Fast Forward* cassette magazine
8116 One Hundred Years (demo)
ORIGINAL RELEASE: Fast Forward 008/009 cassette magazine, December 1981
COMMENTS: To accompany an interview conducted during the Cure's Australian dates, the Cure also handed over an otherwise unavailable demo of the then-unreleased 'One Hundred Years'.

Fast Forward would include an additional Robert Smith interview with issue 13.

1982

LINE-UP #5 (to June 1982) Robert Smith (vocals, guitar), Simon Gallup (bass), Lol Tolhurst (drums)
LINE-UP #6 Robert Smith (vocals, guitar, bass etc), Lol Tolhurst (keyboards), Steve Severin (bass etc – 'Lament'), Steve Goulding (drums – 'Let's Go To Bed').

(RADIO) BBC, John Peel, 4 January 1982 (rec 21 Dec)
   UNR The Figurehead
   UNR A Hundred Years
   UNR Siamese Twins
   UNR The Hanging Garden (incomplete/not broadcast)
ORIGINAL RELEASE: unreleased
COMMENTS: A haunting, haunted session, cut short by time constraints with just three songs in a state fit for broadcast – but what there was, was spectacular. An ultra-aggressive guitar ushers in 'One Hundred Years', with the lingering threat of that opening line ('it doesn't matter if we all die') still resonating in the ears when the song ends, a little over five minutes later.

A deliciously desolate 'Siamese Twins' marks a career-best rendering – sparse and jangly, the guitars and percussion dance behind a vocal that is already weary and lost, but whereas the band's last Peel session was very much a window into a work-in-progress, it is clear that, this time, the bulk of the finished album already exists on paper.

The one exception to this is 'The Figurehead', which kicks off as a continuation of 'Splintered In Her Head', its minute-long intro giving few indications whatsoever of how the next six would resolve themselves; instantly identifiable today, the song is nevertheless patently awaiting a final paring-down.

(TV) *Echo des Bananas* (France) 11 April 1982
   UNR The Figurehead
   UNR Cold
   UNR Play For Today
   UNR Hanging Garden
   UNR A Forest
   UNR One Hundred Years
ORIGINAL RELEASE: unreleased
COMMENTS: A week before the Cure returned to the road with the *14 Explicit Moments* tour (it opened in Plymouth on 18 April), French television was treated to an early taste of the new live set, four 'new' songs interrupted with

a pair of *Seventeen Seconds* survivors.

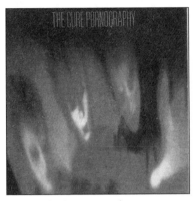

(ALBUM) *Pornography*
　8201 One Hundred Years
　8202 A Short Term Effect
　8203 The Hanging Garden
　8204 Siamese Twins
　8205 The Figurehead
　8206 A Strange Day
　8207 Cold
　8208 Pornography

ORIGINAL RELEASE: Fiction FIX 7, April 1982

COMMENTS: 'I was very proud of *Pornography*, but no-one else liked it" – Robert Smith.

'That's the one album that stood the test of time,' marveled Lol Tolhurst in 2004. 'It's Robert's main touchstone and I know why. We were still reasonably new, even though that was our fourth album, and it was the most pure version of the Cure, of what was there. It was a time when we actually managed to capture, in the best way, what was going on with us. Even though it was the most fractious period, it was quite insane the way things were going; but, looking back at it, despite that, we still managed to capture the soul of what it was about.'

Unfortunately, by the time the Cure came to make the record, that soul was as shattered as it ever could be; and if, as one reviewer claimed, *Faith* had taken no prisoners, *Pornography* would not even recognize its allies. It was going to wipe out everyone.

'My attitude was: it's all rubbish, we're rubbish, so let's go out with a bang,' Smith told *The Guardian* two decades later. 'I wrote all the songs in a windmill over one weekend. We slept very little during the recording, there was a lot of drugs involved, and the stage shows that followed were just brawls between us and the audience. It's strange because that's not my nature at all, and it wasn't even fun. In fact it was really, really awful.'

'The album was about things that have far-reaching effects,' Smith gallantly continued. 'It was far more considered about... some of the horrors that people go through just in everyday living, I suppose.' And it was indicative of just how heavily those horrors had impacted that the Cure felt they faced no alternative but to allow them to affect the band itself, as though they could not truly describe the nightmare unless they dreamed it themselves. It would be some time later before Smith could confess, 'I hate the idea that you'd die for your audience, [but] I was rapidly becoming enmeshed in that around the time of *Pornography*; the idea that Ian Curtis had gone first [the Joy Division vocalist committed suicide in May 1980] and I was soon to follow. I wasn't prepared for that to happen.'

What he was prepared for, however, was the arc that the Cure's career had taken; later, indeed, Smith would admit that, in many ways, the direction the band forged for itself, and the fate that awaited it at the conclusion of that journey, had been planned beforehand.

Even today, it is unlikely whether the Cure will ever escape from the three-headed hydra of *Seventeen Seconds*, *Faith* and *Pornography*. They are, almost unquestionably, the band's greatest albums; they may even rank amongst the greatest albums ever made, triplets of such unrelenting pressure and intensity that the very act of listening to them leaves one feeling both purged and punished. Imagine, then, what it must have done to the people who made them.

Smith continued, 'after *Three Imaginary Boys*, which I hated straight away, to pull off a three-year project like *Seventeen Seconds* to *Pornography*, I realized we couldn't be seen to do it in a half-hearted way, so we threw ourselves into a whole lifestyle that was a vicious circle. By *Pornography* we weren't having any fun, and it seemed pointless because, by then, we were only doing it for other people and it all fell apart.

'The difference between now and then – whenever "then" was – is that it was all pure autobiography, taken exclusively from things that had worked me up to the point where I'd write a song. Now I can take situations which don't really upset my equilibrium, I can hear something we could do musically, and I'll write a song to complement it – which, in the old days I would never ever do. I had no interest in it, I just wanted to put my own point of view across, and say this is how I feel about something, and the music was just a backdrop.'

The very recording of *Pornography*, Smith confessed, was 'horrifying, chaotic... but not in a nice way. It was a very vicious, anarchic way. I seriously don't remember making a lot of it.' The first blow fell when long-time engineer Mike Hedges announced he would be unavailable for the sessions, having already been poached by Siouxsie and the Banshees. (The group turned instead to Phil Thornally, fresh from working with Duran Duran and the Thompson Twins).

The normally supportive Chris Parry was unhappy. Tolhurst continued, "in the early days, if I look back on it, the places Chris Parry took us, the things he gently nudged us towards, they all worked. And even some of the things he nudged us towards that we rebelled against, worked as well. At the time we came up with *Pornography*, that was the last kind of album that he wanted us to do; he always said *Pornography* was this little triangle of people that nobody could get inside; to him he thought it was going straight down the drain.'

Smith tried to justify the downbeat mood of the album by insisting, 'I don't think it's in the human nature to write inspiring material about happiness. It's just meant to be enjoyed. You can really wallow in sadness.' But still he knew that the sheer weight of the new album was going to prove shocking... as he demonstrated with his choice for its title. Indeed, Polydor reacted to Smith's first pronouncement on that subject by insisting, 'whether or not it goes out under that title remains to be seen.'

Neither was the vista to be lightened any when the media finally got its hands on the album. 'I'm hard-pressed to find any redeeming features," grouched *Melody Maker*, a bad-tempered condemnation that was to be echoed throughout a music press which had expected the new Cure album to be a lot of things, but had never even dreamed of such rancour or vitriol. 'Pornography,' *Melody Maker* continued, 'plummets like a leaking submarine into depths unfathomable by man. Frankly, it's unhealthy. "One Hundred Years" is the least depressing track; it's merely gloomy.'

The *NME* described *Pornography* evocatively, if not enthusiastically, as the sound of 'Phil Spector in Hell,' a reference to the wall of unrelenting sound against which the songs banged their heads; and, again, there can be few less marketable openings to an album than those first lines that had already shocked the John Peel listenership.

Nor, as the album continued on, had the pop kids ever been offered a more savage indictment of the human condition than the tales of betrayal, dissolution and ultimately, disgust that permeate *Pornography*'s most dynamic quarters. And, finally, never has an audience been tempted with an album whose most pervasive aura was that of a band purposefully tearing itself into shreds, simply to see how far it could throw the fragments. As Smith himself has said since, when you are only selling 50,000 records worldwide, you have to do something to get yourself noticed. The Cure chose to destroy itself.

Although *Pornography* remains a touchstone to which Smith has continued to refer back to, the writer himself is surprisingly dismissive of the record. 'If you were to be totally dispassionate, which I suppose is impossible... but, if you listen to those [early] albums on merit, they don't stand up to the later albums, not even emotionally and certainly not the song-writing. There's a completeness to the later albums that just isn't there.

'You're not really gonna expect someone who buys *Standing On A Beach* or *Galore* to then buy *Faith*, and sit back and say, "ah my life's changed." I don't think you're gonna buy the *Wish* album, and then think, "I'm gonna check out their back catalogue and pick up *Seventeen Seconds*. They're still good songs, but it's older fans who are gonna like the early stuff best because they were younger when we did it.' And though, perhaps wisely (in view of much of its lyrical content), he stops short of describing *Pornography* as the old lover you never quite got over, somehow the point is made.

The counter to this argument, of course, can only ever be made from a personal viewpoint, simply because the songs themselves are never less than intense and intensely personal. But they are universal too.

STOP PRESS! 2005 BONUS DISC "Rarities 1981-1982"

Details of the 2005 Deluxe Edition were released as this book went to press. Contents are as follows:

PREVIOUSLY AVAILABLE MATERIAL

8211 All Mine

PREVIOUSLY UNRELEASED HOME INSTRUMENTAL DEMO (November 1981)

Break

PREVIOUSLY UNRELEASED RHINO STUDIO INSTRUMENTAL DEMOS (December 1981)

Demise

Temptation

The Figurehead

The Hanging Garden

One Hundred Years

PREVIOUSLY UNRELEASED SOUNDTRACK RECORDING (March 1982)

Airlock: The Soundtrack

PREVIOUSLY UNRELEASED LIVE MATERIAL

Cold (Hammersmith Odeon 5/82)

A Strange Day (Hammersmith Odeon 5/82)

Pornography (Hammersmith Odeon 5/82)

A Short Term Effect (Brussels 6/82)

Siamese Twins (Brussels 6/82)

PREVIOUSLY UNRELEASED ROBERT SMITH STUDIO DEMO (July 1982)

Temptation Two

COMMENTS: Following on from his almost-revisionist approach to *Faith*, Smith again delved deep into the archive to conjure up a fresh face to *Pornography*, although (as with *Seventeen Seconds*), the nature of the beast was already so well-defined in his mind that little about the new material truly shocks the listener... that treat is saved until the very end of the disc, as 'Temptation Two' bounces out of the band's disbandment to herald the dawn of an entire new era. Although 'Let's Go To Bed' (for that is what this demo became) never sounded like this.

Three songs considered for *Pornography*, but ultimately cast adrift, are included here in rough form. The sound across the band's instrumental demos is, typically, raw enough to mask any especially outstanding qualities, although 'Break' is pure Pornography, regardless of the mud and muffles. ('Demise,' on the other hand, is positively shiny, by comparison.)

Alternate lyrics and, to an extent, arrangements flitter through the Rhino Studio demos – a magnificent version of 'The Figurehead' actually rivals the familiar album take. And it is criminal that we've had to wait this long to hear 'Airlock,' a stark slab of discordant piano atmosphere that takes its lead from the three-year-old 'The Final Sound,' but goes so much further than that –

imagine Philip Glass performing in a wild west saloon. The full 13 minutes probably won't demand too many repeat listens, but once or twice will clean you brain out nicely.

(LIVE) Manchester Apollo, 27 April 1982
    8209 Killing An Arab
    8210 A Forest
ORIGINAL RELEASE: bonus 45 included with Fiction FICG 15, July 1982
COMMENTS: Two old warhorses given an energetic, but somewhat perfunctory run out, five nights before the conclusion of the UK tour.

(LIVE) London 1 May 1982
    8211 All Mine
ORIGINAL RELEASE: *Curiosity* – Live 1977-1984, Fiction FIX 10, October 1984
COMMENTS: Taken from the final night of the British tour, 'All Mine' is one of those rare numbers that have occasionally frequented the Cure's live set, but were never taken into the studio. However, it does offer up some very valid suggestions as to how the fifth Cure album might have sounded, had the band not broken up instead. Clearly unformed, a lyric in search of a thrashing accompaniment, and suffering from a too-abrupt ending, it is impossible to predict how dramatically the number might have ultimately shaped up, but its inclusion on *Curiosity* (alongside the similarly under-exposed 'Forever') at least confirmed that Smith had not forgotten it.

(RADIO) Paris Olympia, 7 June 1982
    UNR Figurehead
    UNR M
    UNR Drowning Man
    UNR Short Term Effect
    UNR Cold
    UNR At Night
    UNR Splintered In Her Head
    UNR Three Imaginary Boys
    UNR Siamese Twins
    UNR Primary
    UNR One Hundred Years
    UNR The Hanging Garden
    UNR Play For Today
    UNR A Strange Day
    UNR A Forest
    UNR Pornography
    UNR 10.15 Saturday Night
    UNR Killing An Arab
    UNR All Mine

IN BETWEEN DAYS

ORIGINAL RELEASE: unreleased

COMMENTS: This French Radio 7 recording captures the first of two nights at the Paris Olympia, just four days before the scheduled end of the tour... and the unscheduled end of the 'original' band's lifetime; and the tensions that had been drawn out across the past two months are present for all to hear. The somewhat murky sound of the bootleg translations of this show are *not* a drawback... this is what the band actually sounded like now, and the screaming discordance of the near-eleven minute 'All Mine' that closes the show, all echo and angles, offers up an epitaph that most bands would need to die for.

Even with the original set jumbled somewhat by the broadcast and the bootlegs, from the pounding overture that leads 'The Figurehead' into view, this is an amazing document. The set-closing 'Pornography' is truly suffocating; 'Splintered In Her Head' is grinding and painful, while the versions of 'Three Imaginary Boys' and '10.15 Saturday Night' are searing shards of sound that are scarcely recognizable even after they've resolved themselves into familiar themes – indeed, the roar of relief that oozes out of the audience as the latter kicks in travels so far beyond celebration that you wonder how they'd ever managed to sit through the rest of the show.

Twenty years later, Smith and Gallup would revisit these same pastures within the *Trilogy* series of concerts, recreating the entire *Pornography* album for the benefit of an audience that, for the most part, was barely even alive when this concert took place. But neither, as this recording makes plain, was the band.

Pornography was a harrowing album, but the accompanying tour has gone down in rock 'n' roll folklore as one of the most disastrous, in personal terms, any band has ever undertaken. 'The tour was like a rerun of the worst movie you've ever seen,' Gallup shuddered later. 'We were cracking up, so all the people offstage began to fall apart as well. Twenty-three people reverting to primitive is not a pretty sight.'

On another occasion, Smith recoiled, 'everyone involved in that tour disintegrated somehow, their characters became distended. They seemed to revert back to something horrible inside them, and there was a lot of physical violence. We just took our lives up onto the stage. It was a distressing time, and it made me go quite odd for about eighteen months. It all got too intense and depressing, everything was wrong, we were stagnating, me and Simon were fighting and we hadn't got anywhere.'

Audiences were another disappointment, as Tolhurst explained. 'I think about this. In the early days, the tours started off with a few people, then the next time a few more people, and the third time it was house full everywhere. And that had been the point up until *Pornography*. Every time we went out, slightly bigger venues, more people. And when we did *Pornography,* we hadn't actually released it when we went on the road, so we were just playing *Pornography* to people in these huge halls that were about ... less than half full, tiny amounts of people, and that kind of made it look absurd.

'That was the first and probably the only time I remember that happening with the Cure. We started off with two or three hundred people, then a thousand, then three thousand, and it seemed okay, another album, another tour and it'll be bigger. And that kind of happened with *Pornography*, but the other way around. I distinctly remember playing some place in Germany, with about 150 people in a 10,000 seater hall which was kinda weird... we sat on the edge of the stage and invited everybody up and they sat in the first couple of rows and we just sort of did it like that, played to an intimate audience in this huge cavern.'

It was in Strasbourg, on 27 May, that Smith and Gallup fell into the fight that would precipitate the end of the latest line-up. Tolhurst recalled, 'we went out that night, to a club; we had an Irish band opening for us, Zerra 1, and they came out with us and I was sitting in the corner of this club with them, and suddenly there was this big commotion at the bar. Then somebody came up and said "oh, Robert and Simon just had this big fight," and I was oh, okay... they'd gone by that time so I just carried on, stayed at the club for a couple more hours, went back to the hotel, then woke up the next morning to find that both of them had got on a plane back to England. Robert had left a very cryptic note at the front desk for the tour manager, something about not being able to laugh.'

Attempts to find out what was happening were fruitless; neither Gallup nor Smith's phones were being answered, and it was still too early to catch anybody in the Fiction offices. 'I was talking to the Zerra 1 guys, saying "we've got a show tonight and tomorrow, and I don't know what we're going to do....So I thought, maybe what we could do was – we'd recorded a few of the shows, so we'll play the tape of the show, put wigs on the Zerra 1 guys, turn the lights a little lower and nobody would notice. And we seriously considered that for about two minutes, and then I got a phone call from Fiction, saying Robert wants to take a couple of days off and then he's going to come back. So I said okay... and it was the first time we'd ever cancelled any shows. We missed one or two, now and again, by not getting there on time, but we'd never actually cancelled.'

Tolhurst spent the next few days relaxing by the shores of Lake Geneva, waiting for his errant bandmates to return; but their reunion was but a respite. Tempers held for another fortnight, but the final show in Brussels, Belgium, on 11 June, was Gallup's last. 'There's a lot of things I'd rather do than trek around countries being drunk and playing to drunk people,' he declared.

'The atmosphere between Gallup and Smith had become murderous,' *Mojo* magazine later reflected of that final show. 'Backstage, Smith refused to sing, insisting that he was going to play the drums. Gallup elected to play guitar, drummer Lol Tolhurst played bass. The ensuing racket was further enlivened by roadie Gary Biddles, who staggered on stage, grabbed the microphone, and began shouting about what a cunt Robert Smith was. Another fight ensued. While Smith and Biddles and Gallup punched it out, and the audience whistled and booed, the hapless Tolhurst dutifully kept playing the bass.'

'We weren't in the best of health mentally,' Smith confirmed. 'Night after night playing those songs. Most nights after the show were pretty demented as a response to what we were doing musically. I was in a really depressed frame of mind between 1981 and 1982, and I was taking an awful lot of drugs, anything and everything. We all were. It was all right, because we were young enough to cope with it, but inevitably, it sent your mental equilibrium awry. Looking back, I was really disappointed with what we were doing. I thought we should be going somewhere else, not in success terms, but I thought we should be making music that was on a par with Mahler symphonies, not pop music. I was completely fed up with what the group was, in every way. I thought we were going downhill. I just felt I was not doing what I wanted to do, your classic early twenties crisis.'

'We got home and that was it,' says Tolhurst. 'Robert said "I don't know about all this, I'm off".' Gallup, too, fled immediately, hooking up with Biddles and Matthieu Hartley in a new band, Cry. And the Cure, to all intents and purposes, were no more.

(SINGLE) The Hanging Garden
    8203 The Hanging Garden
    8201 One Hundred Years
    8209 A Forest (live)
    8210 Killing An Arab (live)
ORIGINAL RELEASE: Fiction FICS 15, July 1982
COMMENTS: Released, perhaps, as much out of habit as any need to actually flag *Pornography* with a 45, 'The Hanging Garden' is more memorable for the limited edition bonus live disc that helped inch it up the charts (it reached #34, the Cure's biggest hit since 'A Forest'), than for the record itself. Released around a month after the conclusion of the *14 Explicit Moments* tour, it was less a 'new' single, after all, than a tombstone.

(SINGLE) Lament
    8212 Lament
ORIGINAL RELEASE: Flexipop 022,November 1982
COMMENTS: Smith and girlfriend Mary took off for a camping trip in Wales. Tolhurst took a month's vacation in Europe, then parked his drums to one side, in favour of mastering keyboards: as a child, his music teacher sister had driven him to a certain degree of confidence and competence; now, he was taking formal lessons from 'a little old lady who used to rap me on the knuckles if I got anything wrong.'

Neither he nor Smith could ever imagine the Cure stirring again.

'I despaired about the whole business,' Smith mourned. 'Being in a band, being involved in the music bit. After a while, it takes you over and you can't see out of it. It's important for me to have a sense of myself as a person outside of all this...' and the cold truth was, he had lost that.

Of course, the split was eventually proven to be nothing more than a simple parting of the ways. Refreshed from their breaks, and the wholesale dismantling of their next year's schedule, Smith and Tolhurst would regroup, and that would turn out to be more than sufficient. But things were looking very shaky when *Flexipop* magazine requested an exclusive Cure track for a forthcoming freebie flexidisc. Smith promptly donated the recorder-laden electro-pulse of 'Lament', a song he recorded with Steve Severin, and which was markedly less representative of the Cure, than it was indicative of another looming Smith/Severin side project, the psychedelic Glove.

Neither was he likely to have the time to consider a future for the Cure, as Severin's Banshees bandmates overcame the November 1982 departure of guitarist John McGeoch (who, in turn, had replaced Smith following his last tour of duty) by recalling Smith to active service. And, while Siouxsie was pointedly adamant that he had no creative input whatsoever in the band ('Fat Boy', she sniffed, 'just plays what he's told'), still Smith was moved to ask *Melody Maker*, 'do the Cure really exist anymore? I've been pondering that question myself.'

Years later, he told Banshees biographer Mark Paytress, 'when Severin asked me to come and be in the Banshees, I thought "yes, that's what I want to do." It allowed me to play serious music, big chords and, crucially, I was no longer the focal point. I was just the guitarist. Playing with the Banshees was different to playing with the Cure. It was big music, dead loud on stage.'

Siouxsie, for her part, was simply left to count the cost of publicly describing Smith by a nickname she had long used in private. 'It's really funny. When I called Robert that [in print], there were lots of letters saying "how dare that Siouxsie! Who DOES she think she is?". He calls me... well, we all have unflattering names we use. We're just cartoon characters when we're all together. But it's all nasty fun really. When I'm being nice I tend to bear-hug people, so I don't know which is worse.'

(SINGLE) Let's Go To Bed
   8213 Let's Go To Bed
   8213a Let's Go To Bed (extended version)
   8214 Just One Kiss
ORIGINAL RELEASE: Fiction FICS 17, November 1982
COMMENTS: With Smith having apparently already determined his immediate future, Fiction head Chris Parry finally convened a band meeting in October,

1982, to try and sort out the state of the Cure, and request a new single. Smith and Tolhurst alone attended, but that was enough; encouraged by Parry's own enthusiasm, the pair agreed to make a new record, but vowed at the same time to ensure it would destroy the myth of the Cure forever.

Smith reflected, 'When Ian Curtis died in 1980, I have known that people thought that I was going to be the next one on the list: well, we have been somehow a bit excessive about things at that time, and so it was kind of natural for people to consider things like me dead very soon. But these things kind of bothered me and, meanwhile, the group wasn't working well and I started asking myself what I really wanted, as that lifestyle didn't really fit to me anymore.

'The only thing to escape this monster, that I have contributed to build up, was to destroy it. My reaction towards all those people who thought that The Cure could only be pessimistic and negative, ... and predictable, all the time, was to make a demented and calculated song like "Let's Go To Bed": the purpose was specifically to destroy our image and then somehow start it all again.'

With drummer Steve Goulding – most recently sighted behind Wreckless Eric's band – the pair began work on 'Let's Go To Bed', an unabashed pop song of such buoyancy that, as its release date loomed, Smith himself was stricken by a major dose of cold feet, and suggested it be released instead as a solo Robert Smith single. Parry refused.

Smith told *Flexipop*, '"I don't think it's a Cure song. I wanted it released under a different name like we did with "Cult Hero" a couple of years ago. It's not that Cure songs are a formula but they do share a central core. This single has been released to get major daytime radio play.

'It's disappointing to me, because it's the first time we've been seen to be involved in current trends or fashions. There's probably only a few thousand people who've held us up as an example to themselves but if I were one of them, I'd feel let down. For us to be seen to be bothering to compete in an arena I don't respect upsets me. When you spend time in a band trying to achieve certain goals, you don't want to betray them.'

Today, too, Smith acknowledges, 'I never sit down and think I'll write a song. I can't sit down in a calculating manner and say "I will write a song about...." I have done it, but the songs that come out are like "Let's Go To Bed"... very flat. They're good on a certain level, but they don't resonate.'

But that was the point. Smith wanted to shatter the Cure's dreary image, and the playful 'Let's Go To Bed', with its catchy chorus and doo-doo-doo-doo backing vocals, and a seven-plus minute dance remix for the 12-inch, could not have been further removed from that.

Neither could the video, as Smith was introduced to director Tim Pope, who subsequently admitted to *Mojo*, 'something in my fetid imagination just fitted in with Robert's fetid imagination. For the "Let's Go To Bed" video, he was very, very shy. I don't know whether the videos brought him out of his shell, I just think I happened to be around at a time when he wanted to come out of his shell. To be honest with you, I haven't a clue. We always used to pretend we understood what each other was saying, but I don't think either of us had a fucking clue.'

No matter. The project not only reinvented the Cure, it reinvigorated them, knocking them off the gloom-enshrouded pedestal upon which they had so recently moped, and allowing them a luxury which so few artists are ever granted – the chance to start again with a clean slate, and continue doing so forever more.

By proving so irreverently that there really was no such thing as a 'typical' Cure record (at least until you flipped it over, and heard the *Pornography*-esque 'Just One Kiss'), Smith had conjured for the band an option that only David Bowie, with his own continual self-reinvention, had ever successfully exercised in the past. Keep moving, keep changing, keep confusing people. And, so long as those people cared enough to keep moving and changing with them, the future was theirs for the taking.

(RADIO) BBC, David Jensen, 1 November 1982 (rec 24 Oct)
   UNR Let's Go To Bed
   UNR Just One Kiss
   UNR One Hundred Years
   UNR Ariel
ORIGINAL RELEASE: unreleased
COMMENTS: With Goulding again along for the ride, Smith and Tolhurst turned in relatively straightforward versions of one album track, both sides of the new single, and one song, 'Ariel', that has never reappeared since then, and which has since described by Smith as a song intended for the solo album he has now been threatening for 20 years.

1983

LINE-UP #7 Robert Smith (vocals, guitar), Lol Tolhurst (keyboards), Derek Thompson (keyboards – 'The Walk'), Phil Thornally (bass), Andy Anderson (drums)

(TV) *Riverside Ballet* (UK) 17 March 1983
  UNR Siamese Twins
ORIGINAL RELEASE: unreleased
COMMENTS: Having spent the last three months on tour with the Banshees, venturing as far afield as Australia, New Zealand and Japan, Smith returned to London to meet with Nicholas Dixon, choreographer with the Royal Ballet, initially to discuss scoring *Les Enfants Terrible*. Ultimately agreeing that this might be too grandiose a first step, the pair instead embarked upon a somewhat smaller project, based around *Pornography*'s 'Siamese Twins'. Screened on BBC2's *Riverside*, with Smith and Tolhurst joined by Steve Severin and Marc Almond's Venomettes string section, the ensuing performance was well-received, but did not lead to any further such collaboration.

(TV) *Oxford Road Show* (UK) April 1983
  UNR One Hundred Years
  UNR The Figurehead
ORIGINAL RELEASE:
COMMENTS: Although Smith was now spending most of his time in the studio with Steve Severin, working towards their Glove project, he accepted an invitation for the Cure to appear on the BBC's *Oxford Road Show*, and pieced together another new line-up featuring Brilliant drummer Andy Anderson and SPK bassist Derek Thompson alongside Smith and Tolhurst.

The show's own team requested that the band perform both sides of the 'Let's Go To Bed' single. Smith preferred to unearth two more tracks from *Pornography*. 'It was great being on the same programme as Kajagoogoo,' he enthused afterwards.

(SINGLE) The Walk
  8301 The Walk
  8302 The Dream
  8303 The Upstairs Room
  8304 Lament
ORIGINAL RELEASE: Fiction FICS 18, July 1983

COMMENTS: With 'Let's Go To Bed' having peaked no higher than #44, the second in what the duo was now terming their 'fantasy trilogy,' the synth and beat thumping 'The Walk', was recorded immediately after the *Oxford Road Show* performance and ran, equally swiftly, into a barrage of comparisons with New Order's recently released 'Blue Monday'.

In fact, similarities between the two songs owed more to the technology of the time, then to any musical magpie-ing, as Tolhurst recalls. 'For us... we'd obviously heard that and liked it a lot, but there wasn't a conscious decision to make something like that. I think part of the reason it ended up sounding like that was because we had Steve Nye, the first producer we'd ever worked with, and I can remember we got this big Oberheim set up with a drum machine, a sequencer and the keyboards, and I sat down and read the manual... and it was pretty confusing.' In fact, the very beginning of 'The Walk' is a mistake; 'that first note that starts it off, before everything else comes in, was because we couldn't figure out how to switch the sequencer off at the beginning, when we triggered it. So we just thought "oh well, we'll incorporate it into the track".'

The electronic direction of 'The Walk' was very much Tolhurst's responsibility. As far back as the band's first demos, Smith had nicknamed his best friend the X-factor... 'because I liked all the people like Can, bands who would experiment with different things and approaches, whereas the rest of the band – Robert and Michael, then Robert and Simon – were a bit more Luddite in their approach to everything. Unless you could spank it or hit it to make a sound, they weren't very interested.

'But, in Robert's defence, he was always very open-minded about that. He wouldn't necessarily want to do something, but if I did, he'd let me. Even in the early days, I'd been having little bits and pieces added to my kit, little electronic things... little triggers that would make one particular noise (the percussive swish that sweeps through 'A Forest' is one such) and then fall apart after four months. So I'd always been interested in the electronic side and, having already picked up keyboards again, because that was the direction a lot of the technology was moving in, things just developed.'

The single soared to #12, disturbing Smith with the knowledge that 'ten times as many people bought "the Walk" than did "Charlotte Sometimes." But I don't worry about it. They're not released to compete.' Still he acknowledged, 'I'd rather listen to "One Hundred Years" than "The Walk",' and admitted 'I suspected something was up when my mum liked it. She normally hates any Cure stuff that I play her.'

Of the three b-sides spread between the 7-inch and 12-inch pressings, the most remarkable was probably 'Lament', rerecorded from the *Flexipop* version of the previous year, with Smith subsequently noting, 'I'd had a few weeks to think about it, work out the parts and the words, and it had turned into a really nice song.' 'The Upstairs Room', too, had a Severin link – Smith wrote it while sleeping on the floor in the Banshee bassist's flat, the upstairs room itself.

'The Dream', meanwhile, was recorded with the same Oberheim synth set-up as 'The Walk', with Smith acknowledging former Ariola-Hansa stablemates

Japan as a reference 'because I loved what [Steve Nye] had got on their album *Tin Drum*, and I wanted something along those lines.' The Cure, he laughed, were 'off on a short holiday to Electropopland,' but 'The Dream' should not be overlooked, if only for its similarities to recent (and subsequent) releases by the Thompson Twins.

And, to return to the New Order comparisons... the Mancunians got their own back when they borrowed the descending doll sequence from the accompanying Tim Pope-directed video, for inclusion in their own 'Blue Monday 88' remake video.

(TV) *Top Of The Pops* (UK) 7 July 1983
　　UNR The Walk
ORIGINAL RELEASE: unreleased
COMMENTS: Andy Anderson and Easy Cure-era guitarist Porl Thompson joined Smith and Tolhurst for the Cure's first *TOTP* appearance; *Pornography* co-producer Phil Thornally appeared at the second. Tolhurst explained, 'we did the video for "The Walk" in St John's Wood, which was just down the road from where we'd done *Pornography*, so on our lunch break we went and saw if Phil was around, asked him if he wanted to play bass on the road, and he said yes.' That video, in the meantime, languished largely unaired – the BBC apparently objected to the sight of Smith and Tolhurst in make-up.

Melody Maker reacted bemusedly to the band's sudden pre-eminence. 'The Cure on *TOTP* was an event almost as absurd as Jimmy Saville's inanity. They looked and acted bored but, all across the nation, Cure fans, Cure converts, and folk who can't tell the Cure from Culture Club and couldn't care less, interpreted Smith's stifled yawns as enigmatic arrogance. Such is the power of reputation, such is the impact of dressing in black.'

(RADIO) BBC, David Jensen, 21 September 1983 (rec 26 Aug)
　　UNR Speak My Language
　　UNR Mr Pink Eyes
　　UNR The Lovecats
ORIGINAL RELEASE: unreleased
COMMENTS: August 1983 saw the Cure finally confirm their rebirth, as the new line-up of Smith, Tolhurst, Anderson and Thornally headlined the Elephant Fayre festival in St Germains, Cornwall; then slipped over to the United States for a handful of shows – where, much to Tolhurst's shock, they discovered precisely how big the Cure were becoming, without them even realizing it. 'After we put out "Let's Go To Bed' and 'The Walk', we came over for a short promo tour, and we went onstage at this small club in LA and it was berserk! And I thought "they like this? It was a bit of a joke, and they liked it?"

Both singles were 'simply entertainment,' Smith agreed, but they obviously struck a chord with both fans and band. Immediately upon their return home, the Cure decamped to the Studio Des Dames in Paris, there to record the most fantastical of the entire fantasy trilogy, 'Lovecats' – which was then granted its world première just days later, at a session for the BBC DJ formerly known as Kid.

(SINGLE) The Lovecats
   8305 The Lovecats
   8305a The Lovecats (video mix)
   8306 Speak My Language
   8307 Mr Pink Eyes
ORIGINAL RELEASE: Fiction FICS 19, October 1983; 8305a on *Staring At The Sea – The Images*.
COMMENTS: 'The Lovecats,' Smith insisted, 'fulfilled an idea to put out an amateurish pop song, rather than do an obvious follow-up to "The Walk." A year and a half ago, we wouldn't have released something like that, because it wouldn't have fit in with the idea of the Cure. The area we work in now,' he warned, 'is much looser.'

And 'loose' describes 'The Lovecats' to a tee, a playfully warm, doo-wop-rock-a-silly-billy-backing for a song that was originally inspired by a passage in author Patrick White's *The Cockatoos*, in which a litter of kittens is placed in a sack and thrown into the sea. 'That… was originally the start of the song's chorus,' Smith revealed. 'But when we were doing it, I thought I can't really sing this.'

Although Smith later confessed that 'if we purely did things like "The Lovecats" I'd hang myself,' the knockabout swing flavour of what *International Musician* termed 'their best single to date' was retained for the two b-sides, as the band took full advantage of the studio's own arsenal of unusual instrumentation.

Although Smith claims the harmonica powered 'Mr Pink Eyes' (written after he caught a glimpse of himself in the bathroom mirror) is one of his favourite Cure b-sides, neither it nor 'Speak My Language' are ever likely to make a Cure fan's all-time Top 10. But, as mementoes of a particular mood, that which yowled to effervescent fruition aboard 'The Lovecats', they are wonderfully, wonderfully, wonderfully pretty regardless.

Tim Pope's video for the single, truly one of the greatest collaborations in the two teams' long partnership, is of especial interest in that its soundtrack offers up a markedly different, and deliriously looser take on the familiar single version.

(TV) *Top Of The Pops* (UK) 27 October 1983
   UNR The Lovecats

(TV) *Echo des Bananas* (France) October 1983
   UNR The Lovecats
ORIGINAL RELEASE:unreleased
COMMENTS: Suddenly, the Cure were becoming *TOTP* regulars – a realisation that Smith marked by forgetting the words to the song. He continued to be

disparaging of the Cure's newfound celebrity, however. 'We don't smile enough to fit in [on *TOTP*]. I find it really hard to pretend to see through that camera into the homes of those millions of people who are really going to love you. It's such a farce. I look really bored because I am.'

So, why do you keep doing it then?

'Because, if we didn't, someone else would.'

(TV) *Top Of The Pops* (UK) 25 December 1983

UNR The Lovecats

Dear Prudence (ROBERT SMITH with SIOUXSIE & THE BANSHEES)

ORIGINAL RELEASE:unreleased

COMMENTS: Back in the days when both *Top Of The Pops* and Christmas still mattered, the show's annual Xmas Day bash was an opportunity for all of the year's biggest hitmakers to gather for one long, mad, celebration of their success. But whoever would have expected Robert Smith to turn up twice, with the Cure and the Banshees?

1984

LINE-UP #8 (to October) Robert Smith (vocals, guitar), Porl Thompson (guitar, keyboards), Lol Tolhurst (keyboards), Phil Thornally (bass), Andy Anderson (drums)
LINE-UP #9 (October-November) Robert Smith (vocals, guitar), Porl Thompson (guitar, keyboards), Lol Tolhurst (keyboards), Phil Thornally (bass), Vince Ely (drums)
LINE-UP #10 (from November) Robert Smith (vocals, guitar), Porl Thompson (guitar, keyboards), Lol Tolhurst (keyboards), Phil Thornally (bass), Boris Williams (drums)

(RADIO) BBC, David Jensen, 22 February 1984 (rec 2 Feb)
    UNR Banana Fish Bones
    UNR Piggy In The Mirror
    UNR Give Me It
    UNR The Empty World
ORIGINAL RELEASE: unreleased

(TV) *Oxford Road Show* (UK) 24 February 1984
    UNR Shake Dog Shake
    UNR Give Me It
ORIGINAL RELEASE: unreleased
COMMENTS: With Smith dividing his time between the Cure and the Banshees, commuting between studios in London (Eel Pie) and Henley-On-Thames, it was a wonder that either band's new album was completed as quickly as it was. Nevertheless, by late February the Cure were ready to step out with their latest material, serving up a more-or-less straightforward rendering of four new songs for Jensen, and then (with bassist Norman Fisher Jones filling in for Thornally – himself in Australia, engineering the new Duran Duran album) two for the *Oxford Road Show*.

(SINGLE) The Caterpillar
    8401 The Caterpillar
    8402 Happy The Man
    8403 Throw Your Foot
ORIGINAL RELEASE: Fiction FICS 20, April 1984
COMMENTS: Had there not been a new album on the horizon, 'The Caterpillar' could easily have slotted into the fantasy trilogy, a song whose primary means of propulsion was the repetitious 'flicker-flicker-flicker' hook, and which relied as much on effects-ridden piano, barely audible mumblings and violin-ish squawks for its impact, as on anything so ordinary as a tune. But what a tune it was, a singalong

sing-song that inspired Tim Pope towards a video that was even more surreal than 'Lovecats', as an ornate greenhouse became the setting for a bug-encrusted band performance, and Chinese dragons danced alluringly out on the lawn.

Among the b-sides, 'Throw Your Foot' looked back towards 'Lovecats' in its generally jollity, while 'Happy The Man' borrowed its title from an old Genesis single, but was better compared to the Cure's own 'Descent', over which Smith whispered and even stuttered with absolute disregard for anything else going on around him.

(TV) *The Tube* (UK) 06 April 1984
    UNR Bananafishbones
    UNR Piggy In The Mirror
    UNR The Top
ORIGINAL RELEASE: unreleased
COMMENTS: A tremendous performance that peaked with a magnificent rendering of the sombre 'The Top'.

(TV) *Top Of The Pops* (UK) 12 April 1984
    UNR The Caterpillar
ORIGINAL RELEASE: unreleased
COMMENTS: Reviewing 'The Caterpillar' single, the *NME*'s Julie Burchill placed Smith firmly, cross-leggedly, 'in the garden of English eccentricity'; obviously taking her words to heart, the entire band sat thus for their next appearance on *TOTP*, although nobody was going to credit the journalist with inspiring that decision. 'We were knackered,' Smith explained. They'd been in the studio all night and, besides, 'why should we stand? Next time, I may go on in bed.'

(STUDIO) ROBERT SMITH – TIM POPE, Olympic Studios, April 1984
    8404 New Day
    8405 I Want To Be A Tree
    8406 Elephant Song
    8407 The Double Crossing of Two Faced Fred

ORIGINAL RELEASE: 8404 on *Half An Octopus* (Fiction FICST 23), 8405-07 Tim Pope single Fiction FIC 21, August 1984
COMMENTS: Video director Pope's first (and only) single was recorded in late December 1983, after Pope was asked to produce a new show-reel. He told *Zig Zag*'s Dave Thomas, 'I had to make [this] show reel, so I decided to go right over the top and do an hour and a half, really pretentious job, just to get all these ideas out of my system. I wanted to end it with something really stupid, so there was this song lying around which a friend and I had

written when I was 18.'

'We recorded it over Christmas [1983], then I called up various people who I'd worked with and who were in London at the time.' The original demo was recorded with one Charlie Gray, and the accompanying video, featuring contributions from the Style Council, Talk Talk, Paul Young, Freur (the future Underworld), the Banshees and Soft Cell, alongside the Cure, was screened on *Old Grey Whistle Test* early in 1984.

'It was all a huge joke, but within seven days of the show-reel going out, I'd been offered seven record deals.' He accepted Fiction's offer and set about rerecording the song with a more-or-less complete complement of Cure members behind him: Thompson, Anderson, Tolhurst, and Smith played a scintillatingly fuzz-drenched guitar, and made occasional 'boing'-ing sounds on 'I Want To Be A Tree', (Tolhurst alone provided percussion on 'Elephant Song'). A second video, featuring Pope alone (and dressed as a tree), accompanied the release.

Some down time during the Pope session also gave Smith the opportunity to cut one new Cure number, 'Shout', which in turn became 'New Day' before the evening was out. It was also the last song Smith would record before the madness and mayhem of the past months finally caught up with him. Returning to his hotel from the studio, he collapsed in the street. 'The last thing I remember was hearing someone say "an ambulance is on its way"'.

(ALBUM) *The Top*
  8408 Shake Dog Shake
  8409 Birdmad Girl
  8410 Wailing Wall
  8411 Give Me It
  8412 Dressing Up
  8401 The Caterpillar
  8413 Piggy In The Mirror
  8414 The Empty World
  8415 Bananafishbones

8416 The Top
ORIGINAL RELEASE: Fiction FIX 9, May 1984
COMMENTS: '*The Top* was really...' 20 years on, Lol Tolhurst remains speechless. '*Pornography* virtually finished the band; we came off the tour with that and we weren't going to do anything, but we did the three funny singles, which was fun to do, and then *The Top* was the first time we'd tried to get back as a unit, as the Cure, so there was a certain amount of hopeful experimentation.

'There's still a couple of songs on there, like "Bird Mad Girl," that I still listen to, and there are a few that are heavy going, but it was the middle of winter in Henley-On-Thames and I think a lot of that is reflected in the record.'

Indeed, *The Top* as a whole sat uncomfortably amid the welter of success that now surrounded the Cure; Smith himself described it as 'fucking deranged,' as a ragbag of styles and sounds removed not only from the single-minded themes of its long-playing predecessors, but perched firmly on the brink of a precipice that still possesses the ability to shock and alienate listeners – *The Top*'s reputation today as the 'forgotten' Cure album was not earned by accident.

'I think, subconsciously, I made the decision to make *The Top* different [from our other albums]. It does resemble our first LP more than anything we've done, in as much as there is a variety of moods and styles. But, although it's similar in its diversity, the content is very different.'

Smith claimed that *The Top* was one of two albums he could have chosen to release – the other comprised nothing but 'facile... singles... with really crass choruses' that the likes of Nik Kershaw or A-ha 'would die for.' He chose to keep that one out of sight, however; the rest of the band had heard the tape, but Smith was adamant that, though 'I've thought of releasing them under a pseudonym, I don't want people... you could write a shopping list, but you don't want to be best known for your shopping lists.'

Rather, he aimed for an album of ever-changing textures, and that despite later claiming (in sharp contradiction of the record's own musician credits) 'I played all the instruments except drums, [and] it was easy to get carried away in a dense mixture of sounds.' Still the record looped lushly from the wracked psychedelia of 'The Caterpillar' to the frantic punk of 'Give Me It', through the churning near-dance and demented poetics of 'Bird Mad Girl', and onto the super-playful flute-led 'Dressing Up' – one of the most tender sort-of-love songs Smith had penned to this point: 'Piggy In The Mirror' has a vocal that might have been left on a bus by David Bowie, and the portentous dirge of 'The Empty World', with its stylistic foretastes of 'Lullaby'.

Best of all, though, was a title track that – with Dave Allen's pristine production supplanted by a more melancholy sheen – might have rivalled 'Faith' or 'Siamese Twins' in terms of intensity, and certainly gave 'Three Imaginary Boys' a run for its atmospheric money.

Such broad strokes, Smith has claimed, developed from his own state of mind. 'The album was really incoherent, not just how it ended up, but the actual making of it, in a very dense kind of strange haze... I was totally unfocussed, and I think it shows in some of the songs... that they are a bit dilettante.'

He has come down a little too hard on 'The Wailing Wall' ('I'm not too sure about that one'), when the song's eastern moodiness in fact conjures one of the album's most delightful atmospheres; and, looking back from a decade and a half, Smith admitted, 'I think it's a patchy album. For me personally, it reminds me of a very confused period; I wasn't quite sure what album I was making.

'But I think "Shake Dog Shake" is a great song, and "The Top" is a good song... there are songs on it that figure among the best songs I think I've written. "Bird Mad Girl" is quite good, and "Dressing Up" I like... "The Caterpillar"'s pretty good as well. I do in fact like quite a lot of the songs!

'But it wasn't a heavily promoted album, even in Cure terms. Plus, it was a pretty chaotic period... we swapped drummers three times during that tour, Andy, then Vince Ely, then Boris... the whole period was pretty disjointed.'

(TV) *WWF Music Convoy* (Germany) 02 May 1984
UNR Shake Dog Shake

(TV) *Countdown* (Netherlands) May 1984
UNR The Caterpillar
ORIGINAL RELEASE: unreleased
COMMENTS: European TV appearances, leading up to the launch of the band's next tour.

(LIVE) Oxford, 5 May 1984
8417 Shake Dog Shake
8418 Primary
8419 Charlotte Sometimes
8420 Give Me It

(LIVE) London, 8 May 1984
8421 One Hundred Years

(LIVE) London, 9 May 1984
8422 A Forest
8423 10.15 Saturday Night
8424 Killing An Arab

(LIVE) London, 10 May 1984
8425 The Hanging Garden
8426 The Walk

ORIGINAL RELEASE: *Concert*, Fiction FIX 10, October 1984

COMMENTS: Tickets for the Cure's next tour, running from late April into mid-May, went on sale on 3 March; within three weeks, the band had been forced to add two further nights at London's Hammersmith Odeon, and it was these final shows that would contribute the bulk of tracks to the Cure's first official live album.

Released less than six months after the tour closed, the prosaically titled *Concert* captured what remain dubious highlights of a spectacular show, one that saw them pay due homage to bygone landmarks, as well as fulfilling any expectations of an audience watching the authors of *The Top*. *Concert* may have been a better album had the band either gone for the double LP market, or concentrated less of their attentions on the oldies.

A remarkable 'Three Imaginary Boys' notwithstanding, the concert highlights all drew from *The Top*... 'Wailing Wall' and 'The Top' itself were hypnotic drones, 'Bananafishbone' was a celebration, with a little film projected onto the backdrop to render this most impenetrable of lyrics even more obscure. Even the audience clapalong to 'The Caterpillar' was forgivable.

Concert, however, played it safe and emerged, sadly, a slighter being than it ought to have. But still there are few album openers more impressive than the roaring slab of 'Shake Dog Shake' with which the needle hit side one; and few live albums (at least at that time) that so patently reveled in the warts and all of the actual concert experience. 'It's all been done very plainly,' Smith confessed. 'We only spent four days mixing it, and it's not a very big budget number. It's a very trashy record, it doesn't glisten, it sounds like a concert.'

(LIVE) Paris, 15 May 1984

8427 Forever

ORIGINAL RELEASE: *Curiosity – Live 1977-1984*, Fiction FIX 10, October 1984

COMMENTS: One of the all-time legends in the Cure's back catalogue, 'Forever' has appeared on enough bootlegs, and in enough different forms, that fans could (and have) create entire box sets around it. The Cure, on the other hand, have allowed it just one official airing, and that from the very last days of the song's lifespan – first performed back in 1981, when it glistened out of the pre-*Faith* John Peel session, it was finally retired following *The Top* tour, and closes *Curiosity* with five (edited) minutes of a dramatically impassioned performance, that rockets to a Mach-ten conclusion of honking (Porl Thompson's saxophone) and howling, that remains quite unlike any other in the Cure's repertoire.

(TV) *Rock Around The Clock* (UK) 25 August 1984
  8428 Shake Dog Shake
  8429 Primary
  8430 The Walk
  8431 The Hanging Garden
  8432 One Hundred Years
  8433 Give Me It
  8434 A Forest
  8435 Piggy In The Mirror
  8436 Happy The Man
  8437 Play For Today
  8438 The Caterpillar
  8439 10.15 Saturday Night
  8440 Killing An Arab
  UNR Forever

ORIGINAL RELEASE: *Rock Masters* DVD, Image Entertainment; scheduled for 2005

COMMENTS: To celebrate the 30th anniversary of the record that, historically, launched Rock 'n' Roll, BBC 2 was devoting a full 24 hours to rock programming, in a weekend slot titled (what else?) *Rock Around The Clock*. Broadcast live, the show featured a number of bands in various performance situations, with the cameras pursuing a dapper-looking Cure to Glasgow's Barrowlands, to capture highlights of the show – seven songs from the above (full) set were broadcast live, although the entire show (excluding, infuriatingly, 'Forever') was subsequently made available as an almost-an-hour long TV special, the source for a number of bootleg VHS and DVD versions.

An authorized version of the same show was announced for release in October 2004, but was delayed for unspecified reasons.

(LIVE) Tokyo, 17 October 1984
  8441 Shake Dog Shake
  8442 Play For Today
  8443 Primary
  8444 Wailing Wall
  8445 The Empty World
  8446 The Hanging Garden
  8447 The Walk
  8448 One Hundred Years
  8449 Give Me It
  8450 A Forest
  8451 The Top
  8452 Charlotte Sometimes
  8453 Let's Go To Bed
  8454 The Caterpillar
  8455 Boys Don't Cry

8456 10.15 Saturday Night
8457 Killing An Arab
8458 The Lovecats

ORIGINAL RELEASE: *The Cure Live In Japan* VHS, Toshiba VTS M129 (Japan), 1985

COMMENTS: The final night of the Cure's Japanese tour (following visits to New Zealand and Australia) was also Andy Anderson's last performance with the band prior to his dramatic sacking. In his place, the Cure called in former Psychedelic Furs drummer Vince Ely for the first 11 nights of the forthcoming US tour, before ex-Thompson Twin Boris Williams stepped in to the breach.

Despite the turmoil, Japanese Toshiba went ahead with plans to film the last show for domestic home video release, with the concert footage joined by soundcheck and backstage material, plus an interview. The performance itself is stupendous, and reminds fans of just how much was lost in the pruning of *Concert*. Material from *The Top*, in particular, rings out with a confidence that the studio renderings struggled to attain, while the band has also grown out of the earlier habit of slamming the oldest numbers down at hitherto unimaginable speeds.

The only downside to all this is the sheer obscurity of the release; for many fans and collectors, the first they knew of it was its appearance within Darren Butler's *The Cure On Record* book; since that time, e-Bay has brought a few more copies to light, but prices remain sky-high.

1985

LINE-UP #11 Robert Smith (vocals, guitar), Porl Thompson (guitar, keyboards), Lol Tolhurst (keyboards), Simon Gallup (bass), Boris Williams (drums)

(SINGLE) In Between Days
   8501 In Between Days
   8502 The Exploding Boy
   8503 A Few Hours After This
ORIGINAL RELEASE: Fiction FICSX 22, July 1985
COMMENTS: The feud that may or may not have been ignited by the similarities between 'The Walk' and New Order's 'Blue Monday' continued into 1984, as the Manchester band cut a song that could, were one feeling mischievous, surely be their response to the 'borrowing'. The brutal, percussive 'Murder' instrumental clattered through raw noise and dark cries, to emerge so close to 'Splintered In Her Head' that any perceived past slights were surely remedied.

Or had they? Weeks later, as 'In Between Days' landed in the UK chart, Peter Hook was prompted to admit, 'even my mother got upset. Phoned me up, she'd just heard their "In Between Days", she was like "You've got to sort this out, our Peter!"' (The feud continued when Smith noted the similarities between 'All The Way', from New Order's *Technique*, and his own 'Just Like Heaven'.)

Over on the b-side, the Cure served up 'The Exploding Boy', which rivalled the A-side in its vibrant, acoustic-led romps – with Thompson's sax lending a soupy bonus to the throbbing sound. This song, Smith later enthused, was a celebration of the enthusiasm and expectation that he was suddenly feeling.

'A Few Hours After This', meanwhile, packed all the martial pomp of a central European national anthem and was the latest in the Cure's attempts to do something that was both orchestral and quirky, 'that didn't quite come together.'

(TV) *Top Of The Pops* (UK) 1 August 1985
   UNR In Between Days
ORIGINAL RELEASE: unreleased
COMMENTS: Although the new line-up had already completed the new album, and played live in Spain, Italy and Greece, this was the British public's first opportunity to witness the return of Simon Gallup, as he departed Fool's Dance to replace the departing (to Johnny Hates Jazz) Phil Thornally. The *Top Of The*

Pops appearance also preserved viewers from exposure to quite the most garish video in the Cure's library so far, a straightforward performance over which Tim Pope superimposed an array of fluorescent, hand-drawn socks – an odd interpretation of Smith's original request that the band have 'flashes of colour going between my head when I was singing. [Pope] said "what, colour like my socks?" and I said "yeah". And that obviously stuck in his mind.' The animation team wound up spending £8,000 painstakingly inserting socks into every frame. 'Bloody mental.'

(RADIO) BBC, John Peel, 7 August 1985 (rec 30 July)
    UNR The Exploding Boy
    UNR Six Different Ways
    UNR Screw
    UNR Sinking
ORIGINAL RELEASE: unreleased
COMMENTS: If the lively warmth of 'In Between Days' painted one side of the Cure in colours as bright as those dancing socks, their return to the confines of the BBC studios offered a somewhat more thoughtful side of the band. The grinding attack riff that propels 'Screw' easily detracts from the song's light-hearted hookline; 'Six Different Ways' had a pulsing force that, again, pulled the wool over the eyes of anybody otherwise entranced by the toytown motif that plays scales around the rhythm; and 'Sinking' unashamedly looked back to the textures and tones of *Seventeen Seconds* – on record, the discordant piano that announces it could even have segued straight out of 'The Final Sound'.

Only 'The Exploding Boy', reprised from the latest b-side, reminded listeners that the Cure were now a top pop band – because, lost within this remarkable session, it was easy to forget that fact.

(ALBUM) *The Head On The Door*
    8501 In Between Days
    8504 Kyoto Song
    8505 The Blood

8506 Six Different Ways
8507 Push
8508 The Baby Screams
8509 Close To Me
8510 A Night Like This
8511 Screw
8512 Sinking

ORIGINAL RELEASE: Fiction FIX 11, August 1985

COMMENTS: *The Head On The Door* was titled, said Smith, for a nightmare that plagued him during his childhood, coupled with similarly vintage memories of puppet shows. 'I've always been fascinated with puppets like Punch and Judy, because the tradition is so old..., and there's something about the way a puppet's head will roll off.'

He also claimed that the record's original title was to be *The Head On The Pole*, in memory of the medieval practise of publicly displaying decapitations... 'all your instincts just scream at that. Then I changed it.'

Nevertheless, after the disparate worldview of *The Top*, *The Head On The Door* very much displayed a return to past (pre-split) glories, in terms of musical intensity, if not subject matter. Smith himself agreed, 'I prefer this record to *The Top*... it's a bit easier for me to like, so I imagine it's easier for everybody else to like as well. There's a lot of different songs, but it's got the sort of continuity that those *Disco Beach Party* albums have,' and his choice of analogy was not simply silliness for the sake of it.

There is something quintessentially *summery* about *The Head On The Door*, a consequence of course of its height-of-the-season release, and the sheer inescapability of 'In Between Days' through that July and August; but also because the very instrumentation speaks of Mediterranean climes... the Spanish whoop of 'The Blood', the sultry seduction of 'Kyoto Song', and onto 'A Night Like This', a song that had been around since the days of Malice, but which was so thoroughly revised, so majestically arranged, that it captures the first flush of teenaged romance better than any record since the Bay City Rollers'... you guessed it... 'Summerlove Sensation'. And, if you don't agree, play the pair back to back. Even the hyper-claustrophobia of 'Close To Me', the sound of living your life enveloped within a skein of very thick wool, has a sun-drenched warmth to it, even after Tim Pope re-envisioned it as the sound of a wardrobe full of people falling off Beachy Head.

And there is more. From start to finish, *The Head On The Door* revelled within a naked spontaneity which harked back as far as *Seventeen Seconds*; no less than eight of the album's ten songs were first takes, something that the Cure had not managed since that album.

Later, Smith would complain that *The Head On The Door* 'was a very constructed album. I sort of sacrificed any inspiration that could have come out of the five piece, for the sake of getting the record done.' In fact, *The Head On The Door* emerges as the most relaxed album of the Cure's career, while the simplicity suggested by the first-take feat is itself one of the record's strongest points.

'All the songs were written on one synthesizer, and an old guitar I rediscovered. I thought, "if I can't make these work on these instruments...." The crazier effects, horn parts and so on, that he envisioned complementing the song were all accomplished with voice alone – Gallup later recalled going into the studio to hear the demos for the first time, and spending the entire day in fits of laughter.

Smith continued: 'I wanted to write moody songs and pop songs and put them in the same record, which is what really happened. During that period, the fact that we've been paying attention and efforts in making videos, made the Cure not only a listenable band, but also a seeable one. "Close To Me" helped us in that sense, because it has become one of the most famous videos ever. The kind of pop music that I wanted to do was a mixture of the Beatles and of the Buzzcocks: the basic idea was a three minutes pop song just like "Boys Don't Cry".'

Smith has also described *The Head On The Door* as the first album that actually forced him to contemplate, and confront, his approach to song-writing. 'There was a college in California, and someone sent me a letter saying "could you give me an insight into 'The Blood', because I'm writing a thesis and I can get a certain amount of credit points, because they're running this course and it's called *Robert Smith's Words*." And you wonder why I'm paranoid?'

Reflecting from the late 1990s, Smith continued, 'you have to insert a certain idea of craft into a song, which is an old argument I've had for five or six years. It's not spontaneity, because there comes a certain point when you learn to distil what you've done, add a certain essence. It's an argument I had with... not to drop names, but the Thin White Duke, because he thinks the first thing you write is of the essence, and that's it, that's like the performance, and I don't think it's true. You get that first idea, and distil it.

'You use certain words – its like Dylan Thomas, saying the first poem, the first thing he writes, is going to be the best. Is it fuck. He might have spent weeks refining it and, if someone like that, who's that good at writing words, can spend that amount of time refining words, I don't feel obliged to think, "ooh, the first thing I say...."

'I sing stuff on stage that's the first thing that comes into my head and, at the time, it's incredibly gratifying, it's a huge relief. But afterwards, I'll listen back to the cassette and I'm mortified at how shit it is. To honestly believe that the first thing you do is the best you'll ever do, is so lazy. Or a degree of self-confidence that is manic. It's like the first pot you make, believing it'll be better than the tenth. Although it might be funnier looking....'

(TV) *Mon Zenith a Moi* (France) August 1985
  UNR In Between Days

(TV) *Le Jeu de la Verite* (France) August 1985
  UNR In Between Days

(TV) *Top Of The Pops* (UK) August 1985
UNR In Between Days

(TV) *Saturday Night Live* (UK) 13 September 1985
UNR In Between Days
UNR Close To Me
UNR Kyoto Song
UNR Baby Screams
UNR Sinking
ORIGINAL RELEASE: unreleased
COMMENTS: Again, that song was *inescapable*.

(SINGLE) Close To Me *aka Half An Octopus* EP
8509a Close To Me
8513 A Man Inside My Mouth
8514 Stop Dead
8404 New Day
8509b Close To Me (extended)
ORIGINAL RELEASE: Fiction FICS 23, September 1985
COMMENTS: Having always insisted that the Cure would *never* cull two singles from the same album, Smith was persuaded to break his own rule by his bandmates. '[They were] all saying that, if we release it, it will get to number one.' In fact, in climbing no higher than #24, 'Close To Me' became the Cure's lowest-performing 45 since 'Let's Go To Bed', four years earlier. The accompanying video, on the other hand, remains one of the group's most popular, as the entire group climbed into a wardrobe, which was then hurled from the cliffs at Beachy Head, into the sea below.

'Close To Me' was remixed for this release, and punched up with some proudly thrusting brass overdubs – the six minute extended remix (present on the 12-inch single) is especially pleasing, as the horns take center-stage for a minute-twenty-long overture that sets up an excellent mood of jazzy mayhem.

Flip the disc over, and one swiftly encounters one of the most over-analysed songs in Smith's canon, 'A Man Inside My Mouth'. Although Smith has acknowledged 'the weirder sexual aspects of the lyric,' little about the song prepares the listener for the interpretation offered by *Gothic* author Richard Davenport-Hines, who describes the song as referring to 'mild sexual abasement,' then strengthens his imagery by quoting from Poppy Z Brite's *Lost Souls*, a tale in which a young man reflects upon the sexual practices of a gay friend. (*Lost Souls* itself makes a number of references to Cure songs, within its own labyrinthine exploration of contemporary 'dark wave' lifestyle.)

In fact, Smith eventually explained, 'the "man inside my mouth" was... the stranger who sometimes used my voice – I felt that what I was saying was often at odds with what I was thinking and feeling....'

'Stop Dead', the other b-side, is less open (or otherwise) to interpretation, a thumping howl that has the ghost of 'Let's Go To Bed' dancing around its doo-

doo-doo hook, a cheeky Tolhurst keyboard line, and a growling bass line that has established the song among Gallup's all-time Cure favorites. The song was intended for the *Head On The Door* album until the very last moment, but was pulled, according to Gallup, because Smith was never able to match the lyrics to the music as seamlessly as he hoped.

(TV) *Old Grey Whistle Test* (UK) 19 November 1985
    UNR In Between Days
    UNR Close To Me
ORIGINAL RELEASE: unreleased
COMMENTS: Live broadcast from the Cure's MENCAP charity show at the Camden Palace, London. A full Cure set climaxed with an encore of Gary Glitter's 'Do You Want To Touch Me', but the BBC chose only to air the two singles.

(TV) Oracle text-news service (UK) December 1985
    No music, just a cocktail recipe supplied by Smith. 'Oracle' was so-named for its ingredients – Orange juice, Rum, Apple slices, Calvados, Lemon juice, Everything mixed up – and was by no means a calculated attempt at getting his name on the TV. The drink itself, incidentally, is disgusting.

1986

LINE-UP #11 Robert Smith (vocals, guitar), Porl Thompson (guitar, keyboards), Lol Tolhurst (keyboards), Simon Gallup (bass), Boris Williams (drums)

(TV) *Zenith* (France) 21 February 1986
UNR In Between Days

(TV) *Champs Elysées* (France) 12 April 1986
UNR Close To Me – (voice live)

(TV) *Zenith* (France) 15 April 1986
UNR Close To Me
UNR Six Different Ways
ORIGINAL RELEASE: unreleased
COMMENTS: More continental TV, with 12 April offering up an oddity when, with drummer Williams unavailable, Tolhurst switched to drums for the evening, and his flatmate Martin sat in to mime the keyboards part.

(SINGLE) Boys Don't Cry
7918a Boys Don't Cry (New Voice New Mix)
7813 Pillbox Tales
7814 Do The Hansa
ORIGINAL RELEASE: Fiction FICS 24, April 1986
COMMENTS: With the career-spanning *Standing On A Beach* compilation imminent, March 1986 saw Smith remix 'Boys Don't Cry' for release as a single for the second time in its life – he also rerecorded the vocal, apparently so that

he wouldn't have to try and capture the original, higher, lines in the TV appearances that were lined up alongside the release. (The original version would appear on the album itself).

A Top 20 hit this time around, the single was further distinguished for collectors by the inclusion of two period oldies on the b-side, the 1978-79 demos of 'Pillbox Tales' and 'Do The Hansa'.

(TV) *Top Of The Pops* (UK) 08 May 1986
    UNR Boys Don't Cry

(TV) *Countdown* (Netherlands) 15 May 1986
    UNR Boys Don't Cry
    UNR Close To Me

(TV) *Formel Eins* (Germany) 27 May 1986
    UNR Boys Don't Cry

(TV) *Touites Foles de Lui* (France) 21 June 1986
    UNR Boys Don't Cry
ORIGINAL RELEASE: unreleased
COMMENTS: A new video shot for 'Boys Don't Cry', featuring the original trio of Smith, Tolhurst and Michael Dempsey in silhouette behind three younger (*much* younger) look-alikes, received rotation airplay both across Europe and the United States, where MTV was now climbing very enthusiastically onto the Cure bandwagon. In the meantime, the Cure themselves got on with a string of television performances.

(LIVE) Orange, France, 9-10 August 1986
    8601 Shake Dog Shake
    8602 Piggy In The Mirror
    8603 Play For Today
    8604 A Strange Day
    8605 Primary
    8606 Kyoto Song
    8607 Charlotte Sometimes
    8608 In Between Days
    8609 The Walk
    8610 A Night Like This
    8611 Push
    8612 One Hundred Years
    8613 A Forest
    8614 Sinking
    8615 Close To Me
    8616 Let's Go To Bed
    8617 Six Different Ways

8618 Three Imaginary Boys
8619 Boys Don't Cry
8620 Faith
8621 Give Me It
8622 10.15 Saturday Night
8623 Killing An Arab

ORIGINAL RELEASE: *Cure In Orange* VHS, November 1987

COMMENTS: Taking over the Roman amphitheatre for the closing of the summer-long Beach Party tour of the US and Europe, the Cure turned in a magnificent performance that was captured, with evocative stylishness, by Tim Pope. The Cure were the first rock band to play the venue since Dire Straits in 1984, and Smith explained, 'we wanted to film it ... because every concert we do now reaches a point that has seemed unattainable in the past and I wanted it captured for ever, before we move on or give up.'

Pope's recruitment as director was, of course, inevitable, even though he had little experience at filming such events – indeed, the fact that 'he isn't really a director' worked to his advantage. Smith continued, 'we could have got in some proper director to make a film of any old concert but he wouldn't know what the band was about and I want this to be a Cure film about The Cure."

Pope himself continued, 'the risks, of course, are many. Because of the limited budget, all the live filming had to be done on Saturday, at the concert, with close-ups following during Sunday's mock up. Rain on one or both days would have scuppered the whole thing – £150,000 literally down the rain because they couldn't comprehend their cheapest insurance quote: £50,000. It didn't rain until Monday.'

Comparisons with Pink Floyd's similarly staged 1971 concert at the Roman ruins of Pompeii were inevitable – so much so that the Cure soundchecked with a version of Floyd's own 'Set The Controls For The Heart Of The Sun'.

1987

LINE-UP #11 (to July) Robert Smith (vocals, guitar), Porl Thompson (guitar, keyboards), Lol Tolhurst (keyboards), Simon Gallup (bass), Boris Williams (drums)

LINE-UP #12 Robert Smith (vocals, guitar), Porl Thompson (guitar, keyboards), Lol Tolhurst (keyboards), Roger O'Donnell (keyboards), Simon Gallup (bass), Boris Williams (drums)

(SINGLE) Why Can't I Be You?
  8701 Why Can't I Be You?
  8702 A Japanese Dream
  8701a Why Can't I Be You? (extended)
  8702a A Japanese Dream (extended)
  8617 Six Different Ways (live)
  8611 Push (live)
ORIGINAL RELEASE: Fiction FICS 25, April 1987
COMMENTS: 'Why Can't I Be You?' was, according to producer Dave Allen, always viewed as a potential single, 'because it's short and up-tempo.' That said, it was not until very late in the day that Smith finally gave it the green light, with Allen adding, 'Robert doesn't have any rules about what makes a good single. He'd release anything if he liked it enough.'

A regular in the band's live repertoire even before it was recorded in autumn 1986, 'Why Can't I Be You?' has alternately been described as one of the Cure's most characteristic singles, and one of their most annoying. Another in the line of purpose-built pop songs that Smith insists do not 'resonate' (he regularly cites it alongside 'Let's Go To Bed'), it's horn-led hooks, and the frantic mockabilly backing track pile in around one of Smith's most uncontrolled vocals to paint a picture of absolute absurd jollity, which in turn inspired Tim Pope to craft one of the group's most unexpected videos. 'This it it! This is the video I've always wanted to make! The Cure DANCING! I can't believe I'm seeing this. They're FINISHED!'

Pope may have been right, as well. The single climbed no higher than #21 in the UK – which is odd, because it was certainly garish enough to make the Top 10.

The studio b-side 'A Japanese Dream' was a turbulent epic, one of the Cure's most powerful flips, and was intended as a tribute to one of the band's trips to Japan. Smith later confessed he had fully expected the song to make It onto the finished album – it was certainly one of the strongest of the demos. However, 'when I sung it for real... I knew it wasn't going to make it.'

A bonus 7-inch issued in the UK additionally packaged two live cuts from the *Orange* VHS.

(TV) *Azzurro 87* (Italy) April 1987
UNR Why Can't I Be You?

(TV) *Toccata* (Italy) April 1987
UNR Why Can't I Be You?
UNR Catch
UNR Just Like Heaven

(TV) *The Tube* (UK) 24 April 1987
UNR Catch
UNR Why Can't I Be You?
UNR Hot Hot Hot!!!

(TV) *Top Of The Pops* (UK) 6 May 1987
UNR Why Can't I Be You?

(TV) *A La Folie* (France) 10 May 1987
UNR Why Can't I Be You?

(TV) *The Montreux Rose D'Or Rock Festival* (Switzerland) May 1987
UNR Catch
UNR Why Can't I Be You?
ORIGINAL RELEASE: unreleased
COMMENTS: The run-up to the release of the new album, and the usual string of European TV dates.

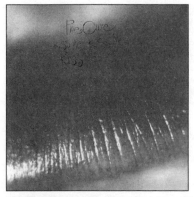

(ALBUM) *Kiss Me Kiss Me Kiss Me*
  8703 The Kiss
  8704 Catch
  8705 Torture
  8706 If Only Tonight We Could Sleep
  8701 Why Can't I Be You?
  8707 How Beautiful You Are
  8708 The Snakepit
  8709 Hey You!!!
  8710 Just Like Heaven
  8711 All I Want
  8712 Hot Hot Hot!!!
  8713 One More Time
  8714 Like Cockatoos
  8715 Icing Sugar
  8716 The Perfect Girl
  8717 A Thousand Hours
  8718 Shiver And Shake
  8719 Fight

ORIGINAL RELEASE: Fiction FIX 13, May 1987

COMMENTS: For many music fans, there comes a time in even the most obsessive relationship when the release, purchase and absorption of a band's new album becomes less a pleasure than a chore.

In most instances, this usually happens around the time of the third LP; the Cure, by that (admittedly subjective) criterion had already done well to double that span to six. But, for listeners who had followed the group since the days of *Three Imaginary Boys*, the point was fast approaching when the Cure had so exceeded every possibility that they once embodied that, to all intents and purposes, they had become a completely different band. This sprawling, diverse double album, released exactly one year after the hits collection, marked that crucial juncture for many.

But their cries of dismay were barely audible, lost beneath the trample of an entirely new Cure audience, drawn from all around the globe.

Britain, Japan, Europe, and finally, the United States all fell to the band. While singles collection *Standing On A Beach* breached the Stateside Top 50, *Kiss Me Kiss Me Kiss Me* stormed the Top 40. Between them, the two albums sold over six million copies worldwide and, at a time when 'alternative music' was still a media hype waiting to be created, and the mainstream muddied everything that crept close to success, the Cure emerged as a self-sustaining anomaly, a band whose audience still regarded them as the world's best kept secret; whose detractors regarded every new hit a fluke; whose own record company essentially despaired of them.

'They only like us when we're selling records,' Robert Smith remarked a decade later and, perhaps, that was true. What was different in 1987 was that the Cure were selling records, and their record company must have liked them very much indeed.

With the wonderful working title of *1,000 Virgins*, demoing kicked off in June 1986, with sessions scheduled around both the European and US tours, and the upcoming World Cup; recording itself got underway later in the autumn, and sped ahead so quickly that, it quickly became apparent that the band had more than enough material to stuff a double album. Producer Dave Allen reckoned there were 40 or so songs in contention when the demo sessions began, of which no less than 32 were still on the band's mind, as they got down to the actual recording.

Smith himself remarked, 'The *Kiss Me* album was mainly an experiment for me: suddenly I was having a lot of freedom and The Cure could literally do anything. We wrote 20 songs and recorded 15 of them and I was just keeping on writing, because we were developing lots of ideas and I thought that the only way to get the best out of it was to never stop writing!'

For many observers, the most shocking aspect of the new sessions was Smith's willingness to allow his bandmates to become fully involved in the songwriting process, a role that he had hitherto kept much to himself – although both Tolhurst and Gallup regularly contributed their own demos (both music and lyrics) to the Cure's repertoire, the remainder of the band seemed to steer clear of such waters.

'The guys had gotten a little lazy, I thought,' Smith explained. 'It was like "why bother if he can do it?" So I told them they'd have to be more involved… or I'd have to humiliate them in public or something.' Every member of the band was asked to present what amounted to an album's worth of songs (or, at least, song ideas), for the group to play through in a series of marathon sessions at Williams' house. The basic shape of the album was then decided upon, before the entire party decamped to studios in Miravel, France, an environment that offered the band a distraction-free environment in which to work. It was, enthused Smith, 'the first time we've been a group since *Pornography*, when we could just sit down and play, and I'd look at Lol or Simon and know what they meant.'

It was the recreation of that mood that prompted Smith to single out two tracks, the James Bond-in-a-field-of-thistles 'Shiver And Shake', and the stuttering 'The Kiss' as songs that 'would've got on [*Pornography*] if I'd written them at that time, because they're the horrible songs that I was looking for then, but couldn't manage.'

Indeed they are, with the remainder of the album's meatiest chunks likewise emerging from within the darker corners. Riding a beautifully mellow bass line, 'The Snakepit' was 'classic' Cure, while the anthemic stomp of 'Fight' was described by Smith as 'the weirdest Cure song that we've ever done', but, surely, only because it was so strangely redolent of Led Zeppelin at their most grandiose and dramatic. It was also singled out by Smith for the out-of-character insistence that 'people should get up and do something'; in the past, after all, he advocated the complete opposite approach. 'I'd never have dreamed of doing a song like "Fight" [for *Pornography*]. "Give In" would have been more like it.'

The semi-acoustic prettiness of 'How Beautiful You Are' (with the opening lyric that so defies that description), the sub-continental atmospheres of 'If Only Tonight We Could Sleep', the symphonic 'All I Want' and the sleepily drifting 'One More Time' all brought further gems to the table and, if *Kiss Me Kiss Me Kiss Me* had ended there, it might well have emerged among the Cure's greatest albums. Unfortunately, it carried on… and on… and on, and so we suffered the gimmick-laden 'Hey You!!!!!!' (mercifully chopped from the CD version of the album) and 'The Perfect Girl' (the Banshees' 'Dear Prudence' meets a melody line left behind by *The Head On The Door*), the mordant sleaze of 'Icing Sugar', the Zeppelin echoes, once again of 'Like Cockatoos' and 'To The Sky', which strangely sounded like something David Bowie might have considered rather good around this same point in the late 1980s.

(STUDIO) *Kiss Me Kiss Me Kiss Me* out-takes etc
    8707a How Beautiful You Are (Bob Clearmountain 7-inch remix)
    8715a Icing Sugar (alternate remix)
    8720 To The Sky
ORIGINAL RELEASE: 8720 on various artists *Stranger Than Fiction*, Fiction promo LP, August 1989; all on *Join The Dots*.
COMMENTS: Celebrating 10 years of the Fiction label, *Stranger Than Fiction* ranks among the rarest of all Cure-related collectibles, a fabulously limited edition that would dominate a complete Cure archive, the rarest of the rare. Both 'I'm A Cult Hero' and 'I Want To Be A Tree' made it onto the album, together with the alluring *Kiss Me* out-take, the rather lovely 'To The Sky'. One of the first songs recorded for the album, it was never completed and Smith admitted he was reluctant to hand the track over for the compilation – 'for the first time in five years, something had been released that wasn't quite finished.'

Of the remixes, 'How Beautiful You Are' was handed to Bob Clearmountain for manipulation into a proposed French single. The release never took place and the track was archived.

(SINGLE) Catch
    8704 Catch
    8721 Breathe
    8722 A Chain Of Flowers
    8606 Kyoto song (live)
    8610 A Night Like This (live)

ORIGINAL RELEASE: Fiction FICS 26, June 1987

COMMENTS: One of the least appealing songs on the entire *Kiss Me* experience was then mystifyingly selected to become of the least appealing singles the Cure have ever issued, a winsome little ballad that limped to #27.

Neither are its studio b-sides, out-takes from the album sessions, much of an improvement, although 'Breathe' at least packs a merry melody line, while 'Chain Of Flowers'... no matter that the drum roll seems convinced it's about to remake 'A Night Like This', somebody once said it sounds *exactly* like you'd expect a Cure b-side to sound, and they are right. It does.

The original UK 12-inch single featured just the three tracks; a second release a few weeks later dropped 'Chain Of Flowers' in favour of two more excerpts from the *Orange* live video.

(TV) *The Roxy* (UK) June 1987
    UNR Catch

(TV) *Top Of The Pops* (UK) June 1987
    UNR Catch

ORIGINAL RELEASE: unreleased

COMMENTS: *The Roxy* appearance was a surprise, if only because the show really didn't seem worthy of such high profile guests. The *TOTP* appearance was one of their least memorable.

(SINGLE) Just Like Heaven
    8710 Just Like Heaven
    8723 Snow in Summer
    8724 Sugar Girl

ORIGINAL RELEASE: Fiction FICS 27, October 1987

COMMENTS: The Cure were back on the road at last, their first dates since a South American tour earlier in the year introduced a sixth member to the band. Former Psychedelic Furs sideman Roger O'Donnell was recruited to ensure that the vast washes of keyboard heard on the new record could at least be approximated on stage – guitar Porl Thompson had hitherto been doing double duty, filling in flourishes around Tolhurst, but the demands of the *Kiss Me* material were so great that a second full-time player became essential.

'There was so much keyboard on that album,' Tolhurst marvelled. 'I remember in the studio in Miravel, I counted them one day, we had 15 keyboards set-up; that's a lot of stuff, a lot of hands, and although there was a lot of connections and MIDI and things, I couldn't do everything by myself on stage. It was just impossible, three or four lines going at the same time on some tracks and, unless you really wanted to strip the song down, you couldn't play it. It was the same with guitar, that's why we had an extra guitarist.'

Neither could he rely upon tapes and technology to fill in around him – more and more bands were going that route, but their own fans could speak of the nightmarish evenings that resulted, as gear broke down, tapes switched off, click-tracks sped up and the entire universe, essentially, collapsed in a heap of electronic soup.

'Very little was sequenced with us,' Tolhurst insists. 'Everything was played, everything was live. There were some little bits here and there that were sequenced... flute sequences, little things.... But nothing along the lines of... for instance, when Boris used to play with the Thompson Twins, he told me how Tom used to do a lot of stuff with a big eight-track machine, and some pedals in front of him. We never did that. We were a live band and we wanted a full live sound. I think the only time we ever used tapes was on the *Pornography* tour, we had a tape of some noises for the song 'Pornography', and a drum machine on 'One Hundred Years".'

Life on the newly-launched Honeymoon Tour of Europe road, Smith laughed, remained rooted in the band's customary, time-honoured pursuits: 'drinking... watching old *Dr Who* videos... Lol-baiting... arguing about the merits of compact discs and how the Luddites would smash them up... crimping... Lol-baiting,... drinking... phoning home... anyone baiting... signing autographs... trying to avoid signing autographs...' – and Tolhurst today reflects on the *Kiss Me* band as one of the two truly essential Cure line-ups ('the other was the three-piece that made *Faith* and *Pornography*'). It was also on the very edge of becoming one of the most successful bands of the age.

Out of British view until December brought shows in Birmingham and Wembley... great big stadium shows, as well... the Cure pulled a third single from the album and, after the dismal disappointment of 'Catch', this time they actually made the right decision. 'Just Like Heaven' not only boasted the cachet of having been written as the theme to a French TV show (the musical showcase *Les Enfants Du Rock*), it also flirts and bounces along like all the best Cure pop songs should... and how can anyone resist an opening line that demands, 'show me how you do that trick, the one that makes me scream.' And people say 'Man Inside My Mouth' was suggestive.

A pair of impossibly irresistible b-sides complete the package – 'Sugar Girl', with its cheeky soundtrack to a toytown traction engine rally; and 'Snow In Summer', which punches the drums so hard up front that it's no wonder the weatherman's brain hurts.

1988

LINE-UP #12 Robert Smith (vocals, guitar), Porl Thompson (guitar, keyboards), Lol Tolhurst (keyboards), Roger O'Donnell (keyboards), Simon Gallup (bass), Boris Williams (drums)

(SINGLE) Hot Hot Hot!!!
    8712a Hot Hot Hot!!! (remix)
    8712b Hot Hot Hot!!! (extended remix)
    8709a Hey You!!! (extended remix)
ORIGINAL RELEASE: Fiction FICSX 28, February 1988
COMMENTS: Hey, hold on a moment. The *fourth* single from *Kiss Me Kiss Me Kiss Me...* with nothing more than a couple of Francois Kervorkian remixes to intrigue anybody who already owned the record. True, it did mark the CD debut of 'Hey You!!!', the song lopped off the original LP 'to facilitate a single compact disc,' but was that intended to be a recommendation? Hmm.

That it foundered at #45... that is, the lowest that *any* Cure single had ever charted... is totally incomprehensible – sure the fans all had the album, but this wasn't a single for the fans. This was a single for everyone who bought 'Lovecats' and 'In Between Days'; for everyone who liked to watch *Top Of The Pops* and wave balloons along with the audience; and for everyone who watched the video and thought, 'oh my, this is their wackiest yet.' Because it was all those things and, as such, was the best of all the singles culled from the LP. Shame they left it till last, then.

Releasing it *only* on 12-inch and CD in the UK was a dirty trick as well, although it reflected how the market was beginning to move, and maybe the extended running time was required for what (all concepts of taste and decency notwithstanding, of course) was certainly a strong single, all punchy rhythms, twisting signatures, elaborate flourishes and lunatic vocals.

(STUDIO) Rough mix listening party, RAK Studios, London, December 1988
ORIGINAL RELEASE: unreleased
COMMENTS: The Cure had been in the studio for little more than two months when they hosted a listening party for the new album-so-far. But dominating far more of the proceedings (and ensuing commentary) than the music were the awful scenes that exploded between Smith and Tolhurst. It was no secret that the recent sessions had been fraught, with the battle between the band's two founders only one of several conflicts ripping through the group. But this one looked more serious.

'[Lol] slagged off everything to do with the album, the group and me, and just got drunker and drunker," Smith complained afterwards. He later claimed that Tolhurst barely played on either this new album or its predecessor, and continued, 'we'd grown apart too much to work together anymore. It had been building up, or I suppose breaking down, for two years really and I said if he didn't come around I couldn't stand it. I wanted there to be a kind of intensity within the group, try and work ourselves back up to the emotional level we haven't really had for a few years. He didn't want to be there, didn't accept it. On the *Disintegration* sessions, he sat and watched MTV during most of it.'

Tolhurst countered, 'it's funny, because on *Disintegration* I actually played on more things than I had for the last couple of albums. But it did get to the point with me where I didn't feel excited enough by things to feel I wanted to contribute. It was about halfway through *Disintegration* that things weren't working out too great. I wasn't feeling that well in myself and I guess the Cure psychosis struck again. Big time!

'I think what happened with *Disintegration* was, number one – I was pretty much disintegrating, and number two – we got to the point where, all the things that we always said we hated, we'd started to become. We spent over a year making it, which is just so unnecessary; we did a whole load of demos for it, then we went and recorded it all again... I think something like *Kiss Me*, where we spent the same amount of time, but produced twice the amount of music, was much more fulfilling for everybody.

'The whole ethos of the Cure had become slightly warped as far as I was concerned. It became very undemocratic, and a lot of people around the band, like the record company, found it better that way because they only had to deal with one person, and that was a bit upsetting as over the years I'd put a lot of my life into it.' Two months later, Tolhurst left the Cure. He took the *X*-factor with him.

1989

LINE-UP #13 Robert Smith (vocals, guitar), Porl Thompson (guitar, keyboards), Roger O'Donnell (keyboards), Simon Gallup (bass), Boris Williams (drums)

(SINGLE) Lullaby (UK)/Fascination Street (US)
   8901a Lullaby (edit)
   8901b Lullaby (extended remix)
   8902 Babble
   8903 Out Of Mind
   8904a Fascination Street (edit)
   8904b Fascination Street (extended remix)
ORIGINAL RELEASE: UK Fiction FICS 29, April 1989/US Fiction 69300 USA – April 1989
COMMENTS: The Cure's first new release in two years, 'Lullaby' (in Europe) and 'Fascination Street' (in the US) trailed the new album in devastating style, by unveiling two of the strongest songs on the record. Indeed, 'Lullaby' ranks among the most distinctive, and creepy, songs in the Cure catalogue, a corollary to the joyous likes of 'The Lovecats' and 'The Caterpillar', as Smith contemplates being eaten alive by spiders.

'Spiders are one of the phobias I've not been able to overcome,' Smith told *Melody Maker*. 'Fat spiders with long thin legs that look like they're going to burst make me go really weird. When I was young, I was really scared of spiders and they always used to be in my bed. They weren't actually there at all, but I imagined they were. I'd try to get over the phobia the way you get over any phobia. I'd approach them and force myself to pick them up. I can hold spiders now, even the big hairy ones. But I wouldn't let them near my face.

'Tim Pope wanted to do that. He was trying to persuade me to fill the bed with spiders in one of the videos. These horrible, bird-eating spiders. I refused, and he thought I was being petty. He knew this spider-keeper from London Zoo. Tim thought they were pretty and kept holding them up by the legs and poking them. When we were touring South America a couple of years ago, I remember turning the light on in the bathroom in Brazil and this huge spider disappeared behind the cabinet on the wall. I kept thinking him and his friends are going to join me in bed. Didn't sleep all night.'

For all Smith's misgivings, the theme – if not the physical beasties – became the focus of the accompanying video, with director Tim Pope saying of the 70s horror shtick storyboard that he and Robert devised, 'you can't fuck that up. The basic structure of the idea is in the song, even if you could go off in two million different directions.'

'Lullaby' remains the Cure's most popular, and most successful, video, scooping a prestigious British Phonographic Institute BRIT award for Best Video in 1990, although Smith later shrugged, 'it was a kind of throwaway video.'

'Fascination Street', on the other hand, fascinated because, as Smith later pointed out, it really didn't fit into the overall thematic shape of the forthcoming album... although 'it's the only one that doesn't really fit. I like all twelve songs on the record, and told the [American] label they could have any one of them for the single. But in fact, it would have been my choice as well.'

The extended versions of both a-sides offer little more than... well, an extension... to the original recordings, although there is something deliciously mantra-like about being stalked across the floor by eight bubbling, percolating minutes of 'Lullaby', all the more so since you're forced to wait through some three minutes of sighs and breathing before the vocals finally come in.

'Fascination Street' is expanded to even greater lengths... almost nine minutes... although very little happens that requires pointing more than a cursory ear in its direction. The reappearance of this same mix on the *Mixed Up* collection works far better.

The b-sides shared between the two releases both hailed from the *Disintegration* sessions, although these, too, would have sounded peculiar on the LP. Rather, 'Out Of Mind' would have been better suited to a tribute to David Bowie's *Low* album, as its minute-plus intro swept through the same sonic pastures as the Thin White One's 'Speed Of Life'. For Smith, however, the song's greatest asset is the mention of his favourite animal, the lemur, in the lyric. 'I'd always promised myself I'd do it.'

The slightly shrill 'Babble' is itself a babble of experimental tape effects, and includes the recorded debut of Boris Williams' dog, with his paws up on the keyboard; it quickly kicks in, however, to the kind of soundscape that the Mission might have been proud of – and it would have sounded great on *Kiss Me Kiss Me Kiss Me*. Incidentally, more than one set of ears have suggested that elements of 'Babble' can be found within the marathon version of 'Faith' performed in Turin, on the night of the Tiananmen Square massacre.

(TV) *Top Of The Pops* (UK) 20 April 1989
   UNR Lullaby
ORIGINAL RELEASE: unreleased
COMMENTS: The next Cure album was still pending when the new-look Cure debuted, turning out on *Top Of The Pops* for the first time since the departure of Lol Tolhurst. Filmed just days after Smith's 30th birthday, it was to prove a controversial appearance, as the band donned make-up based upon the cobwebs and all-round strangeness of the accompanying video, at which point the show's producers flipped, deeming the disguise 'too frightening' for the show's youngest viewers. A tense stand-off ensued and, at one point, the Cure threatened to walk off the show altogether. Ultimately, they agreed to remove the make-up, but the band members could only marvel at such strictures being

imposed by a show whose historical appreciation of the bizarre – Arthur Brown with his blazing head, Roy Wood with his Glam Hag warpaint, Gary Glitter with his Michelin bulge – had long since established it among the most daring visual experiences on British TV.

Smith himself was especially perturbed by the entire affair, although not necessarily because of the band's climb-down. 'It's a real shock to come to *Top Of The Pops*, thinking that I'm going to be facing people again. I wonder why I'm doing it. Horrible. I genuinely feel like that. I find it quite frustrating that I'm sometimes so easy-going about this group, and that I sometimes let it slip. But at least I let it slip upwards.'

The agonies of the appearance, of course, quickly proved worth the trouble: 'Lullaby' became the Cure's biggest hit ever, even eclipsing 'Lovecats' as it rose to #5 in the UK. Indeed, one can only wonder what might have transpired had Fiction followed their American counterpart's lead, and held the release back a few months – 'Lullaby' was released in the US just in time for Halloween.

(ALBUM) *Disintegration*
   8905 Plainsong
   8906 Pictures Of You
   8097 Closedown
   8908 Lovesong
   8901 Lullaby
   8904 Fascination Street
   8909 Prayers For Rain
   8910 The Same Deep Water As You
   8911 Disintegration
   8912 Untitled
CD/cassette bonus tracks
   8913 Last Dance
   8914 Homesick
ORIGINAL RELEASE: Fiction FIX 14, May 1989
COMMENTS: The Cure started work on their eighth album late in 1988, at drummer Williams' Cornwall home. Demoing completed, the party then moved

on to the residential Outside Studios, a 48-track operation in the heart of the Berkshire countryside. Smith confessed to be shocked that the band was back at work so quickly – 'I thought it was all over after *Kiss Me*, when we had a very long lay-off. It gets to the point where it takes so much effort to get going again.

At the same time, however, Smith had a lot to write about. His 30th birthday was swiftly approaching, on April 21 1989, and the looming event was weighing heavy on his mind – he later claimed that what would become the new record's title track, 'Disintegration' itself, was actually written on that fateful day, while the remainder of the lyrics all stemmed from a time 'when I was feeling completely awful. I was very aware that I was reaching my 30th birthday, I realized that I didn't want to go on juggling my different personalities. I didn't want to keep on worrying about the difference between the public me and the private me. I felt a bit weird coming off the back of the *Kiss Me* period, particularly in America, where I wasn't really prepared for that level of mayhem... I wasn't prepared for the amount of attention we were getting.'

One of the key moments in this process was the evening when Smith sat down and listened to *Faith*. It was the first time he had immersed himself in that album in some years, and he confessed 'it disturbed me. I realized I hadn't resolved anything. I reached the point a long time ago where I don't have any kind of spiritual faith and so I have to find something else, some form of release otherwise everything would become unbearable.'

Initially, Smith insisted that he was writing towards that on-again off-again solo album that he had been threatening for some years, and which he actually started seriously contemplating shortly after marrying long-time girlfriend Mary – the couple tied the knot at Worth Abbey, Surrey, on 13 August, 1988, after a 16 year romance.

He quickly noticed, however, that the songs he regarded as too 'personal' for the Cure were, in fact, direct descendants of those that once epitomised the band, back in the days of *Faith* and *Pornography*; and, as the writing continued, so he began to describe the new material as something of a missing link between the two – a link, incidentally, which he had once believed never existed: 'apart from my voice, which is quite constant, *Faith* and *Pornography* are like two different groups.'

Having arrived at that understanding, he devoted himself to maintaining it. 'The things that bother me seem to crystallize, rather than go away. The same things still disturb me [now as then] but I scream in private now, rather than in public. The group is there for me to scream. I didn't want any songs that didn't conform to that mood. It will be compared to those records, but I think it's better.'

Thus resolved, Smith took the songs 'to the rest of the group, knowing that if they were resistant to the ideas of going back to the Cure of eight years ago, I would use them myself. I would have been quite happy to make those songs on my own.' The theme of most of the songs, he continued, 'is age... what happens with age, and your inability to feel as keenly, and that sense of loss all the time. Which either depresses you or it doesn't. I've always felt the perfect age was 17, and I don't wander about crying about it all the time, but those things do bother me.'

Once again, Smith encouraged his bandmates to collaborate in the songwriting, his only condition being that all the music had to be targeted in the same direction as his lyrics. 'I had a key song to motivate me, a strong instinct to start with, then an idea of what I wanted, and went to the group so that we could mutate it.' He reminded them that the album was called *Disintegration*, Williams recalled, 'so everyone knew the mood it should have, and the framework.'

Of the songs which the rest of the band presented at the sessions, 'the most depressing ones got onto the album. Everybody's come in with demos [Tolhurst's offerings included the demo that became 'Homesick'), then we all [sit] around, listen to them, play around with them and decide which are best. Those are the ones we used. It's all very enjoyable. We really are a band now."

Smith continued, 'what we create as a group is far more important than what people think of us as individual players. Having said that, I'd like to add, everyone is good. Boris is a brilliant drummer, who can play everything. Porl is concerned with his guitar playing and has become quite good. Much better than me. Simon is a much better bass player than he ever was. And, by default, I'm a better guitar player. Our standards for ourselves have gone up with each record. We've become good.'

And, with that improvement, there came the confidence to stretch the group's musical boundaries. From the outset, Smith insisted that the group take full advantage of the still-new (ish) CD format by constructing an album that was no less than an hour long, 'which we've never done before,' the ensuing lack of time constraints permitting the band to record 'eight or nine minute songs, long, strong, atmospheric pieces. If you've got an idea you should allow it to develop. If we play something and it sounds a bit rough, but it captures the idea I want, we'll keep it.'

Pre-empting the critics who would inevitably rail at the protracted meanderings of several of the numbers, he continued, 'some of our songs go on because they're exploring the mood. You need a certain amount of time to express that. You can't just say "this is sadness," and play it in one note. We play the kind of music I like to listen to. I don't think I need to justify it.'

But there *were* other thoughts at work, as producer Dave Allen explained, 'for *Disintegration*, we were trying to knit it into one long entity so it's obsessively non-diverse.' *Disintegration* was intended to prove a difficult album, too, to shake off those fair-weather fans who maybe picked up on the Cure as a result of their recent pop successes, and had no appreciation or understanding of the group's inner being. 'I want people to like the Cure for the right reasons,' Smith sniffed, 'because it's different to everything else, and not really accessible. It's a bit of a crass generalization, but people whose favorite Cure albums are *Pornography* and *Disintegration* are generally more alert, and have thought about things.'

That same generalization might also explain the record company's opinion –

the first time the assembled bigwigs heard *Disintegration*, they professed it akin to commercial suicide. 'I thought it was our masterpiece,' Smith mourned. 'They thought it was shit.'

Smith's own determination notwithstanding, a number of other events shaped the record, not least of all the breakdown of relations between Smith and Tolhurst. Other members of the band, too, were fighting, while October almost ended the entire affair in tragedy, when fire broke out in one of the bedrooms, and destroyed almost everything Smith owned.

An electric heater short-circuited, and, because the band was in the studio for the long haul (four months of sessions yawned before them), 'I'd bought all my worldly goods with me. We saved my lyrics, crawling along the floor with wet towels around our heads. We had to make a chain and hold hands and, because I was the only one who knew where they were, I was the last in the chain.' He admitted ruefully, 'we got really told off by the firemen, it was like being back at school. They were saying "your life is more important than your words," and I was like, "what do you know?" They were the only thing that was irreplaceable, I thought.'

Around the distractions and disasters, *Disintegration* took on a life of its own. Many nights, the band stayed up until dawn simply playing, something they hadn't done since they were making *Pornography*. In the studio itself, Smith deliberately made life difficult for himself, just to force himself to breach new frontiers. 'Things got very intense. We put songs like "Disintegration" into a key I can't sing, so it hurt me. It sounds really good from a physical point of view.'

Disintegration reached #3 in the UK. It was in the United States, however, that the true measure of the Cure's popularity could be taken. Even before the band's tour reached American shores, *Disintegration* had smashed into the album chart at #12, provoking an outbreak of Cure mania which saw their faces adorn seemingly every even vaguely music-oriented magazine throughout that summer.

(LIVE) Wembley Stadium, London, 24 July 1989
    UNR Plainsong
    8915 Pictures Of You
    8916 Closedown
    UNR Piggy In The Mirror
    UNR Catch
    UNR A Night Like This
    UNR Just Like Heaven
    8917 Last Dance
    8918 Fascination Street
    UNR Primary
    UNR The Drowning Man
    UNR Lovesong
    UNR Charlotte Sometimes
    UNR The Walk

UNR A Forest
UNR In Between Days
UNR The Same Deep Water As You
8919 Prayers For Rain
8920 Disintegration,
UNR Lullaby
UNR Close To Me
UNR Let's Go To Bed
UNR Why Can't I Be You?
UNR Shake Dog Shake
UNR Siamese Twins
UNR One Hundred Years
8921 Homesick
8922 Untitled
UNR Faith
UNR M
UNR Three Imaginary Boys
UNR Fire In Cairo
UNR Boys Don't Cry
UNR 10.15 Saturday Night
UNR Killing An Arab

ORIGINAL RELEASE: *Entreat* Fiction FIX 14 (France), FIX 17 (UK), 1990

COMMENTS: The *Disintegration* tour kicked off under the Prayer Tour banner, at the Roskilde Festival on 1 May 1989, the first date of what promised to be a gruelling thirteen-week trip around Europe's most gargantuan sports arenas – shows in France, Spain, Portugal, Yugoslavia, Hungary and Greece were included and Smith confessed, 'if this tour had been six weeks, it would have been perfect.' By July, however, he was acknowledging, 'we're moving into the state where it's physically quite demanding. Travelling every day, never being settled, never really doing anything normal... being stared at is a bit of a bind as well."

Then again, he boasted that the group had only had one major row in ten weeks, which was 'pretty good considering we're all living together day-in, day-out. Always on the previous tours, we've never gone beyond the fifth week without someone hitting someone else. That hasn't happened.'

Still the strain was intense and, in October (with the group now in the US), Smith complained to *Sounds*, 'this is the last time I'm gonna tour. It's reached the stage where I can't personally cope with it. I just don't feel comfortable any more with the attention I've been getting. It's purely the number of people that want a bit of the Cure, or a bit of me. We were in some of the most beautiful cities in Europe, and I couldn't go out without my entourage. I tried a disguise and it didn't work. I had no make-up and my hair flat and a hat on, but people recognized me. When I asked them how they knew it was me, they said it was my shoes, so the second time I did it, I changed my shoes and I was still recognized.'

'The concerts were brilliant, but the problems with touring have always been there. Because of the way the group is, because of the type of songs we play, and the make-up within the group, it generally leads to a kind of excess on tour. Not excess in the rock 'n' roll sense, but the feeling that you're there not only to perform as well as you can, as if it's going to be your last concert, but also to experience everything as if it's your last day on earth.

'It tends to become very emotionally and physically exhausting. And, as I get older, I find it takes me longer to recover. Touring's not intrinsically tiring, it's what you make of it. Unfortunately, when we're together, we encourage each other to excess, it becomes very wearing. It's also very gratifying, but I'm just worried that we'll reach a point like so many bands, when the concerts become secondary to actual touring. That's when the rot sets in.

'There are some older acts that still make it. Neil Young's still good, but [David Bowie's] Tin Machine thing is a complete waste of time. There's definitely a performance drug that people will suffer any indignity to hold onto. The Rolling Stones are so hideous it's almost funny. I don't want to be something I've already started making fun of. This is most definitely our last tour.'

The European leg of the tour ended with three nights at London's Wembley Arena, with the third and final show, July 24, ranking amongst the longest Cure gigs ever – three and three-quarter hours, all of which was recorded for future use. At the time of writing, only a fraction of the set has emerged, the eight songs featured on the *Entreat* live album, but still it was a mark of the band's triumph that even this brutal abbreviation was described, by *Melody Maker* as 'possibly the finest live album ever.'

It was also destined to become one of the most controversial. The original release was planned for French consumption only, a limited edition featuring live versions of six songs from *Disintegration*, and intended as a free gift for customers purchasing three or more back catalogue Cure albums.

With a change in jacket colour, from pink to yellow, and the addition of two further tracks, the album was then released in the UK as part of a similar giveaway organized by the HMV records chain; this time, two purchases were necessary, from a twelve-album *A Complete Cure* offer.

Smith himself had approved the French release alone and, when the promotion crossed the channel, he admitted he could have prevented it. Unfortunately, 'the trouble is, I give up. I think "what is the fucking point of doing this?", then everyone rushes through this nonsense and then I think, "oh no, I spent so many years making sure everything's right," and then I rush back into the fight again.'

The full UK release of *Entreat*, in March 1991, was geared towards those collectors who had balked at the high prices already attached to the French and HMV versions of the album, but whose collections would remain incomplete without them; released at a budget price, the album became an instant hit, peaking at a most impressive #10 on the British chart. Unfortunately, it still misjudged the Cure's devoted following, who now found themselves with three

Photo: Gabor Scott, Redferns

The Cure, 11 November 1979: (l-r) Robert Smith, Lol Tolhurst, Simon Gallup, Matthieu Hartley

Photo: Andre Csillag / Rex Features

Another day, another festival, 1981 – (l-r) Robert Smith, Lol Tolhurst, Simon Gallup

*The Cure, 1983: (l-r) Phil Thornally, Porl Thompson, Robert Smith,
Andy Anderson, Lol Tolhurst*

*Italian TV 1987: (l-r) Porl Thompson, Boris Williams (behind drums), Robert
Smith, Lol Tolhurst (with trumpet), Simon Gallup*

Robert and Mary, 1986

Photo: Richard Young / Rex Features

Photo: Bleddyn Butcher / Rex Features

A Relaxed Robert in 1987

An unusual portrait from 1989

Photo: Everett Collection / Rex Features

A classic pose, also from 1989

IN BETWEEN DAYS

Live at Glastonbury, 1995

Robert Smith on stage at Las Vegas, 1996

Photo: Action Press / Rex Features

Late night TV, 1996: Perry Bamonte, Roger O'Donnell, Robert Smith, Jason Cooper, Simon Gallup

Photo: Brian Rasic / Rex Features

Robert Smith and David Bowie at an aftershow party for the Meltdown 2002 festival that Bowie curated

Photo: MB Pictures / Rex Features

Robert Smith and Simon Gallup, 2004

Photo: Rex Features

Hollywood Walk of Fame, 2004: Jason Cooper, Simon Gallup, Robert Smith, Roger O'Donnell, Perry Bamonte

separate versions of the album to try and hunt down for the sake of completeness.

All in all, it was a very botched exercise, and one that was only exacerbated by the ready availability of 50% of the album on the b-sides of various singles. 'Last Dance', 'Prayers For Rain', 'Disintegration' and 'Fascination Street' all appeared as b-sides across the various permutations of 'Pictures Of You'; in addition, 'Homesick' and 'Untitled' were featured on the American 'Lullaby' CD single. This left 'Pictures Of You' and 'Closedown' alone to compensate the Cure fan for the price of admission.

Despite such failings, however, it is not difficult to agree with *Melody Maker*'s enthusiastic response, as *Entreat* offers up the opportunity to hear almost an entire studio album in its live state, after several months of previous shows have already seen the songs reach what could be termed their ideal state of development.

(SINGLE) Love Song
    8908a Love Song (remix)
    8923 2 Late
    8924 Fear Of Ghosts
    8908b Love Song (12" extended remix)
ORIGINAL RELEASE: Fiction FICS 30, August 1989
COMMENTS: Smith wrote 'Lovesong' as a wedding present for Mary. 'The main reason we got married was to have a day we got married on,' Smith explained. 'But actually, it was the best day we ever had. It was brilliant to have all the family there. It would have been wrong if we hadn't done it. It means quite a bit, but we both still think of each other as boyfriend and girlfriend. In fact, that's what we still call each other.'

As a UK single, 'Lovesong' scarcely performed. Even with its lilting melody doubled in length, and a pair of out-take b-sides that could readily have fallen onto *Disintegration* itself, this most lovely of Cure singles peaked at a meagre #18 in September. Across the ocean, however, it became one of the year's most memorable American hits, as it soared to #2, aided by MTV's furious love affair with the accompanying video – a video, incidentally, that Simon Gallup described as 'a bloody travesty.'

Tim Pope, he complained, 'took two days to make those stalactites.'

Smith responded, 'but hang on, that was number two in America. And the video made me look glamorous, and it's the only one ever to do that. It was a poor video, but it made the song.'

But Gallup wouldn't let go. 'We all looked like we don't look like.'

And that was true. (Robert Smith, glamorous?) But did that matter? In a year that had already made American superstars of Love and Rockets (the Peter Murphy-less remnants of Bauhaus), New Order, Depeche Mode and Morrissey, it was suddenly very apparent that *looks* no longer counted for very much. 1989, the dawning of what future historians quickly came to call the age of Alternative Rock, had held a lot of musical surprises in store. But none could be so great as the sudden elevation of a band for whom the term 'Cult Heroes' might well have been invented, as they revisited the musical and motivational scene of a sonic crime that had driven them to the brink of self-destruction less than a decade before.

(TV) *MTV Video Music Awards* (USA), Universal Amphitheatre, 6 September 1989

UNR Just Like Heaven

ORIGINAL RELEASE: unreleased

COMMENTS: The video industry's annual back-slapping beanfeast is most cogently remembered today for comedian Andrew Dice Clay's routine – foul-mouthed enough to earn him a ban from MTV itself. This was also the year when Bon Jovi performed an acoustic set, to answer the critics who accused them of being talentless noise-makers, Motley Crue's Vince Neil punched Guns n'Roses Izzy Stradlin, and Neil Young won the Best Video gong for 'Rockin' In The Free World'.

Amid so much fun, is it any wonder that few people even noticed the weird looking Brit band playing a poppy ballad around the midway mark?

1990

LINE-UP #13 (to May 1990) Robert Smith (vocals, guitar), Porl Thompson (guitar, keyboards), Roger O'Donnell (keyboards), Simon Gallup (bass), Boris Williams (drums)
LINE-UP #14 Robert Smith (vocals, guitar), Porl Thompson (guitar, keyboards), Perry Bamonte (keyboards), Simon Gallup (bass), Boris Williams (drums)

(SINGLE) Pictures Of You
   8906a Pictures of You (remix)
   8906b Pictures Of You (remix)
   8917 Last Dance (live)
   8918 Fascination Street (live)
   8919 Prayers for Rain (live)
   8920 Disintegration (live)
ORIGINAL RELEASE: Fiction FICS 34, March 1990

(TV) *Top Of The Pops* (UK) 12 April 1990
   UNR Pictures Of You
ORIGINAL RELEASE: unreleased
COMMENTS – OR, THE CURE ARGUING: 'When we did the video for "Pictures Of You",' Simon Gallup mourned, '*the Chart Show* wouldn't show it.'

   'That's because it was a rubbish song,' Smith shot back.

   'No it wasn't. They wouldn't show it, because the video wasn't up to a "professional standard," because it was shot on Super 8. But then you get these bands with all these digital bollocks, and they'll show them because it looks posh. No-one ever looks at the entertainment value.'

'I thought it a bloody fine video,' mused Roger O'Donnell.

'Yeah,' Smith agreed. 'I thought it was one of the best five we ever made, and it never got shown anywhere because the song wasn't a single. If that had been the video for "High," we would have had a hit. "Close To Me," people remember the video and the song comes with it. If that video had gone with one of less catchy songs, it wouldn't have been shown so much.'

'Pictures Of You' was written after the fire that struck the studio, and destroyed so many of Smith's possessions. 'I genuinely felt happy about the fire, I didn't feel upset, I felt relief in a very banal way.' The song was about shrugging off past burdens. 'I realized that I'm clutching old pictures of things, even taken before my birth, to give me a sense that things went on.'

Edited down from its original 7.24 minute length (and then pushed back up to 6.43 for the extended remix), 'Pictures Of You' would prove to be one of the most controversial singles in the Cure's entire catalogue, as Fiction released it in a total of twelve different formats, a barrage of different coloured sleeves and vinyls, alternate b-sides (drawn from the 1989 Wembley Stadium concert) and fresh mixes, all aimed at outrageously milking the band's long-established coterie of die-hard collectors.

Such crass commercialism was to receive its just rewards, however. Not only did the single falter at a paltry #24, it also prompted the British Phonographic Institute to announce that, henceforth, only four formats of a specific single could be counted towards its chart placing – ideally, 7-inch and 12-inch vinyl, cassette and one CD. Smith himself has since confessed, "we were sort of misled, because I was probably tired at the time, and we got sucked into the idea that it would be good to do twelve different versions. It was pretty dumb.'

Yet 'Pictures Of You' was only the latest manifestation of a limited edition craze that swept the Cure's catalogue in the wake of *Disintegration*, as a slew of 'exclusive limited editions' were foisted upon the band's completist public. The first of these, available on the day of release only, was a specially autographed copy of the album, available only from branches of Britain's HMV records chain on May 5, 1989. Each shop is estimated to have received no more than four copies of the album, to be sold on a first-come first-served basis. Promoted only via an ad campaign in the *New Musical Express* that same week, this version of the album offered the first sign that Tolhurst was no longer a member of the Cure – he was the only band member whose autograph was missing.

A *Disintegration* vinyl picture disc was also issued, a year after the original album release. In August 1989, 10,000 individually numbered *Lovebox* packages appeared, to help promote the newly released 'Lovesong' single, each comprising the regular 7-inch single, plus a linen print of the cover art. All four singles, meanwhile, were incorporated into *Integration* (Elektra 966633-2), a limited edition US release, issued in CD long-box format, with a tinted detail from the regular album cover as its jacket. A sticker on the front claimed the package featured "17 rare Cure tracks" – in fact, the box merely brought together the four regular US singles, plus a none-too-impressive poster.

The aforementioned *Entreat* album, of course, fits into this same period, while a neat promo release was the *Thirteen Doses: An Incomplete Video Cure* VHS sampler, which replicated the *Entreat* jacket photograph in black and white, and included '10.15 Saturday Night', 'Play For Today', 'Primary', 'Hanging Garden', 'The Walk', 'The Lovecats', 'The Caterpillar', 'In Between Days', 'A Night Like This', 'Why Can't I Be You?', 'Just Like Heaven', 'Lullaby' and 'Pictures Of You'.

Alongside the so-convoluted mass of 'Pictures Of You' variations, these releases marked the culmination of the Cure's flirtation with 'limited edition' versions of releases, a tangled jungle of collectible heartache that, Smith acknowledged, he was more-or-less unaware of until the publication of Daren Butler's priceless *The Cure On Record* book.

'He introduced me to a world that I was totally unaware of. I honestly was totally unaware that that kind of mania even existed. A lot of that book was related to what goes on globally, because if you seriously think we have any control over a handprint and a bit of squiggle on the Brazilian cover of *Kiss Me*, it doesn't happen like that. They do what they like, everywhere except Europe and America. There's stuff comes out of Australia, New Zealand, still, that bears no resemblance to what we're doing, and there's African things... we've been on albums with the Specials and Joy Division, whoever they can get their hands on, and it really is stuff they've just taped off the radio, and remastered back onto vinyl.'

(STUDIO) Mixed Up sessions, May-June 1990
    8101a Primary (Red mix, June 1990)
    8213b Let's Go To Bed (Milk mix, June 1990)
    8401a The Caterpillar (Flicker mix – by Brian 'Chuck' New, May 1990)
    8501a In Between Days (Shiver mix – by William Orbit, June 1990)
    8509c Close to Me (Closest mix, June 1990)
    8509d Close To Me (Closer mix by Paul Oakenfold, June 1990)
    8710a Just Like Heaven (Dizzy mix, June 1990)
    9005 Never Enough
    9005a Never Enough (Big mix, June 1990)
    9006 Harold and Joe
    9007 The Walk (Everything mix – rerecorded June 1990)
    9008 A Forest (Tree mix – rerecorded June 1990)
ORIGINAL RELEASE: Fiction FIX 18, November 1990 and associated singles
COMMENTS: Sessions for the forthcoming Cure remix project (see appendix one, *Mixed Up*)

(LIVE) Glastonbury Festival, 23 June 1990
    UNR Shake Dog Shake
    UNR A Strange Day
    UNR A Night Like This
    UNR Catch
    UNR Pictures Of You

UNR Fascination Street
UNR Lullaby
UNR Dressing Up
UNR The Same Deep Water As You
UNR Lament
9001 Just Like Heaven
UNR The Walk
UNR Primary
UNR In Between Days
UNR A Forest
UNR Disintegration,
UNR Close To Me
UNR Let's Go To Bed
UNR Why Can't I Be You?
UNR 10.15 Saturday Night
UNR Killing An Arab
UNR Never Enough

ORIGINAL RELEASE: *Glastonbury Broadcasts Volume One* (*NME* freebie), June 1999

COMMENTS: Although the show was remarkable for the appearance of 'Never Enough', several months shy of its eventual release, the BBC broadcast featured only a dozen songs, of which just one, 'Just Like Heaven', was subsequently culled for release on an *NME* freebie.

The show itself was not especially amazing. Passing helicopters drowned out much of 'Fascination Street', while Smith later complained, 'Glastonbury was ok, but its organisation does leave an awful lot to be desired. There should have been crush barriers in the main field.' One particular incident close to the front of the stage, which led to a girl requiring the kiss of life 'shocked us a bit too much to really get into the set.'

(ALBUM) various artists *Rubaiyat*
9002 Hello, I Love You
9003 Hello, I Love You (A Short Return)

9004 Hello, I Love You (Psychedelic Mix)
ORIGINAL RELEASE: Elektra 960940 (U.S.), 1990
COMMENTS: Celebrating the 40th anniversary of Elektra Records, *Rubaiyat* rather uniquely turned to its current roster to reinterpret songs from the label's illustrious past, a somewhat hit-and-miss operation that nevertheless turned up in some remarkable jewels.

The Cure's version of the Doors' 1971 classic 'Hello I Love You' was certainly destined to fall into that category, although it was later revealed that the song was, in fact, the band's second choice. Smith originally intended covering (and got so far as demoing) Wendy Waldheim's 'Pirate Ships', taken from her 1973 album *Love Has Got Me*... the Elektra connection was conjured by songstress Judy Collins, who covered the song on 1975's *Judith* album. Turning to harmonium, seagulls and crashing waves, Smith created a beautifully atmospheric piece. But it was also unrecognizable as the Cure in *any* of their guises. 'It didn't feel quite right,' Smith mourned.

A joyous, raucous and frantically leering 'Hello I Love You', on the other hand, could not have been anyone but, and that despite the Cure recording no less than three versions of the song, a three minute run through and a 13-second reprise of cacophony for inclusion on *Rubaiyat*, and the contrarily, dramatically, lurching six minute 'psychedelic mix' that was aired on the band's private Cure FM radio station, then archived until *Join The Dots*.

For their own not inconsiderable contributions to the Elektra story, the Cure themselves were covered on *Rubaiyat*, as one John Eddie took on 'In Between Days'.

(SINGLE) Never Enough
   9005 Never Enough
   9006 Harold and Joe
   8213b Let's Go To Bed (milk mix)
   9005a Never Enough (Big Mix)
ORIGINAL RELEASE: Fiction FICS 35, September 1990

(TV) *Top Of The Pops* (UK) 27 September 1990
   UNR Never Enough
COMMENTS: The lurching 'Never Enough' was originally conceived as a one-off single, to help wipe away the taste of the *Disintegration*-era overkill. In the event, it became the herald of a new album, as a specially commissioned new mix of 'Let's Go To Bed' was added to the CD release – an eye-catching partner to Simon Gallup's peculiar 'Harold And Joe', a song whose original demo was titled for characters from the TV soap *Brookside* – and which Smith never got round to renaming.

'Never Enough' itself is a magnificent single, a swirling mass of noisy guitars and squelching Smiths, flirting through the same kind of psychedelic stew that the band had already inflicted upon the Doors' 'Hello I Love You', and demanding *precisely* the kind of maniacal remix that Mark Saunders would serve up for the extended version.

(SINGLE) Close To Me (Closest Mix)
   8509c Close to Me (closest mix)
   8509d Close To Me (closer mix)
   8710a Just Like Heaven (dizzy mix)
   8101a Primary (red mix)
ORIGINAL RELEASE: Fiction FICS 36, October 1990

(TV) Top Of The Pops (UK) 1 November 1990
   UNR Close To Me
ORIGINAL RELEASE: unreleased
COMMENTS: A heavier taste of what the new album portended was served up by this hastily issued follow-up single, and it has to be admitted that the wheels are already coming off the project – both via Paul Oakenfold's surprisingly lifeless tampering with the deep-set majesty of the original version, and a Tim Pope video that attempted to tell the story of what happened next... after the wardrobe fell into the sea. Looking much like a dry-run pre-sentiment of *Spongebob Squarepants*, the result simply couldn't compete with what had gone before.

Lest any hint of Luddism should seem rife in such sentiments, however, it should be pointed out that the b-side mixes, whirling up 'Just Like Heaven' and positively terrorising 'Primary', were as good as such things could ever get – and, maybe if we all wish real hard, the rest of the album will be as stunning? Altogether now....

1991

LINE-UP #14 Robert Smith (vocals, guitar), Porl Thompson (guitar, keyboards), Perry Bamonte (keyboards), Simon Gallup (bass), Boris

(LIVE) T&C2, London, 17 January 1991
9101 The Big Hand
UNR Pictures Of You
UNR Lullaby
UNR Fascination Street
9102 Away
UNR A Letter To Elise
UNR Just Like Heaven
UNR Dressing Up
9103 Wendy Time
UNR The Walk
9104 Let's Go To Bed
UNR Why Can't I Be You?
UNR In Between Days
UNR A Forest
UNR Disintegration
UNR A Strange Day
UNR In Your House
UNR Primary
UNR Never Enough
UNR Three Imaginary Boys
UNR Boys Don't Cry
9105 10.15 Saturday night
9106 Killing An Arab

ORIGINAL RELEASE: 9101-04 *The Cure Play Out* VHS/DVD (Windsong WIV 007) + 9105-06 on promo VHS

COMMENTS: Billed as the Five Imaginary Boys, the Cure stunned fans with a handful of new songs, which Smith later said were recorded with a view towards a live EP. This never transpired, but four tracks from the performance – new numbers 'Wendy time', 'The Big Hand' and 'Away', plus 'Let's Go To Bed' would be included on the *Play Out* video collection. Two further tracks, '10.15 Saturday Night' and 'Killing An Arab' were included on promotional copies of the same VHS.

Play Out itself would emerge a fascinating collection, its contents documenting a fortnight in the life of a functioning rock band at the top of the world, tracing the Cure through two gigs (one club, one arena), a TV show, an *Unplugged* session, a pair of rehearsals and an awards ceremony – as detailed below. And, of course, the completed package has its critics – fans would rather have seen more of the club show, and less of *Unplugged*; more behind-the-scenes and less in-front-of-the-cameras and so forth.

Some future DVD release may deliver as much. For now, however, *Play Out* is one of those very rare releases that really does seem to have been compiled more for the fans than for the money; and, as such, can probably be recommended higher than any other single live Cure document.

(LIVE) The Great British Music Weekend, Wembley, 19 January 1991
    9107 Pictures Of You
    9108 Fascination Street
    UNR Just Like Heaven
    9109 Lullaby
    UNR The Walk
    UNR Let's Go To Bed
    UNR Why Can't I Be You?
    UNR In Between Days
    9110 A Forest
    UNR Never Enough
    UNR Three Imaginary Boys
    UNR Boys Don't Cry,
    UNR Disintegration
ORIGINAL RELEASE: *The Cure Play Out* VHS/DVD (Windsong WIV 007)
COMMENTS: Several of the bands appearing at this festival, the Cure included, were recorded for a Radio One live broadcast; in addition, four songs were included on *Play Out*: 'Pictures Of You', 'Fascination Street', 'Lullaby' and ' A forest.'

(STUDIO) E-zee Hire rehearsal studio – London – 22nd January 1991
    9111 The Blood
    9112 The Walk
ORIGINAL RELEASE: *The Cure Play Out* VHS/DVD (Windsong WIV 007)
COMMENTS: Rehearsals for the forthcoming MTV *Unplugged* broadcast.

(TV) *The Jonathan Ross Show* (UK) 23 January 1991
    9113 Harold And Joe
    UNR Hello I Love You
ORIGINAL RELEASE: *The Cure Play Out* VHS/DVD (Windsong WIV 007)
COMMENTS: Accompanied by a handful of clips, the *Jonathan Ross* performance of the b-side 'Harold And Joe' was included within the 'Day Three' portion of the *Play Out* video.

(TV) *MTV Unplugged*, 24 January 1991
   UNR Lullaby
   9114 Just Like Heaven
   UNR Let's Go To Bed
   9115 If Only Tonight We Could Sleep
   UNR The Caterpillar
   UNR In Your House
   UNR The Walk
   9116 A Letter To Elise
   UNR The Blood
   UNR Time Has Told Me
   UNR M
   9117 Boys Don't Cry

ORIGINAL RELEASE: *The Cure Play Out* VHS/DVD (Windsong WIV 007)

COMMENTS: A suitably eccentric selection of songs heralded the Cure's much-anticipated appearance on MTV's *Unplugged*, in the days before the series... indeed, the entire unplugged concept... became a by-word for artistic over-endeavour and artlessness. A lovely cover of Nick Drake's 'Time Has Told Me' notwithstanding, there were no real surprises, of course – the Cure have frequently acknowledged the vitality of acoustic performance, although it is possible to snipe at both the truncated version that was aired on MTV, and the even-briefer (four song) showcase that appeared on *Play Out*: 'Just Like Heaven', 'A letter to Elise', 'If Only Tonight We Could Sleep' and 'Boys Don't Cry', plus rehearsals of 'The Blood' and 'The Walk' (see 22 January entry). The MTV broadcast featured 'Let's Go To Bed', 'Just Like Heaven', 'The Caterpillar', 'The Blood', 'Boys Don't Cry' and 'The Walk'

(STUDIO) rehearsals for the BRIT Awards, Dominion Theatre, London, 9 February 1991

(TV) the BRIT Awards, Dominion Theatre, London, 10 February 1991
   9118 Never Enough

ORIGINAL RELEASE: *The Cure Play Out* VHS/DVD (Windsong WIV 007)

COMMENTS: Wrapping up both the *Play Out* video, and a hectic few weeks, the Cure crowned a triumphant year with a brilliant performance at the BRITs – and, of course, a gong, for Best British Group.

1992

LINE-UP #14 Robert Smith (vocals, guitar), Porl Thompson (guitar, keyboards), Perry Bamonte (keyboards), Simon Gallup (bass), Boris Williams (drums)

(SINGLE) High
> 9201 High
> 9201a High (higher mix)
> 9201b High (Trip Mix)
> 9202 This Twilight Garden
> 9203 Play
> 9204a Open (Fix Mix)

ORIGINAL RELEASE: Fiction FICS 39, March 1992

COMMENTS: The first single to be taken from the forthcoming *Wish* album was… shall we say… just a little misleading. It was really rather good – indeed, 'High' could probably take its place in any Cure-career-spanning Top 30, a bouncy pop number filled with intriguing rattles and 'Why Can't I Be You?'-shaped gurgles. A deserved UK #8.

Flip it, and 'This Twilight Garden', a session out-take, was so great that even Smith now mourns 'I cannot believe I left it off the album,' as it rolls in on languorous rhythms, the vocals echo off the studio walls, and Smith's vocal lapses into a tenderness that he doesn't always pull off so well. 'It's my most quintessentially English song,' Smith insists… he wrote it shortly after he and wife Mary moved to the south coast, to a home with its own garden, Smith's first. 'I was trying to capture that feeling of late summer dusk, the colour of the sky, the smell of the grass, the sound of the last bird singing. I think it's one of the best love songs we've ever done.'

The sort-of-just-like 'Just Like Heaven'-ish 'Play', too, bodes well for the main attraction, which means only the sundry remixes spoil the show – but that's hardly a problem that's confined to the Cure. The scarcity of the limited edition 12-inch pressing featuring 'Open (Fix Mix)', incidentally, was addressed by the song's subsequent appearance on the *Select* magazine cassette freebie *Maximum Bliss*.

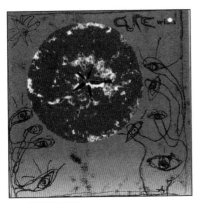

(ALBUM) *Wish*
   9204 Open
   9201 High
   9205 Apart
   9206 From The Edge of the Deep Green Sea
   9207 Wendy Time
   9208 Doing The Unstuck
   9209 Friday I'm In Love
   9210 Trust
   9211 A Letter To Elise
   9212 Cut
   9213 To Wish Impossible Things
   9214 End

ORIGINAL RELEASE: Fiction FIX 20, April 1992

COMMENTS: Looking back on *Disintegration*, Smith explained, 'hitting 30 was a real benchmark. I wanted to change everything about the way I was doing things, and that was the album. After that, it changed, it became a much easier going group. Whether you think the albums suffered or not is irrelevant. The way it worked within the context of the group was immeasurably better than the albums leading up to being 30.'

As the first full scale example of this new egalitarian regime, *Wish* remains perhaps the most contentious, and certainly the most misunderstood album in the Cure's repertoire. Its success simply cannot be argued with – it soared to #2 in the US, dragging the 'Friday, I'm In Love' single into the Top 20 in its wake, and sending the band out on a world tour which seemed to last forever.

'*Wish* was our most successful album ever,' Smith remarked a decade later. 'I was really surprised, I was looking back at the figures and I was really shocked; *Wish* was the one Cure album that has sold constantly over time. It went to #1 in virtually every country, but then it dropped and I thought that was it. But it gained this strange second wind that we'd never had before, and will probably never have again, probably from people hearing "Friday I'm In Love," and wondering "which album is that on?"'

IN BETWEEN DAYS

Was it a good Cure album, though? In places, yes: 'From The Edge Of The Deep Green Sea' certainly merited all the applause that was poured down upon it, while 'To Wish Impossible Things' and 'End' close the album in eloquent fashion. 'Open' worked well as well. Indeed, Smith later revealed that *Wish* 'was supposed to follow on from *Disintegration*, in a similar kind of mood. But I ended up putting on songs like "Friday I'm In Love" and "Doing The Unstuck," the more upbeat pop ones, and that made it an altogether lighter album.'

It also transformed it into a patchier affair, with the impossibly saccharin pop of 'Friday I'm In Love' representing a nadir from which even Smith's 'tongue-firmly-in-cheek' defence could not salvage it. Five years on, playing the *Galore* hits collection, it was still very easy to wear out the Fast Forward button, simply anticipating the onset of 'Friday I'm In Love'.

How much of that patchiness existed only in the eye of the beholder, however? Answering that question, Smith recapped the band's recent history. 'Coming off the *Kiss Me* album and tour, there was a lot of anticipation of what we were going to do next. We were becoming a really successful band, playing stadiums, and there was that sense that, whatever we were going to do next, it was going to be something big. So *Disintegration* became a fantastically big album in every sense of the word.

'*Wish* never had that kind of dramatic impact on peoples lives, because we'd already done one *Disintegration*. But the weird thing about Cure fans is, the amount of revisionism that goes on. *Mixed Up*, which came after *Disintegration*, was unanimously slated by critics and fans alike, but now it's been accepted as a pretty cool album because there was a fear that we were going to become a dance band... "what's going on?"... and there was this real sense of disappointment. Whereas now, people know we weren't becoming a dance band, so they can look at the album in a different way, and think "some of these mixes are great takes on songs I like".

'And it's the same thing with *Wish*. People thought it was going to be the follow-up to *Disintegration*, and that *Mixed Up* was just an aberration... "well, maybe they took too many of the wrong kind of drugs... and let's hope they get back on track." But we came out with what they saw as another aberration. *Disintegration* is still perceived as an event, one of those albums that comes out and makes much bigger waves. But there are Cure fans now who like *Wish* just as much.'

And others who still term it the least palatable record in the band's entire catalogue, and here's why. *Wish* wasn't challenging, like *Seventeen Seconds* and *Faith*, it wasn't scary, like *Pornography* and *Disintegration*; it wasn't even endearingly all over the place like *The Top*, *The Head On The Door* and *Kiss Me Kiss Me Kiss Me*. But it was extremely quirky, enduringly memorable and enticingly romantic, which was precisely what people expected from the Cure. Which, in turn, means it was pure flummery, a paint-by-numbers idiot guide to everything that the band once held precious, but was too 'on edge' to transport into the arenas.

What do you want from the Cure? Angst? It was here ('True'). Danceable joviality? Yep ('Wendy Time'). 'Forest'-like creepiness? That's here as well ('Deep Green Sea'). *Wish* had everything that the Cure ever promised, all neatly packaged into Top 40 bite-size portions. And, if it really was a distillation of all that the Cure were legendary for, then where did that leave the legend? Running for cover, of course, before it, too, was turned into 'Friday I'm In Love', a song of such crushingly crippling lameness that *Alternative Press*'s review of the album fervently hoped that it wouldn't be released as a single. 'If it wasn't the Cure, you'd despise it without question. As it *is* the Cure – well, go ahead and despise it anyway. They didn't write it for you.'

'Some songs are very particular to a particular moments, others are very general,' Smith explained. 'Which is why I write about the stuff I write about, which goes on year after year after year. I'm ranging from things that happened to me, things that I've experienced, things I've observed, and other people's points of view altogether.

'That's the difference between now and then – whenever "then" was. It was all pure autobiography, taken exclusively from things that had worked me up to the point where I'd write a song. Now I can take situations which don't really upset my equilibrium, I can hear something we could do musically, and I'll write a song to compliment it, which in the old days I would never ever do. I had no interest in it, I just wanted to put my own point of view across, and say this is how I feel about something, and the music was just a backdrop.

'It's changed around, I've tried... to enhance the music, that will push you towards thinking in a certain way, which I don't think I'd really... it devalues the song a little for me personally, as the singer, but in other ways it enhances it immeasurably as a member of the group. And *Wish* was the first time I tried that, where I wrote [songs] that had nothing to do with me at all, where I was trying to encapsulate something that I was seeing.'

(STUDIO) *Wish* album out-takes
    9215 Uyea Sound
    9216 Cloudberry
    9217 Off to Sleep...
    9218 The Three Sisters

ORIGINAL RELEASE: *Lost Wishes* EP, Fiction FICCS 50, November 1993

COMMENTS: A cassette-only release of such obscurity that, when the American *Alternative Press* magazine included it in a Cure discography in early 1996, the switchboard creaked beneath the weight of angry fans insisting that the writer had invented it. Wrong. He just wished he had.

Smith explained: 'we hit on the idea of a separate album of purely instrumental things,' making it available only through the fan club. A fifth track was scheduled for the EP, but remains unavailable... Smith continued, '[it] sounded like a Cure backing track without me singing. That seemed a bit pointless, so we shelved it for the moment but we'll probably get back to it."

(SINGLE) Friday I'm In Love
    9209 Friday I'm In Love
    9209a Friday I'm In Love (strangelove mix)
    9219 Halo
    9220 Scared As You
ORIGINAL RELEASE: Fiction FICS 42, May 1992

(TV) *Top Of The Pops* (UK) 30 April 1992
    UNR Friday I'm In Love
ORIGINAL RELEASE: unreleased
COMMENTS: Once again, the out-take b-sides – the symphonic 'Halo' (with backing vocals from Shelleyann Orphan's Caroline Crawley) and the lumpy apologia of 'Scared As You' – served up a far grander treat than the bulk of the album from which they were expunged, although the horror that was 'Friday I'm In Love' was so difficult to recover from, that actually ploughing deeper into the single was a fairly onerous task.

But somebody must have liked it, as the Cure overcame their traditional inability to follow up one big hit with another, and saw 'Friday I'm In Love' soar to #6, two places better off than 'High' and, incredibly, their second-highest placing ever ('Lullaby' reached #5.)

(LIVE) Auburn Hills, Detroit, Michigan, 18-19 July 1992
    9221 Tape (intro)
    9222 Open
    9223 High
    9224 Pictures Of You
    9225 Lullaby
    9226 A Night Like This
    9227 Trust
    9228 Doing The Unstuck
    9229 Friday I'm In Love
    9230 In Between Days
    9231 From The Edge Of The Deep Green Sea
    9232 Never Enough
    9233 Cut
    9234 End
Cassette bonus tracks/*Sideshow* CD EP
    9235 Just Like Heaven
    9236 Fascination Street
    9237 The Walk
    9238 Let's Go To Bed
VHS bonus tracks
    9239 To Wish Impossible Things
    9240 Primary
    9241 Boys Don't Cry

9242 Why Can't I Be You?
9243 A Forest

ORIGINAL RELEASE: *Show* CD Fiction FIX 25, September 1993; *Sideshow* EP
Fiction 6627502, September 1993; *Show* VHS Polygram 087742-3

(LIVE) Zenith, Paris, 19-21 October 1992
    9244 The Figurehead
    9245 One Hundred Years
    9246 At Night
    9247 Play For Today
    9248 Apart
    9249 In Your House
    9250 Lovesong
    9251 Catch
    9252 A Letter To Elise
    9253 Dressing Up
    9254 Charlotte Sometimes
    9255 Close To Me

ORIGINAL RELEASE: *Paris* CD, Fiction FIX 26, October 1993
COMMENTS: The above notes only the tracks included on the officially

released recordings of these shows. Cure sets at this point were stretching towards the three hour mark on a regular basis, with between 28-30 tracks performed nightly: among those absented from the *Show* and *Sideshow* double-header were 'A Letter To Elise,' from the main set, and the encore performances of 'Lovesong', 'Close To Me' and 'Charlotte Sometimes', all of which subsequently made it onto *Paris*; plus 'M', 'Three Imaginary Boys' and 'A Strange Day'. Missing from the three nights in Paris that were highlighted for *Paris* itself were versions of: 'It's Not You', 'Faith', 'Shake Dog Shake', 'The Big Hand' and the now-seldom performed 'Forever'.

There were, Gallup explained, some very concrete reasons for the decision to follow-up *Wish* with two new live albums. 'With the *Wish* tour, we knew Porl [Thompson] was going to leave... we didn't, at the time, know Boris [Williams] was also going to, but it seemed like a good way to end that chapter. And, to be quite honest with you, we didn't know if we were going to do another record; we're not that clever that we think "in two years time we're gonna do another record." We tend to get together and get excited if someone's got a tune, just like we did with *Wish*.'

The twin departures shocked Smith, although he admitted, 'I admire them both for stepping away. It's really unusual; most of the time I've had to kick people out. I've got a reputation for being horrible but I hate being around people who don't want to do the same things that I do. I've always believed that there is a natural lifespan for a group. At the end of the tour, we'd been together for so long, we'd run out – not of things to say, but of ways to talk to each other.'

Of the two albums, *Show* (and the *Sideshow* EP that swept up the overflow of tracks from the CD... the cassette album contained all 18 songs) was described by Smith as the 'official' set, with *Paris* aimed exclusively at the old time fans who were demanding an airing for the sometimes stunning versions of older, 'more obscure' songs that the band was occasionally capable of unleashing. '*Show* is a fantastic album,' he enthused. 'It's the Cure live at their best. There's no better collection of songs ever in our history, than that tour. Everyone was playing so well, I just wanted to capture that. I just thought "I want this, this is like my testament, this is what we were like when we were doing this stuff".

'*Paris* came out because there was actually fan demand; I didn't want to put stuff like "Drowning Man" and that on a live album that I thought was a showpiece album [in fact, he didn't!], but a lot of people wanted our interpretations, in a good setting, recorded well, of some of the older stuff, the more hardcore fan stuff, so that's what *Paris* was. It honestly had nothing to do with me, in a funny sort of way, I really didn't mind if it was out or not. We didn't promote it, it had no advertising, it was just sort of there, and it sold a handful of copies.

'It was unusual to bring two live albums out at once,' he conceded, 'but they were such totally different records.' And he adds, with understandable incredulity, 'afterwards, we got criticized by people, saying "well, there's so many bootlegs, why did you bother?" It has nothing to do with me if there's a lot of bootlegs of the Cure; I've never objected to them, no-one's ever had their tape recorder confiscated at a Cure show, it doesn't bother me in the slightest. But, at the same time, I find it incredible that I should be dissuaded from releasing my version of events, just because everybody else has released theirs!'

Smith had originally intended releasing only a tour film, and even that was a half-hearted ambition at first. 'My... reluctance about making the film was that it was another period of looking back, a retrospective,' he told *Vox*. 'I just sort of worry, because that's what record companies do to groups when they've run out of ideas!' There were further difficulties once the film was shot, and editing awaited. A director had been engaged, Smith explained, and a schedule worked out. 'I don't remember the director's name,' he claimed in *Q*, 'but he was supposed to present us with the finished version. Instead he was already working on Paul McCartney's next project, so we had this severely bastardised version of what was a good concert.'

He could have panicked. Instead, he decided to finish the job himself: 'Rather than treating it like something to be done in a hurry, I thought I'd learn about film editing, so the whole exercise was like a three-month film-editing night school. The strangest thing about editing the film was that I really hated the group. [And] I hated myself more than anyone else.'

'For a band whose primary stock-in-trade is atmosphere, intrigue and studio flim-flammery, the Cure have a remarkably high opinion of their concert work. [But] you know how [Robert Smith] loves word games? Let's play one of our own, make up little anagrams and see if we can divine (or even define) the band's future. There's Crue, for instance, or even [B]ruce. But my favourite, deferring to Smith's burgeoning guitar godhood, is R.U.E.C (as in Clapton, dummy). I can't think of anyone else whose made so many live albums.' (*Alternative Press*).

(SINGLE) A Letter To Elise
  9211 A Letter to Elise
  9256 The Big Hand
  9257 A Foolish Arrangement
  9211a A Letter to Elise (blue mix)
  9208a Do The Unstuck (Mark Saunders remix)
ORIGINAL RELEASE: Fiction FICS 46, October 1992; 'Unstuck' on *Join The Dots*
COMMENTS: The Cure adamantly opposed the release of 'Letter To Elise' as the third single from *Wish*. Smith explained, 'We had "Doing The Unstuck" [lined up]... we'd already commissioned the remix... it was the best single... and Polydor and Elektra wouldn't release it. It was a great pop song, I was saving it for the third single and, when we got there, they said "what the market needs is...," and I said, "great! A song you have to listen to, which doesn't have a hook, and which will never get played on the radio. That's a really good idea".

The Saunders remix of 'Do The Unstuck' was unceremoniously shelved until *Join The Dots* hauled it out of oblivion, and the Cure resigned themselves to 'Elise'. 'It was a really good song,' Smith continued, 'but it wasn't a single. That was the one mistake, where I let go of the reins of power, and I allowed the record company to pick what they thought would make a good single.'

The video was no picnic, either. 'That was the worse thing we ever did, it got shown on MTV once. We had a bearded cameraman and he was in more of the video than I was. Nothing against bearded cameramen, of course....'

The b-sides for this benighted release do salvage it somewhat, of course. 'The Big Hand' was the first song recorded for *Wish* and, right up until the very last minute, was intended for inclusion... even the album's artwork includes a pictorial reference to the song. Smith, however, was never convinced by the number and, over the protesting howls of his bandmates, he filed it away for a b-side instead. He was wrong.

'A Foolish Arrangement', meanwhile, was one of the last songs the band recorded – indeed, while the backing track dated from the last weeks of the *Wish* sessions, the lyrics and vocal weren't put down until the band was informed that they were one b-side short, just weeks before the release. Smith and Gallup completed the song in Sydney, Australia, immediately after coming offstage.

1993

LINE-UP #14 (to October) Robert Smith (vocals, guitar), Porl Thompson (guitar, keyboards), Perry Bamonte (keyboards), Simon Gallup (bass), Boris Williams (drums)
LINE-UP #15 Robert Smith (vocals, guitar), Perry Bamonte (keyboards), Simon Gallup (bass), Boris Williams (drums)

(LIVE) Great Expectations, Finsbury Park, London, 13 June 1993
    UNR Shiver And Shake
    UNR Shake Dog Shake
    UNR One Hundred Years
    9301 Just Like Heaven
    UNR Push
    UNR Fascination Street
    UNR Open
    UNR High
    UNR From The Edge Of The Deep Green Sea
    9302 Disintegration
    UNR End
    UNR Friday I'm In Love
    UNR Three Imaginary Boys
    UNR It's Not You
    UNR Boys Don't Cry
    UNR Fire In Cairo
    UNR A Forest
ORIGINAL RELEASE: various artists *Great Xpectations Live*, XFM XFMCD 1, 1993
COMMENTS: Playing their only concert of the year, the Cure headlined a benefit concert for the radio station XFM (Smith and Chris Parry were numbered among the station's directors), alongside Carter USM, Belly, the Frank & Walters, Catherine Wheel, Senseless Things and the Family Cat. Two songs from their set were included on the subsequent souvenir live album, a so-so 'Just Like Heaven' and a magnificent 'Disintegration'.

(ALBUM) various artists *Stone Free: A Tribute To Jimi Hendrix*
    9303 Purple Haze (Virgin Radio mix)
    9303a Purple Haze
ORIGINAL RELEASE: Reprise 45438, 1993

COMMENTS: Although Virgin 1215am Radio played a version of this as only the second song it ever broadcast, in April 1993, the longer mix made available on the actual *Stone Free* tribute album was a rerecording/remix undertaken by Smith and producer Brian 'Chuck' New alone. The original version remained unavailable until its inclusion on *Join The Dots*.

Reiterating the band's age-old fascination with Hendrix (remember 'Foxy Lady'?), the Cure's take on the American's second single remained recognisably 'Purple Haze', but was slowed down in much the same spirit as the 'psychedelic mix' of 'Hello I Love You'. Indeed, the Cure completely underplayed the signature guitar riff, an omission that was compensated for by an echo-drenched vocal, and a lasciviously trip-hop influenced rhythm.

(TV) *Sean's Show* (UK) 29 December 1993
    UNR High
ORIGINAL RELEASE: unreleased
COMMENTS: By the end of 1993, the Cure had reconvened in the studio, albeit one man short. Gallup explained, 'we started doing demos, but because we didn't have a drummer, it's a bit weird rehearsing with a drum machine, so there was a lot of things going on. All the time Robert and I were writing, but there's always things to do... like Robert had to mix *Show*... I was there, but when you see videos of bands sitting round the mixing desk joining in, it's all a lie. Perry and I were there for moral support really.'

1994

LINE-UP #15 (to late spring) Robert Smith (vocals, guitar), Perry Bamonte (keyboards), Simon Gallup (bass), Boris Williams (drums)
LINE-UP #16 Robert Smith (vocals, guitar), Perry Bamonte (guitar), Roger O'Donnell (keyboards), Simon Gallup (bass)

(ALBUM) various artists *The Crow Original Soundtrack*
   9401 Burn
ORIGINAL RELEASE: Atlantic 82519, 1994
COMMENTS: The film-makers' original scheme was to incorporate 'The Hanging Garden', from *Pornography*, into the soundtrack – lyrics to the song are quoted in *The Crow* comic itself. Smith rejected their overture, offering instead a new song cut in precisely the same sonic mould as 'The Hanging Garden'... the rumbling percussive intro, the guitars that dangle from meat-hooks, the vocal torn from the soul. 'Proof', as *Alternative Press* put it, 'that Smith can still make great records when he wants to.'

Sadly, the prominence that the song was intended to enjoy in the movie was sliced following the death of star Brandon Lee – several scenes were cut or shortened, including that for which 'Burn' was planned. A mere fraction of the song thus appears in the film.

1995

LINE-UP #17 Robert Smith (vocals, guitar), Perry Bamonte (guitar), Roger O'Donnell (keyboards), Simon Gallup (bass), Jason Cooper (drums)

(ALBUM) various artists *Judge Dredd Original Soundtrack*
   9501 Dredd Song
ORIGINAL RELEASE: Epic BK 67220, 1995
COMMENTS: An extraordinarily epic sounding production for a less than stellar song, 'Dredd Song' was later dismissed by Smith as 'an example of us over-reaching ourselves with an orchestra. We were trying to do something that was very grand, but it somehow turned into something grandiose.'

(ALBUM) various artists *104.9 XFM*
   9502 Young Americans
ORIGINAL RELEASE: XFMCD 2, October 1995
COMMENTS: Another benefit for the beleaguered XFM station, as it continued its battle to be granted a full broadcast license. Smith originally intended turning in a simple acoustic version of the Bowie song... one of his own all-time favourites... but, with the band's latest album sessions now in full (wild mood) swing, he brought the remainder of the band in, together with a fractured sound that, perhaps surprisingly, worked out rather well.

(TV) *MTV's Most Wanted* (UK) 15 December 1995
   UNR Just Like Heaven
   UNR Mint Car
   UNR Friday I'm In Love
ORIGINAL RELEASE: unreleased
COMMENTS: New drummer Jason Cooper's UK debut as a member of the Cure. 'They found me in *Melody Maker*, August 94... the ad said "very famous band needs drummer, no metal heads," and there were numerous auditions, about four, before they decided they wanted me to join the band. Then they sent a questionnaire, and I guess I kind of cheated because the return envelope was "Fiction, Charlotte Street," and I thought, "well there's only one very famous band on Fiction."

'The next audition was just in a room with a video camera; you didn't get to meet the band, you just heard two songs from the new album, and played whatever came into your mind. They recorded that, then you played a little drum solo, and that was it. Then they viewed the tapes.

'What they did was, a huge amount of drummers auditioned, then they narrowed it down to six or seven and they couldn't decide, so they had us down one at a time to record two songs. I was third and I came down and played on quite a few, and it was just to see how we'd get on with everyone really, because that's quite important… it's who you are, as well as what you play. But it was a really good relaxed atmosphere, they made it as easy as possible.'

Cooper did not have a yawning track record… his best-known past project was the admittedly magnificent My Life Story, while Smith was most impressed to discover he had written a film score with Oliver Krause 'for a black-and-white animated film a couple of years ago, which I'd seen; it's really, really good. And Jason did this really very grand orchestral music for it.'

Cooper continued, 'I joined officially in January 1995, then it was carry on doing tracks, recording, doing the vocals… we toured during the summer; the first gig was in Athens, a big football stadium, 20,000 people something like that. It was great, I was unused to such good treatment that the band obviously get. We came back, then did some gigs in Brazil, that were organized by the Brazilian fan club. They sent us a book of 20,000 signatures saying "please come play here", and it was fantastic. It's been really good – obvious the first gigs were kind of daunting because they were so huge.'

Cooper was a long-time Cure fan… 'when I was 13, I was heavily into albums like Seventeen Seconds and Faith, so it was great. I'd been in other bands before, which were alright, but to play this type of music, with such a catalogue of songs… for the festival tour we did, we learned – I dunno how many songs it was… two and a half hours, 25 or 30 songs, and we rehearsed others, so we maybe had 45 songs. But I knew a lot of them anyway, they were kind of embedded in my mind since childhood….'

'I think it's difficult for the fans to have someone else come in, after Boris [Williams] who played so long and played so well, but they've been really nice. Hopefully… I just have to be musically sensitive to what's gone of before, and the legacy of the Cure; and, obviously I have to bear in mind what the band is about, what's gone on before.

Williams did, in fact, come round to visit the band as they laboured towards the new album, with Smith confessing, 'I'm still not sure why Boris left and I don't think he is. He's come to see us recording… and he actually played with Jason. We did a Gary Glitter jam with two drum kits, which was dead good, so there's no ill feeling.'

1996

LINE-UP #17 Robert Smith (vocals, guitar), Perry Bamonte (guitar), Roger O'Donnell (keyboards), Simon Gallup (bass), Jason Cooper (drums)

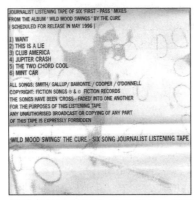

JOURNALIST LISTENING TAPE OF SIX 'FIRST - PASS' MIXES
FROM THE ALBUM ' WILD MOOD SWINGS ' BY THE CURE
(SCHEDULED FOR RELEASE IN MAY 1996)

1) WANT
2) THIS IS A LIE
3) CLUB AMERICA
4) JUPITER CRASH
5) THE TWO CHORD COOL
6) MINT CAR

ALL SONGS: SMITH/ GALLUP/ BAMONTE / COOPER / O'DONNELL
COPYRIGHT: FICTION SONGS ® & © FICTION RECORDS
THE SONGS HAVE BEEN 'CROSS - FADED' INTO ONE ANOTHER
FOR THE PURPOSES OF THIS LISTENING TAPE
ANY UNAUTHORISED BROADCAST OR COPYING OF ANY PART
OF THIS TAPE IS EXPRESSLY FORBIDDEN

'WILD MOOD SWINGS' THE CURE - SIX SONG JOURNALIST LISTENING TAPE

(EP) *WILD MOOD SWINGS* – JOURNALIST LISTENING TAPE
  9601a Want
  9602a This Is A Lie
  9603a Club America
  9604a Jupiter Crash
  9605 The Two Chord Cool (working title for The 13th)
  9606a Mint Car
ORIGINAL RELEASE: Fiction promo cassette (no cat), February 1996
COMMENTS: Sessions for the new album eventually wound up in a rented West Country mansion, the home of actress Jane Seymour, and it was there that *Wild Mood Swings* began taking shape. It would finally appear in early 1996, although the four-year lay-off between albums concealed a lot of behind-the-scenes activity. Less a band, more a commune, the line-up had now undergone two major shifts, as Cooper was followed into the nucleus of Gallup, Smith and Perry Bamonte, by the returning Roger O'Donnell. It could not help but affect the dynamic as a whole, as Smith told journalist Jack Rabid.

'The first concert Jason did with us, last summer in Athens, when we came off, he was really amazed that the audience really wanted to listen to us. He had never been in a band that the audience was like really, really seriously into what the band were doing. And I kind of thought, "I've always taken for granted, for years and years." And its just things like that, that he has a very different take on what we do. And he has actually made a difference on the way I look at what we do, that's true.

'I think having Roger back in the group has also reintroduced a kind of sensibility that was in the group around the time of *Disintegration*. He's had five years away from the band, and I think he's been unsatisfied with what he's been doing. He made a solo album, but it didn't really work for him. And he's determined that this is going to work, that this is the best thing that we've ever done, so that if people remember the Cure, they remember this line-up and this album. There's a really good atmosphere in the band at the moment. I just hope that it doesn't kind of dissipate, because it has in the past.'

By the New Year, the album was sufficiently in shape for journalists to be treated to a sneak preview, in the form of six first-pass mixes, totaling a shade under 19 minutes – that is, around three minutes worth of each of the featured songs. Neither, as these things so often are, was the tape drawn only from the type of songs you'd expect to hear, as the overture of 'Want' and the sorrow of 'This Is A Lie' was followed by a cod-American accent, lifted bodily out of Blur's bleating 'Rednecks', exhorting us to visit 'Club America'.

'Apparently, they call it a novelty song,' choked *Alternative Press*: '"I ride into a town on a big white Trojan horse, I'm looking to have some fun...." What is this, the new Beach Boys album?' No, but it was very nearly the album's first single and, if you listen really carefully, you can hear a little guitar lick out of David Bowie's 'Man Who Sold The World' in there.

Though the 25 songs completed so far still weren't sequenced into a final album, elements were already in place: 'Want', with its vast, symphonic sweep, had already been established as the band's set-opener during the Brazilian jaunt, and Smith enthused, 'that song, I sat down and wrote as quickly as any song I've ever written in my life, I literally sat down outside my house two summers ago, and I was dissatisfied, so I just made a list of everything I've ever wanted and as, I went on, it made me laugh, and with very few changes....'

'Two Chord Cool', too, fascinated; months later, it would be revealed as a prototypical version of 'The 13th', with sufficient lyrical variations to deem it an altogether different performance, as opposed to the mere mix that marked the rest of the journalist listening tape.

Delve deeper into the sessions, meanwhile, and a wealth of further gems emerged: 'Bare'... 'I sat there and wrote it in less than an hour, and it wasn't about something that was happening to me, but it was something going on very close to home.' There was 'Patel Shout', a beautifully sloppy instrumental, with Smith's guitar a slithering, blathering blurge, and there was 'Get Up, Get Out, And Get Gone', another in the band's long line of warped showtunes, 'the same thing,' grinned Gallup, 'as "Hot Hot Hot!!!" (The song was ultimately issued as plain 'Gone!').

'The thing about it is, we always did things in an almost cabaret-type fashion, and that's meant... well it's not meant to do anything, it's a jazz-type song, but we're not jazz musicians. There's an image people have that we're a dour bunch of people, that sit around and practice, but we actually get pissed and try things just for the fun of it.'

(SINGLE) The 13th
    9607a The 13th (swing radio mix)
    9607b The 13th (killer bee mix)
    9608 It Used To Be Me
    9607c The 13th (two chord cool mix)
    9609 Ocean
    9610 Adonais
ORIGINAL RELEASE: Fiction FICCD 51, April 1996

(TV) *Top Of The Pops* (UK) 18 April 1996
    UNR The 13th
ORIGINAL RELEASE: unreleased
COMMENTS: The early 'Two Chord Cool' had now mutated into 'The 13th', a mock Mexican percussion routine that Gallup described as 'a funny song really, because it was only a half-realized idea when we started recording. But then Jason [Cooper] joined, and he started doing certain percussion bits to it, and we thought, "well, we'll add more bits to it," and now it's really good fun, it's like having Lego, playing about with things. When we started doing it, I thought it'd probably be a B-side, but that really is the fun of doing it."

It was also fun imagining people's faces the first time it Latin-loped out of the speaker, like – what's this? Sergio Mendes? But mention that the Cure are possibly the only band around who could step so far out of type and still get away with it, and the chorus goes up that they're not trying to 'get away' with anything.

'Doing things as a departure makes it sound like it's contrived,' Gallup cursed. 'If I looked at "13th" and wasn't involved in it, I could say, "oh look, it's got a Latin beat in it, it's got all this stuff"; but, because we've all been involved, we all think it's a good song. And I'll be thoroughly honest, we're not trying to break new ground with it, because it's actually quite a sleazy song in a way. But if we were to go out tonight and we heard that song, we'd dance to it.'

'I think we lost our belligerence years ago,' Smith continued. 'I think people have become used to the fact we'll do what we do, we're not trying to upset or shock or amuse anyone, we just want people to think it's fun.'

So why did it become the A-side?

'Because I wanted to marry a transvestite on video,' Smith confessed. 'That's the only reason. I don't think anything on this album is going to be a hit. "13th" might be remembered if the video's good, but it won't be a hit.' And here's why. 'I don't have any delusions about our standing in the market. Our record companies love us when we're selling records, but they hate us when we're not. And, while we've got a history of having good videos, so that's in our favour, if it's not a good video they won't flog us, which disturbs me because they will flog other people's videos which are shit.'

The video for '13th' marked the first occasion bar one that the Cure worked apart from Tim Pope, since the pair joined forces in 1982. And it was impossible to tell if the parting was amicable. 'The whole point of me saying I can't work with Tim Pope anymore,' insisted Smith, 'is that I can't be the "Why Can't I Be You?" Man again. I'm not that person and I won't be, but we can do stuff that's infinitely better, but on the same level, that's done like we want, and as big as we want to.

'The advantage we had when we first started doing things with Tim Pope, was that no-one had really done that much, and in the world of video anything you thought of was new. And now....'

Simon Gallup: 'Roger and I were talking the other night, about how Tim Pope always goes down for making these really weird videos, but the videos that he's come up with ideas for, without the group, have been pap.' Smith won't disagree. 'Some of the videos he's done with other people have been boring. So now we're making a video that doesn't rely on the stuff we used to rely on.'

Pope and the Cure would soon reunite but, for now, the band was intent on enjoying the change in scenery. The transvestite wedding was only part of the thrill; Smith was adamant, 'if you haven't got the ability to step outside of what you're supposed to be, and do something that's really dumb, you're fucked. It's like you're saying, "ooh we can't go near that, our idea is to go Nick Cave style, where I'm just reinforcing endlessly my idea of a goth god." In the next video you'll see us looking more stupid than we have in any other video.'

Of the b-sides, 'Adonais' dates from a holiday Smith spent in the Lake District, with his nose buried in a book of Shelley poems (the poet's 'Adonais' was a tribute to Keats), and was once described as Smith's personal favourite among all the new songs, while 'Ocean' is 'a sad song about someone I loved a lot, who I knew was slipping away....'

Best of all, however, was 'It Used To Be Me'. The song started life as 'See Through', a number that the Cure jammed with one of the drummers filing through the audition room two years earlier, Louis Pavlou, and builds the suspense like a piece of *Pornography*. Smith explained, 'I figure most Cure fans are going to buy the first single just to see what it's like, which means it's going to be heard by everyone who buys the single because there's no such thing as a B-side anymore. You buy a CD single, or a cassingle, you're not really gonna play one song and not the other.

'But the reason it's a b-side is because it doesn't fit on the album. It's not a bad song, it really is a good song, but I found it impossible to work it in. There again, if people hear it and think that, because it's a b-side, it wasn't good enough to be on the album, you start to think it must be a great album!'

(TV) *Later With... Jools Holland* (UK) 11 May 1996 (rec 23 April)
UNR Club America
UNR This Is A Lie
UNR Gone!
ORIGINAL RELEASE: unreleased

(TV) *TFI Friday* (UK) 26 April 1996
UNR Friday I'm In Love

UNR The 13th
ORIGINAL RELEASE: unreleased

(TV) *Top Of The Pops* (UK) 2 May 1996
UNR The 13th
ORIGINAL RELEASE: unreleased

(TV) *Saturday Night Live* (USA) 11 May 1996
UNR Mint Car
UNR In Between Days
ORIGINAL RELEASE: unreleased

(TV) *TFI Friday* (UK) 31 May 1996
UNR Mint Car
ORIGINAL RELEASE: unreleased
COMMENTS: A wealth of extremely enjoyable TV appearances included the band's debut on American TV's *Saturday Night Live*, and a rare second appearance on *Top Of The Pops* – rare, because the single itself climbed no higher than #15.

(ALBUM) *Wild Mood Swings*
9601 Want
9603 Club America
9602 This Is A Lie
9607 The 13th
9611 Strange Attraction
9606 Mint Car
9604 Jupiter Crash
9612 Round And Round And Round
9613 Gone!
9614 Numb
9615 Return
9616 Trap
9617 Treasure
9618 Bare
ORIGINAL RELEASE: Fiction 5317931, May 1996
COMMENTS: 'Wild Mood Swings was just a complete mess,' Smith reflected from half-a-decade on. 'I had no idea of what we were doing while we were doing it, I had no idea we'd finished it until we'd finished it.' And, once it reached the stores, people had no idea what to do with it.

From the outset, it was clear that *Wild Mood Swings* was catching the Cure in an odd position, bouncing back after an aeons-long lay-off, wondering whether the mass applause which catapulted *Wish* into the US chart at a still-stunning #2 was still intact. In England, their star had already dipped alarmingly – *Loaded* magazine had recently described them as an utter irrelevance, or words to that effect, a sure sign of how absolutely the Britpop phenomenon had wiped people's brains clean.

The hiatus between albums did not, of course, seem that long to the Cure themselves. 'We've just been being us, really,' Gallup mused. 'Once we finished the *Wish* tour, we all went away and realized we all had personal lives to get on with, and a lot of things to sort out. When you're in your early 20s, it's like "fuck everything." When you're in your thirties, you kind of think – "what's going on?"

'It's never mattered to us if it's a year between albums or ten years. The only criteria is, do we like it and, fair enough, we're meant to be in a situation where we shouldn't care, but the thing is, we do actually care what we're doing, and that comes down to the songs. That's what excites us about doing something'

Smith agreed. 'Right from the off, the only time I've made albums is when I've written songs that I think are good enough to turn into songs for public consumption. The motivation to actually go into a studio environment and make an album of new songs is either there or it isn't. But, if I get writer's block, it doesn't bother me in the slightest. I either have something to say or I don't. And, if it takes another five years for me to write an album, it'll take five years. I don't agonise over it, because the whole point of me doing this was to express my feelings and, if I have no feelings, then there's no point in expressing them.'

Wild Mood Swings did not mark a spell of writer's block. Rather, Smith confessed, 'I'm definitely slowing down.' He once calculated that, throughout the 1980s, 'I spent less than a year actually at home, waking up in the same bed. Through the 1990s, I'd say I woke up in my own bed for four years. It's very much a change of emphasis for me; we've done things in the '90s like *Mixed Up* and *Show*, that took three or four months of editing together and learning the process, things that have taken longer but haven't been new studio projects. But I've had a lot more fun in the 90s than the 80s! I've become a much happier individual.'

By past mighty standards, *Wild Mood Swings* did not do well. Uniformly disregarded by the press, it did enter the US charts at #1, but it then plunged straight down from there. Subsequent reports had sales bottoming out at around half of whatever *Wish* did.

But was Smith downhearted? 'Nah. It kind of reflected a trend, I suppose. I was told "oh, it was the lack of hits and blah blah blah," but I think really, we took too long making it and, even though I wouldn't go back and make it in any other way, because it was really good fun, I did accept the criticisms. But I've never yet evaluated a Cure album by what it's done globally. *Seventeen Seconds* did something like 25,000 worldwide, but it couldn't take away from what it meant to me. So I'm not going to worry about the Cure slipping down into the second division; it doesn't bother me, because I never expected to be in the first division anyway'.

If the album had any faults, he argued, they were those that he built in himself. 'The others were confused by a couple of songs on the sessions – "Gone!" was one that everyone was thinking was one step too far, "The 13th" was another and, for me, those two songs were the least successful on the album... "The 13th" I was kind of satisfied with, but "Gone!," I thought was pretty disastrous. With hindsight, I'd have left that song off and it would have been a much better album.

'There were elements with *Wild Mood Swings* that, if I'd wanted to bring out something a bit heavier, all the elements were there – most of the b-sides were songs that didn't go on the album, but did have that heavier element to them. But I wanted to make an album that swung from one wild mood to another. So I did. And I do think *Wild Mood Swings* is in the Top Five Cure albums that we've ever done. It's a vastly under-rated album. It was just too long. I should have left those two songs off, and it would have been much better received.'

(ALBUM) various artists *Volume 16*
    9603b Club America (Roxy Mix)
ORIGINAL RELEASE: Volume 82430, 1996
COMMENTS: Still sounding like the best idea for a single, 'Club America' was subjected to a handful of preparatory remixes. This, obviously, is one of them... but it's not especially great.

(SINGLE) Mint Car
    9606b Mint Car (radio mix)
    9619 Home
    9606c Mint Car (busker's mix)
    9606d Mint Car (electric mix)
    9620 Waiting
    9621 A Pink Dream
ORIGINAL RELEASE: Fiction FICCD 52, June 1996
COMMENTS: On album, 'Mint Car' is one of those absurdly effervescent songs that can trace its lineage all the way back to 'Let's Go To Bed', but which was truly nailed to perfection during the *Kiss Me Kiss Me Kiss Me* period. Still it made for a thrilling 45, its opening screech and flourish an unforgettable shock whenever it leaped out of the radio – which, sadly, was not often enough. 'Mint Car' peaked at #31

Of the b-side remixes, the acoustic 'busker's mix' is an unalloyed joy; while the pure pop 'electric mix' and 'radio mix' versions really don't deviate from the album's proven path. The three 'new' songs, meanwhile, continued drawing from the out-takes, and were highlighted by 'A Pink Dream', a song that Smith started writing in 1983, during his Siouxsie and the Banshees period, when a flight to Australia had a lay-over in Alaska. A dozen years later, during the Cure's Brazilian sojourn, 'I had a very weird, extended déjà vu experience... extrapolated from the original song idea, and finished it on the plane home.'

(RADIO) *Lovin' Fun Radio* (France) 20 June 1996
    UNR This Is A Lie
    UNR Just Like Heaven
ORIGINAL RELEASE: unreleased

COMMENTS: An entertaining acoustic performance.

(TV) *Nulle Part Ailleurs* (France) 20 June 1996
UNR Club America
UNR Mint Car
UNR Boys Don't Cry

(TV) *Harald Schmidt Show* (Germany) 25 June 1996
UNR Mint Car

(TV) *Pula Arena Festivalbar* (Croatia) 2 July 1996
UNR The 13th
UNR Mint Car

(TV) *Late Show With David Letterman* (USA) 5 July 1996
UNR Mint Car

(TV) *120 Minutes – MTV* (USA) 14 July 1996
UNR Strange Attraction
UNR Fascination Street

(TV) *Late Night With Conan O'Brien* (USA) 17 September 1996
UNR Strange Attractions
UNR Boys Don't Cry

(TV) *Lappel de Couette* (France) 29 October 1996
UNR This Is A Lie
UNR Boys Don't Cry

(TV) *Nulle Part Ailleurs* (France) 6 November 1996
UNR This Is A Lie
ORIGINAL RELEASE: unreleased
COMMENTS: A world of television performances.

(SINGLE) Gone! (UK)/Strange Attraction (US)
9613a Gone! (radio mix)
9613b Gone! (critter mix)
9613c Gone! (ultra living mix)
9613d Gone! (spacer mix)
9602bThis Is A Lie (ambient mix)
9607d The 13th (feels good mix)
9611a Strange Attraction (strange mix)
9611b Strange Attraction (Adrian Sherwood mix)
ORIGINAL RELEASE: (UK) Fiction FICCD 53, (US) Fiction/East West (USA) 63999-2, November 1996

129

COMMENTS: There really was no need to release a third single from *Wild Mood Swings*, and the ardent collector truffles in vain to find one – only to meet Robert Smith coming the other way, equally perplexed over the entire affair. With no more releasable out-takes in the archive, the remix brigade was called in instead, to turn in a jumble of rejigs that, Smith sniffed, were 'so unbelievably bad that I thought the people were taking the piss. Even the ones that were released were uniformly hopeless, and these are people who've got massive club hits, and suddenly seem to lose all concept of how to walk when presented with a Cure song.

'It's really weird. I knew it was going to turn out badly, I just didn't know how badly.'

(LIVE) Sheffield Arena, Sheffield, 13 December 1996
9622 Mint Car

(LIVE) Nynex Arena, Manchester, 14 December 1996
9623 Trap

(LIVE) Birmingham NEC, 16 December 1996
9624 Want
9625 Club America
9626 Treasure

ORIGINAL RELEASE: *Five Swing Live* EP, Fiction FICD.COM 1, June 1997
COMMENTS: Kicking off in London at the end of May 1996, the attendant seven month *Swing Tour* was not to be resolved without a string of problems, most notably the technical hiccups which resulted in the entire British leg of the jaunt being postponed for six full months.

The *Five Swing Live* live EP drawn from three of the rescheduled UK shows, however, sold out its limited edition run of 5,000 within days; available only through the band's website, it did in fact show off the recent material in far stronger surroundings than the actual album.

The full band set during this tour also included the following: 'Plainsong', 'Fascination Street', 'Push', 'Lullaby', 'This Is A Lie', 'The Blood', 'The Walk', 'Cold', 'Strange Attraction', 'Never Enough', 'Prayers For Rain', 'In Between Days', 'Funeral Party', 'One Hundred Years', 'The Figurehead', 'From The Edge Of The Deep Green Sea', 'Bare' and 'Disintegration', with encores pulling out the likes of 'Dressing Up', 'Friday I'm In Love', 'Just Like Heaven', 'Why Can't I Be You?', 'If Only Tonight We Could Sleep', 'Charlotte Sometimes', 'Lovesong', 'Grinding Halt', 'Play For Today', 'Boys Don't Cry', 'Subway Song', 'Let's Go To Bed', '10.15 Saturday Night' and 'Killing An Arab'.

The EP was dedicated to former Fiction colleague Billy McKenzie – the frontman for the Associates took his own life earlier in 1997.

1997

LINE-UP #17 Robert Smith (vocals, guitar), Perry Bamonte (guitar), Roger O'Donnell (keyboards), Simon Gallup (bass), Jason Cooper (drums)

(LIVE) ROBERT SMITH – DAVID BOWIE 50th Birthday Concert, Madison Square Garden, NY, January 1997
    UNR The Last Thing You Should Do
    UNR Quicksand
ORIGINAL RELEASE: unreleased
COMMENTS: David Bowie, Smith admits, 'is the only living artist involved in music who's ever had a real impact on me... despite the fact I've said I don't like a lot of what he's been doing, particularly things like Tin Machine.'

Bowie hit the Big Five-Oh in January 1997 and marked the occasion by arranging a massive New York knees-up, stuffed with superstar guests. Most appeared to have been selected with at least one oddly-coloured eye on their own current bankability (can *you* spell 'wasted opportunity'?), but, among the handful who could be said to enjoy a truly symbiotic relationship with Bowie and his music, Smith was a genuine highlight – for himself as much as for the audience. 'I grew up idolising Bowie and I really do respect what he does.'

Smith joined his host on two songs. Professing himself a fan of Bowie's most recent album, *Earthling*, he was quite happy to play and sing along on 'The Last Thing You Should Do', and later reflected, 'I really liked *Earthling*, I thought it was a really good album. The songs are great songs, they really stand up to be listened to *as* songs, and the fact that he worked in a particular genre and tried to capture a certain sound [Bowie was toying with jungle and drum & bass at the time] is neither here nor there. The songs are really well put together.'

The meat of the moment, however, came immediately after. The routine of the show demanded each guest play one new song, then one oldie and Smith hoped to convince the star to unearth 'Young Americans'. Instead he was handed 'Quicksand' (from 1971), and he acknowledged it felt 'weird getting up there and singing one of the *Hunky Dory* songs.' Smith was a 13 year old fan when he first heard that album; it lived on as one of those peculiar psychic touchstones that everybody accumulates at such an impressionable age; and now he was onstage, alongside Bowie, singing a song he had previously only ever performed in front of his bedroom mirror.

He pulled it off with great aplomb; indeed, listening back to the performance now, Smith's voice actually sounds more in tune with the lyric's original quizzicality that Bowie's own.

(SINGLE) Wrong Number
  9701 Wrong Number
  9701a Wrong Number (Single Mix)
  9701b Wrong Number (Digital Exchange Mix)
  9701c Wrong Number (Analogue Exchange Mix)
  9701d Wrong Number (Dub Analogue Exchange Mix)
  9701e Wrong Number (p2p Mix)
  9701f Wrong Number (Crossed Line Mix)
  9701g Wrong Number (ISDN Mix)
  9701h Wrong Number (Engaged Mix)

ORIGINAL RELEASE: 9701 on Galore CD, remainder FICCD 54, October 1997

COMMENTS: A new song for a collection of oldies, the *Galore* singles compilation, 'Wrong Number' was recorded by Smith alone, with just guest guitarist Reeves Gabrels (moonlighting from David Bowie's band) for company, and some overdubbed drums when the whole thing was finished.

It was born of a defenceless little song called 'Lime Green', that Smith had had kicking around for some months, without ever finding anything to do with it. Having befriended one another during the rehearsals for the Bowie Birthday concert in 1997, Smith and Gabrels 'started pulling ideas apart and then putting them back together again.' Then, selecting 'Lime Green' as one of their earliest victims, it swiftly became apparent that the process was a lot more valuable than it might initially sound.

Arguably, if there was any lacklustre element to the Cure's most recent work it was that it sounded too much like what people thought the Cure should sound like – with all the quirks and surprises that that entailed. 'Wrong Number', on the other hand, didn't sound like anyone until the vocals came in and, with a 40-second intro to get through first, that was more than enough time to make up your mind. Like it, then find out who it's by. Oh, and watch out for the video, reuniting the band with Tim Pope, whose own masterful grasp on their personal imagery was responsible for some of the best videos of their career, but whose absence seriously scarred the *Wild Mood Swings* era.

In fact, just one thing spoiled this most wonderful of singles. Too many remixes, including a few that, once again, Smith admitted were not brilliant. But he was also able to excuse the indulgence. 'The whole point of what we do.... it's not, we don't think, "oh we're in a group, so whatever we do is good," and everyone who's in the group understands that. And that's the difference, because having been in and around a lot of groups over the years, a lot of people have reached the point where they think because they're in a group, whatever they do is great.

'It's tragic, it really is. You always have to think about what you're doing, why you're doing it, why is it working, why isn't it, and a lot of it isn't put into such obvious terms, but there are times when we have to think, "well we could get away with this but do we really want to?" And we don't, because that's a very slippery slope.' They still stretched out the shitty remixes, though.

(RADIO) *Modern Rock Live* (USA) 26 October 1997
UNR Lovesong

(TV) *Tonight Show with Jay Leno* (USA) 29 October 1997
UNR Just Like Heaven

(RADIO) K-ROQ acoustic session (USA) 31 October 1997
UNR Friday I'm In Love

(RADIO) XFM acoustic session (UK) 5 November 1997
UNR Lovesong
UNR Just Like Heaven
UNR Friday I'm In Love
UNR Catch

(TV) *TFI Friday* (UK) 7 November 1997
UNR Wrong Number
UNR Fascination Street (not broadcast)
UNR Why Can't I Be You? (not broadcast)
UNR A Forest (not broadcast)

(TV) *Jack Docherty Show* (UK) 10 November 1997
UNR Wrong Number
UNR Just Like Heaven
ORIGINAL RELEASE: all unreleased
COMMENTS: A lengthy string of promotional appearances, geared around the release of *Galore* and 'Wrong Number'. The US dates tied in around a pair of live shows during October: Los Angeles on 26 October, and a memorable Halloween gig at New York's Irvine Plaza, that was broadcast live on the Internet. Home again, the band continued the promotional routine before slipping back to the US at the end of November, for the Radio Festivals tour.

Several of these were apparently broadcast in part by the sponsoring local radio stations; other highlights included guest appearances from Reeves Gabrels at several of the shows, performing on 'Wrong Number', 'Never Enough', 'Cut' and 'Disintegration'.

(LIVE) WKQX (Chicago) Twisted Christmas Festival, 11 December 1997
UNR Plainsong
UNR Shake Dog Shake
UNR Torture
9702 Fascination Street
UNR Push
UNR Just Like Heaven
UNR The Holy Hour
UNR One Hundred Years

UNR The Same Deep Water As You
UNR Pictures Of You
UNR In Between Days
UNR From The Edge Of The Deep Green Sea
UNR Never Enough
UNR Wrong Number
UNR Cut
UNR Disintegration
UNR Untitled
UNR 10.15 Saturday Night
UNR Killing An Arab
ORIGINAL RELEASE: various artists *Retro 101 Volume One* (Q101), September 1999
COMMENTS: An American radio giveaway CD, featured the night's version of 'Fascination Street'.

(RADIO) WXRT (Chicago) session 12 December 1997
UNR Lovesong
UNR In Between Days
UNR Friday I'm In Love

(TV) *Jack Docherty Show* (UK) 31 December 1997 (rec 16 Dec)
UNR Doing The Unstuck
UNR Friday I'm In Love
ORIGINAL RELEASE: both unreleased
COMMENTS: The WXRT broadcast, and that evening's show at the WPLT Hootenanny marked the conclusion of the Festivals tour; the Cure then returned to the UK for two nights at the Shepherds Bush Empire, 16-17 December. Their appearance on the New Years Eve edition of the *Jack Docherty Show* was recorded on the afternoon of the first Empire show.

The winding down of activities for the year was certainly welcomed by Smith. 'I was feeling quite fatigued about the group with the *Galore* project, and I didn't really enjoy doing the few live shows we did, that were based around the singles. It was a very unemotional experience; I don't think the audience was really into it, I don't think the band was really into it, and I started to question what am I doing with this group?'

That thinking, he would later admit, led him towards the conclusions with which he closed the 20th century – the Cure had reached the end of the road, and all that was now required was to turn in a farewell that would allow them to go out with a crash.

Once they'd got a few other odds and ends out of the way first, of course.

1998

LINE-UP #17 Robert Smith (vocals, guitar), Perry Bamonte (guitar), Roger O'Donnell (keyboards), Simon Gallup (bass), Jason Cooper (drums)

(TV) *South Park* (USA) 18 February 1998
  Mecha-Streisand
ORIGINAL RELEASE. *South Park Volume Three* (Rhino Home Video 05902)
COMMENTS: When... after a lot of other stuff has happened, of course... Barbra Streisand is transformed into the ravenous, town-destroying Mecha-Streisand, there is only one thing left to do... movie critic Leonard Maltin asks Chef to contact Robert Smith. Voicing his own animated character, Smith transforms himself into a massive moth-like creature that... after even more other stuff has happened, of course... successfully launches Mecha-Streisand into outer space, where she explodes.
  'Disintegration is the best album ever!' – Kyle.

(ALBUM) various artists *The X-Files: The Album*
  9801 More Than This
ORIGINAL RELEASE: June 1998
COMMENTS: Not a cover of the old Roxy Music number, although an eerily lush production really doesn't make that seem such an unlikely prospect. Smith himself confessed to being a major fan of the *X-Files'* weekly investigations into the world of conspiracies and Forteana.... 'I'm a huge fan. To the point where I have to wait until the whole series comes out on a video collection, and then I watch it all in one go, I watch them all back to back. Because I'm never around, I never know where I'm going to be, I can't guarantee that I'm going to be able to see it. And I hated the idea of, because again it does actually follow on, there's like an internal logic to the whole series, I think it's like brilliantly done. There's a lot of self reference, and so if you've missed out on too much of it, you don't really understand who's playing what part, or you know, who's supposed to be the bad guy kind of thing. So I am, yeah, a huge fan.'
  Apparently confirming Smith's decision to retire the Cure, 'More Than This' was recorded by Smith and co-producer Paul Corkett alone, and was inspired, he said, by Khachaturian's *Gayaneh Ballet*. It's a beautiful comparison, and a lovely song whose mood ties perfectly into the show that inspired it.

(ALBUM) various artists *For The Masses: An Album of Depeche Mode Songs*
  9802 World In My Eyes

IN BETWEEN DAYS

ORIGINAL RELEASE: August 1998

COMMENTS: Another solo Smith shot, after the entire band's attempt at 'Walking In My Shoes' went nowhere. Recorded in one night, 'using loops and stuff,' the end result sounded exactly like it ought to – the Cure play Depeche Mode, without actually sounding too much like the Cure; indeed, the entire *For The Masses* album proved a surprisingly successful project, as Depeche proved they had written more good songs (and gathered more worthwhile admirers) than a lot of critics give them credit for.

Smith explained his enthusiasm for the project. 'We've bumped into Depeche over the years, a lot. And they've bumped into us. They've been to see us play quite a few times, we've been to see them play, and there's lots of other connections kinda behind the scenes. Perry, our guitarist, went to school with most of Depeche, so he has known them from the days when they were, uh pre-New Romantic or whatever the hell they were when they started. So, yeah, we've known each other for a long, long time. In fact they were probably among our very few showbiz friends.

'They occupy an unusual position in that they've developed out of what I would consider to be a pretty... I don't know how to put this nicely, but there are some things that they did when they first started out in the first couple of years, kind of image wise and musically, which live and haunt and then have lived and haunted many other groups.

'And most groups don't recover from that kind of beginning. I think they've done really well in that they've managed to kinda develop into a critically acclaimed group but one that is also hugely popular, and there's very few groups that manage that. I think a lot of that ties into how they've kinda manipulated their image... I think it's very clever the whole kind of way it's put together. It's not contrived, it's just like a very natural kind of thing that comes out of the members of the band and personalities, but its worked really well.'

As for the final song decision, 'For me it was a straight choice between "World in My Eyes" and ["Walking In My Shoes"] 'cause that's very much my favorite song really. And I thought they, both those songs I could kinda get into them lyrically... they'd suit my voice and I thought I could do an interpretation that would sort of at least throw another light on the song. And I went for "World in My Eyes" in the end, because it felt more natural, I tried both of them at home and that just worked straight away.

'I think what makes this tribute album as good as it is, is that most of the bands aren't trying to sound like Depeche, they're actually trying to sound like themselves doing Depeche songs, and that's why it works. But I think probably like a lot of the bands on there have got more identity, 'cause there's a lot more recognizable bands on this, so they've kind of established an identity for themselves, so I think it's easier. Whereas the couple of albums that have been done so far for us have mainly been kinda fan based, so it's not really the same thing.'

(ALBUM) ROBERT SMITH – COGASM: *Orgasmo Original Soundtrack*
  9803 A Sign From God
ORIGINAL RELEASE: original soundtrack *Orgasmo*, October 1998
COMMENTS: Another collaboration with Reeves Gabrels, although this time, Smith was joined by one other Cure member, drummer Cooper. Recording under the one-off pseudonym Cogasm, the trio turned in a suitably dislocated-sounding portent.

1999

LINE-UP #17 Robert Smith (vocals, guitar), Perry Bamonte (guitar), Roger O'Donnell (keyboards), Simon Gallup (bass), Jason Cooper (drums)

(ALBUM) ROBERT SMITH – REEVES GABRELS: *Ulysses (Della Notte)*
   9901 Yesterday's Gone
ORIGINAL RELEASE: on-line only 1999, E-Magine 1050, October 2000
COMMENTS: Gabrels' masterful solo album was originally released on-line only during 1999; its mainstream release was arranged only after the download was nominated by Yahoo as "Best Internet Only" album of the year. It was an excellent journey not only through Gabrels' own musical strengths, but also those of sundry famed collaborators – Bowie donated the remarkable 'Jewel' to the set, while Smith's lilting ballad 'Yesterday's Gone' was so viscerally opposed to the duo's past unions that it could not help but grab the attention.

   According to Smith, the song was written and recorded in an eight-hour span – one that also included visits to an off-license and a park. 'We wrote the music hand-in-hand, and then I wrote the words to a story he told me.'

(TV) VH-1 *Hard Rock Live* 19 October 1999
   UNR Out Of This World
   UNR Want
   UNR Club America
   UNR Fascination Street
   UNR Just Like Heaven
   UNR The Last Day Of Summer
   UNR In Between Days
   UNR From The Edge Of The Deep Green Sea
   UNR One Hundred Years
   UNR Boys Don't Cry
   UNR Bloodflowers
   UNR Wrong Number
ORIGINAL RELEASE: unreleased
COMMENTS: Speaking around the time of *Galore*, Smith promised the band's next album, then scheduled for an April 1998 release, would be 'such a different step away from what we've been doing that, hopefully, it will be comparable to *Disintegration* and *Pornography*.

   'I've set up my own mini studio at home, and I'm putting together songs at home that are real. I'm putting together performances, rather than just songs which are demo ideas. And I don't take them to the group and ask them to interpret it. I don't have to go through the interminable process of starting off with something, then going all around the houses and ending up with something that's almost the same, but maybe not quite as good. I've kind of gone back to the benign dictatorship of old. Essentially what I'm doing this year is purely to please myself.'

He also insisted that the band should make the most of even these limited opportunities: *Bloodflowers*, he was adamant, would be the final Cure album. 'I hit 40 in April 1999, and I decided a long time ago that I'm not going to be sitting there at 47, strumming an acoustic guitar thinking about what the next single's going to be.'

Sessions for the new – and final – Cure album commenced in January 1999, with Smith intending to have the album completed by April, in time for his 40th birthday ' and I pretty much did. The mixing spilled over into May-June, but I'd pretty much wrapped it up.' The release would then follow towards the end of the year – coinciding, in fact, with the *Hard Rock Live* show. Unfortunately, the record companies deemed otherwise.

'I wanted it coming out at Halloween, because it's a kind of looking-back record. It's nostalgic, it wraps up the '90s for me, and I wanted to start the Naughties, or whatever they're called, with something which wasn't a Cure album.

'But, after all the fights I had over *Galore*, what went on it and when it came out... I got my own way in the end, but they made me pay in their own way, because they didn't market it, didn't advertise it, didn't promote it, and it didn't do very well at all. So, this time, it was like dealing with small kids; they're going "see, you didn't do what we said last time, this is what happens...."' – and they wanted to hold the album over until the New Year, to avoid competing with... of all things... the Millennium.

'They thought advertising space would be more expensive, fewer holes in the racks, blah blah fucking blah, so in the end, I thought "this is pointless – okay, when do you want to put it out?" And they said "February 2000", and my jaw just dropped. But there again, I wouldn't have expected everyone to throw it away on New Year's Eve if it had come out in October, so when it comes out... I don't really mind. Plus, in some ways, it has given me quite a nice brain-cooling-off period between finishing it and... I've had a couple of months of quite normal life, whereas it's normally a mad scramble.'

More than two years had elapsed since the Cure's last American shows; indeed, a short summer 1998 tour of European festivals, and a couple of gigs at the end of that year notwithstanding, the Cure had been off the road for so long that, when the *Hard Rock Live* show was announced, the furore for tickets effortlessly overwhelmed the few hundred that were available for the Sony Studios, New York, event. Similarly, in the days (make that hours) after the show ended, the Internet was swamped by postings... Robert Smith later wondered whether there was anybody at the show who *didn't* post a review of it, but he admitted that he was glad they all did.

'That show… was unanimously acclaimed as the best Cure show people had seen in years,' he mused a few weeks after the event, 'and the reason for it is: first, we were all sober; secondly, we rehearsed for three weeks beforehand; and thirdly, I said to everyone beforehand, "if you fuck this up, that's it. I'm going home and I'm never going to see you again." And afterwards… it was an hour-long show and I was drained, it was a really great feeling, it was like "the old days," in inverted commas'.

When the notion of the Cure playing *Hard Rock Live* was first raised, Smith demurred. 'They said traditionally, everyone who comes on the show does their hit singles, and I said "well, we can't do that, because I don't want to," so they said "well, you can't do it, then," and I said "fine." And then a week later, they phoned back and said "well, actually, if you could do just two hit singles…" and I thought ok. So we did "Just Like Heaven" and "In Between Days," and the rest of it was new songs, and old songs from *Pornography*'.

The VH-1 broadcast, later in the month, spotlighted just five songs from the set; among the absentees was a version of 'From The Edge of the Deep Green Sea' that, Smith shuddered, was responsible for the only sour note of the entire evening. A lot of the Internet postings, he noticed, complained that he had forgotten… or, even worse, flubbed, one particular lyric. In fact, 'I didn't actually forget it. I just like to sing it differently sometimes. I change it… I swap it around so it has the opposite meaning. The thing is, when I do that, it doesn't rhyme any longer, so it isn't quite as powerful'.

2000

LINE-UP #17 Robert Smith (vocals, guitar), Perry Bamonte (guitar), Roger O'Donnell (keyboards), Simon Gallup (bass), Jason Cooper (drums)

(ALBUM) *Bloodflowers*
  0001 Out Of This World
  0002 Watching Me Fall
  0003 Where The Birds Always Sing
  0004 Maybe Someday
  0005 The Last Day Of Summer
  0006 There Is No If
  0007 The Loudest Sound
  0008 39
  0009 Bloodflowers
Australian/Japanese bonus track
  0010 Coming Up
ORIGINAL RELEASE: Fiction FIX 31, February 2000

(STUDIO) *Bloodflowers* out-take
  0011 Possession
ORIGINAL RELEASE: *Join The Dots*, Fiction FIX 31, February 2000
COMMENTS: Smith undertook his first *Bloodflowers* interviews in November 1999, a full three months before the album's release, and the subject of the Cure's impending demise was paramount on every lip – except his. Indeed, he poured considerable scorn on the record companies' insistence upon using the end of the band as a marketing tool. 'Rather than telling everyone it's the last

Cure album, just because they need some sort of angle to hang it off, I said, "no, make the campaign 'the Best Cure album'." Because it may not be the last one.'

Nevertheless, he happily expanded on the reasons behind his decision to disband the Cure, and acknowledged that the imminence of his 40th birthday was the key element – just as the onset of his 30s had fired a similar crisis back in 1989. Back then, he resolved his demons with the recording of *Disintegration* and, though he was adamant that he would not be led astray so easily this time, still he sat his bandmates down to listen through *Pornography* and *Disintegration* before they started recording. 'I told them I want an album that equates with these, on this kind of level of being a classic Cure album. And the only way this line-up can prove to me that it's the best Cure line-up is to make an album which I think matches those.

He was not worried about seeming to repeat himself. 'I used those two albums as touching points, if you like, but I didn't want to emulate them. Besides, it would be impossible for me to make an album like *Pornography* again.

'But I've come to terms with the fact that the Cure do have a sound and, far from fighting that like I used to, I've embraced it. It's quite a cool thing for people to recognize it's us before we've played more than 15 seconds. So I think, with this album, we're playing to our strengths. I wanted it to sound like the Cure; I didn't want it to sound like anybody else. No fucking about in different styles, no pop music. It is the Cure – the heavier, weightier, atmospheric, moodier stuff. That's the album I wanted to make, and that's the album we've made, and it compares very well with what I think are the two best Cure albums of them all.'

Clues about the album's inspirations and influences littered the landscape – indeed, fans quickly fell into the spirit of the occasion, by organizing their own private competitions around how many past reference points they could discern as the band wound their way through the album's nine tracks. 'Lyrically I'm referring back a lot,' Smith acknowledged, 'and musically as well. I've used a couple of classic Cure chord changes, where you think, "where've I heard that before?"' Simon Gallup certainly felt that way when Smith brought 'There Is No If' into the sessions – the bones of the song, the title and the opening lyrics, first appeared during the *Faith* sessions, and Smith laughed, 'he remembered them from back then.

'I'd always gone back to that song for every album, I've always thought "I really love this song, this idea," but I'd never done anything with it. But this time, I thought I will, because I had a guitar piece that I thought would work.' The finished performance was barely altered from Smith's original demo, after attempts to add bass and a drum pattern to the song fell through, and that adds to its desolate beauty... 'it doesn't sound complete to me,' Smith confessed, 'it sounds unfinished, which is probably the charm of it.' Nevertheless, its inclusion on the album was a close-run thing – for a long time, Smith intended placing 'Coming Up' in its place, and confining 'There Is No If' to no greater glory than a bonus track on the Japanese and Australian versions of the album. Sense prevailed, and the roles were reversed at the next-to-last minute.

If Smith had any doubts about the album, they came – and were dispensed with – before the recording sessions were even booked. 'I wanted to express how I felt about certain things, turning from 39 to 40, for example.' The first song composed for the album, in fact, was written at the beginning of that milestone year. '"39" was written on my 39th birthday, and that started the whole project going – I thought I'd have this very quiet on-my-own birthday (because I thought 40 would end up with a horrible surprise party), so I wanted to write myself a birthday song and it wasn't coming out right. It was twee and shit basically. So then I thought I'd write a song about not having anything left inside me to write about, because that's how I was feeling; and, when I listened back to it a week or so later, it was quite good and, in a strange way, it got me going again.'

Nevertheless, he remained uncertain about the direction of the project. 'At first, I thought it was going to be boring if the songs were only going to be about me, because it was the first time in 10 years that I'd sat down and done that. Who cares? So I had to get over that hurdle.' It was his own return to those earlier albums that pushed him over the hump, the realization that the two albums that are unanimously regarded as 'quintessential' Cure were also quite essentially personal.

There was another departure from the norm, in Smith's new-found fascination with the guitar... in particular, lead guitar. 'I wanted the last song on the last Cure album to be a title track, a "Faith" or a "Disintegration," and a mixture of all the bits about the Cure I like, the *Pornography*-style drumming, the *Disintegration*-style six string bass strumming, it's all there. But the new ingredient is my "highly developed" lead guitar style, that I've been practicing for at least a year.

'Over the past couple of years, I've shed all these shackles of what I think things mean... over the years, solos meant "hippy"; Hendrix plays solos and nobody else can. That's not quite true... Neil Young plays fantastic solos as well. But Cure guitar solos have traditionally been melodic, a little voice singing an alternate melody. They haven't really been rampaging... they're riffing and tuneful, they're not really heads down.' This time, he decided to 'kick some ass.'

The sessions themselves were wrapped up in near-record time, at least by the Cure's recent standards. 'I already knew the songs that book-ended the album, I'd written all the words before we recorded the first note, and I had a very good idea of the sounds we were going to use in each song. I did have a concept almost of this album, as I did with *Disintegration* and *Pornography*. The big difference was, the way of working wasn't the same. I wasn't quite so deranged. I wasn't standing there screaming at people. I encouraged everyone to join in with me and create a kind of atmosphere.'

The band returned to St Catherine's, the scene of the protracted *Wild Mood Swings* sessions, 'because there were nights there... the way we lived, dinner was more important than recording, it was the process of living together. The difference was, this time, we had three months from beginning to end. I told the others that I wanted it pinned down in six weeks, and then they could all go home. So, in that way, I was a little bit harsher than I have been for the last few albums, but I felt I needed it to be done without any intrusion and anyone saying "well what about doing it this way...."'

But was this really the final Cure album?

'I don't really care. I've reached that point – if it's the last thing we do, great, it's the perfect place to stop. But if we do another album, if the Cure do make another album, if I do a solo album and don't enjoy it and want to do something again with the Cure, I'm not signing anything that says I can't. I'll be phoning them up again to say "do you fancy..."'

'But I somehow doubt that's going to happen, because historically, for whatever reason, there's never been a line up of the Cure that's made more than two albums together. So history is against that happening.'

Indeed, as early as November 1999, Smith was able to look forward over the next nine months and rejoice in the knowledge that, once they were over, his calendar was completely clean. And that was when he would begin work on the solo album he'd been mulling over since he first realized that anyone might be interesting in hearing such a thing.

The songs were already written, and he had no doubt that they were not suitable for the Cure. In fact, 'the two most important factors that have pushed me into doing something on my own: one is the instrumentation that I've got in my mind from my demos, because they require instruments that no-one in the band can play, including string and wind instruments, and I want them to be played live, I don't want them coming out of a machine. And secondly, at this stage, I don't intend singing on it.

'So, it would be quite strange for me to bring out an album that's driven by strange instrumentation, that has no lyrics... unless I get someone else to sing on it... it wouldn't be fair for me to bring that out as a Cure album. I do have a very strong emotional attachment to the body of work that the Cure has done and I'd hate to start abusing it.

'I'm not naïve; it will still be "Robert Smith of the Cure", whatever I do, but it will, in my mind, distance it from the body of work. And I will try very hard to make people know that.

'The whole point of what I'm doing is... it will be driven by a storyline that is an imaginary film, with a cast of characters... whether I become one of those characters or not... and right now, it's easier for me to think of the voice being taken by an instrument, in the way that *Peter and The Wolf* is put together. But I may end up thinking that's really stupid and sing it after all.'

The other obstacle to this remarkable sounding project becoming a new band album, he laughed, was their own response to the new material. 'I played it to the others... and they're not that impressed. The form of it is not really like Cure songs. For me, it's an experiment and, if it works, I'll be really pleased. And if it doesn't, I'll make another Cure album.'

(SINGLE) Out Of This World
0001a Out Of This World (radio edit)

0001 Out Of This World (album version)
0001b Out Of This World (Paul Oakenfold mix)
ORIGINAL RELEASE: Fiction CURE 2, February 2000

(SINGLE) Maybe Someday
0004a Maybe Someday (radio edit)
0004b Maybe Someday (Hybrid Mix Radio Edit)
0004c Maybe Someday (Dance Mix)
0004d Maybe Someday (Acoustic Mix)
ORIGINAL RELEASE: Fiction CURE 3, February 2000
COMMENTS: 'Out Of This World' was only the second song Smith wrote for the new album, in the months before he realized that there was even an album gestating. 'There are usually two or three songs that hold an album together for me and, once I've got them, I think "okay, it's time to start thinking about it." "Out Of This World"… I wrote it and I knew, immediately, this was the opening track.'

He did not know it was going to be a single; indeed, he was adamant, 'there won't be any singles off this album.' It was the American label's idea to farm a song or two out to radio, to which Smith responded, 'pick whichever one you want, it makes no difference to me because we aren't making a video. We're not doing pop shows, we're not doing videos, the album is an album. I want to get away from that side of things. I don't want to do the single stuff at the moment, I want the emphasis to be on the "big side" of the Cure.'

Reacting, perhaps, to the ghastly surfeit of remixes applied to other recent releases, Smith arranged for just one 'Out Of This World' remix, by Paul Oakenfold – and then decided not to release it. (It finally appeared on *Join The Dots*.) The thus horribly unadorned single was then restricted to a promotional issue only, a fate that also awaited the near-simultaneous 'Maybe Someday'.

That song, described by Smith as the only track on the album that has a 'light side,' was a reflection on the looming end of the Cure. 'It's about me and the others; it's about the group, and it's driven by me saying "this is it, make the most of it, I don't want to do this anymore…" and them turning around and saying "yeah, maybe," because that is kind of part of me… I've said that twice before and meant it, and at least ten times before and not meant it.'

Here the remixes did flow, with Smith smiling, 'the idea of the remixes was to be played on whichever radio format we don't get played on.' Of the ensuing crop, the most fascinating was the 'acoustic' version that reunited the Cure with first-few-albums engineer/producer Mike Hedges.

(TV) *Nulle Part Ailleurs* (France) 8 February 2000
UNR The Last Day Of Summer
ORIGINAL RELEASE: unreleased
COMMENTS: A memorable performance, in that the Cure unveiled a song that nobody could have expected them to play. Born from one of the 15 demos that Gallup came up with in the lead-up to the new album, 'The Last Day Of Summer' is a characteristically beautiful, if sparse, number, built around

Smith's own suggestion that he, Gallup, create a song with an autumnal feel. 'The chord sequence just jumped out at me straight away,' Smith said; 'I'd written the other eight songs for the album, and I was just waiting for something in that particular mood.... There's a particular thing that Simon does, that's a very clever way of mixing a pop sensibility with a very sad sound, and often when I try and write a song like Simon does, it winds up sounding very twee. But he does it.'

(TV) *Mad TV* (USA) 18 February 2000
  UNR Maybe Someday
  UNR In Between Days

(RADIO) K-ROQ session (USA) 29 February 2000
  UNR Out Of This World
  UNR Maybe Someday

(TV) *Late Night With Conan O'Brien* (USA) 29 February 2000
  UNR Maybe Someday
  UNR A Forest
ORIGINAL RELEASE: all unreleased
COMMENTS: Gearing up for the next tour, a rush of high profile media appearances.

(ALBUM) *American Psycho* original soundtrack
  0002a Watching Me Fall (Underdog Remix)
ORIGINAL RELEASE: Koch 8164, 2000
COMMENTS: The album's undisputed epic, eleven minutes of 'Watching Me Fall' originally stretched to 20 minutes in demo form, as Smith envisioned, 'my "Seven Ages Of Man" song... my life in the Cure. But, in the end, I felt I was writing something that Meatloaf might have been singing, so I cut down the scope of it.'

The song was based around 'something that happened to me last time we were in Japan, and a short story by Catherine Mansfield that was strangely similar to something that happened to me, about getting lost in Tokyo – which is not a good city to get lost in. Plus, deep down, I wanted to write an epic rock song. I even practiced guitar for a few months, because I wanted to pull off a couple of big rock guitar solos. And this was my big guitar moment!'

Not in the Underdog's hands it wasn't, as 'Watching Me Fall' was pruned down to a shade under eight minutes, although it still sounded great wedged between David Bowie's yearning 'Something In The Air' and a new Stephen Hague take on New Order's 'True Faith'. In fact, it was a damned good soundtrack all round. (The movie's not so hot, though.)

2001

LINE-UP #17 Robert Smith (vocals, guitar), Perry Bamonte (guitar), Roger O'Donnell (keyboards), Simon Gallup (bass), Jason Cooper (drums)

(TV) *Arte* (France) 26 October 2001
UNR Just Like Heaven
UNR Close To Me
UNR Lullaby
UNR In Between Days
UNR Let's Go To Bed
UNR Lovesong
UNR A Forest
UNR Friday I'm In Love
UNR Boys Don't Cry
UNR Just Say Yes
UNR The Walk
UNR Why Can't I Be You?

(TV) *Europe 2*, 23 November 2001
UNR The Lovecats
UNR Mint Car
UNR Just Like Heaven
UNR High
UNR Lullaby
UNR Cut Here
UNR Friday I'm In Love
UNR Why Can't I Be You?
UNR Boys Don't Cry
UNR Lovesong
UNR A Forest
UNR High
UNR Fire In Cairo
UNR Boys Don't Cry
UNR In Between Days
ORIGINAL RELEASE: unreleased
COMMENTS: The *Bloodflowers* tour came and went… Smith's 1 August start date for the solo project too. October 2000 saw the Cure play a smattering of Australian dates – notable for the cover of Joy Division's 'Love Will Tear Us

Apart' that they first worked up in Canberra ('it's hard to cover such a fantastic original,' Smith later shrugged); the new year saw a return to the Roskilde Festival. *Bloodflowers* was nominated for a Grammy. There was a flurry of excitement over the suggestion that some kind of live documentation of the tour might be imminent... a series of CDs, perhaps, a video, *something*... And then... silence, until October brought a sudden burst of activity.

The live project was on hold, and the solo album was in abeyance once again. 'I enjoyed last year with the band a lot,' Smith confessed. 'Any doubts I had about the validity or "purpose" of the group were dispelled, and most of the new songs I've written this year have turned out sounding like they should be played by us, not by me.'

All that remained, then, was to wipe out the last vestiges of the group's existing record contracts, by approving the release of a *Greatest Hits* collection... the same one Smith had fought so furiously to scupper back in 1998. Then, to help promote it, the Cure also agreed to reverse another of his declarations, Smith's hatred of 'only the hits' type concerts, and play a pair in France, at the Parisian clubs Le Resevoir (26 Oct) and Le Scene (23 Nov).

With the set drawn exclusively from the forthcoming CD, surprises were few and far between. However, Republica vocalist Saffron appeared at Le Resevoir, to preview her duet on the solitary new song, 'Just Say Yes', while sharp-eyed viewers at the same show also caught Ray Cockes adding guitar to 'Boys Don't Cry'. The TV broadcast of that show omitted one track, 'Let's Go To Bed'; the *Europe 2* broadcast of the second gig screened just six songs.

(SINGLE) Cut Here
    0101 Cut Here
    0102 Signal To Noise
    0101a Cut Here (Mixxing Remix)
    0101b Cut Here (CD Rom video)
    0103 Signal To Noise (acoustic version)
ORIGINAL RELEASE: Fiction FICCD 55, November 2001
COMMENTS: One of two new songs recorded for inclusion on the forthcoming *Greatest Hits* album, 'Cut Here' marks a full-blooded return to the *Head On The Door/Kiss Me* era of the Cure – all the stronger for the 15 years or so that this style of playing had receded into the background. That said, it came very close to being relegated to the b-side of the new single, as Smith found himself favouring the FX-fed, and gargantuan guitar soloing 'Signal To Noise' for some time... even going as far as recording an acoustic version for inclusion on the album's bonus disc, before reverting to his original plan.

(TV) *CD: UK* (UK) 10 November 2001
    UNR Friday I'm In Love

(RADIO) *Janice Long* (UK) 12 November 2001
    UNR Boys Don't Cry

UNR In Between Days
UNR High

(RADIO) XFM Session (UK) 13 November 2001
UNR Lullaby
UNR Lovesong
UNR Pictures Of You

(TV) *Top Of The Pops* (Germany) 15 November 2001
UNR Cut Here   (playback)

(RADIO) Simon Mayo (UK) 26 November 2001
UNR A Forest
UNR Just Like Heaven
UNR Friday I'm In Love
UNR Cut Here

(ALBUM) *Acoustic Hits*
0104 Boys Don't Cry
0105 A Forest
0106 Let's Go To Bed
0107 The Walk
0108 The Lovecats
0109 In Between Days
0110 Close To Me
0111 Why Can't I Be You?
0112 Just Like Heaven
0113 Lullaby
0114 Lovesong
0115 Never Enough
0116 High
0117 Friday, I'm In Love
0118 Mint Car

0119 Wrong Number
0120 Cut Here
0121 Just Say Yes

ORIGINAL RELEASE: Polydor 5894342, November 2001

COMMENTS: The main attraction of the *Greatest Hits* album was the array of classic singles that were on show. Early copies, however, came with a bonus disc reprising the entire album with newly recorded acoustic versions – as madcap and mercurial as only the Cure could be. From the claustrophobic depths of 'A Forest', to the arachnid quickstep of 'Lullaby', and onto unexpectedly triumphant reinventions of 'Never Enough' and 'Wrong Number', it also served as a reminder that the Cure don't simply make great records. They write great songs as well.

A *Greatest Hits* DVD was released alongside the CD; it, too, featured an acoustic set, albeit somewhat shorter in length: six performances were included: 'A Forest', 'The Lovecats', 'Close To Me', 'Lullaby', 'Friday I'm In Love' and 'Just Say Yes'.

(SINGLE) Just Say Yes

0122 Just Say Yes
0121 Just Say Yes (acoustic version)
0122a Just Say Yes (Curve Mix)

ORIGINAL RELEASE: Fiction FICCD 56, December 2001; 0112a on *Join The Dots*

COMMENTS: 'The original demo [of 'Just Say Yes'] had everything a great pop songs needs,' Smith enthused, explaining that the song was conceived as a rallying point for everybody who was tired of being told 'Just Say No'. 'I wanted something different, and I had the idea that this could be the time for a vivacious duet, which is why the single version has Saffron on it.'

The result, if one overlooks the distinctly modernistic backing track, is a vocal that oozes punk adrenalin and rage (whether it was deliberate or not, there is something about the blending of the two voices), an intoxicating flashback to the heyday of the Rezillos, with Eugene and Fay fighting for supremacy both somehow coming out on top. A magnificent single – damn it, it might even be the Cure's best in a decade.

The original single was backed by nothing more exciting than the regular acoustic version of the song; however, Smith also arranged for a Curve remix ('a pretty strange take on the original song, and pretty fab with it'), which ultimately surfaced on *Join The Dots*.

2002

LINE-UP #17 Robert Smith (vocals, guitar), Perry Bamonte (guitar), Roger O'Donnell (keyboards), Simon Gallup (bass), Jason Cooper (drums)

(TV) *This Is Dom Joly* (UK) 16 May 2002
   UNR In Between Days
   UNR A Night Like This

(TV) *Recovered* (UK) 25 May 2002
   UNR Lovesong
   UNR Don't Believe A Word
   UNR A Forest
ORIGINAL RELEASE: unreleased
COMMENTS: You had to love *Recovered* – the only British rock show of the millennium with the balls to ask bands to admit what they really like, as opposed to trotting out the usual array of hip references that they normally do.

For the Cure, the question left Smith reaching back to his mid-70s youth and settling on Thin Lizzy, the Anglo-Irish-American band whose street-smart fighting swagger actually saw them flirt with the earliest strains of the nascent punk scene – what single, after all, better conjures up the summer of 76 than 'The Boys Are Back In Town'? And what mood would better be crystallised at the end of the year?

Back in 1997, Smith confessed to 'listen[ing] to the first two Thin Lizzy albums and I just started crying, but in a good way. It showed me that I still like the same things. In some ways I've changed dramatically and in some ways I've stayed exactly the same as when I was 15 – emotionally retarded.' Now he was returning to those roots (and that realisation?) once again and, though 'Don't Believe A Word' wasn't, in fact, one of Lizzy's better songs... a bit too faceless *lumpen*rock, a bit too clumsy in the lyrical department... what the hell. We loved 'em anyway.

(LIVE) Tempdrom, Berlin, 11-12 November 2002
   0201 One Hundred Years
   0202 Short Term Effect
   0203 The Hanging Garden
   0204 Siamese Twins
   0205 The Figurehead
   0206 A Strange Day

0207 Cold
0208 Pornography
0209 Plainsong
0210 Pictures Of You
0211 Closedown
0212 Lovesong
0213 Lullaby
0214 Fascination Street
0215 Prayers For Rain
0216 The Same Deep Water As You
0217 Disintegration
0218 Untitled
0219 Homesick
0220 Out Of This World
0221 Watching Me Fall
0222 Where The Birds Always Sing
0223 Maybe Someday
0224 The Last Day Of Summer
0225 There Is No If
0226 The Loudest Sound
0227 39
0228 Bloodflowers
0229 If Only Tonight We Could Sleep
0230 The Kiss
UNR M
UNR Play For Today
UNR A Forest
UNR Grinding Halt
UNR Boys Don't Cry

ORIGINAL RELEASE: *Trilogy* DVD, Eagle Vision EV 30036-9

COMMENTS: The Cure surfaced once again for a string of summer 2002 festival dates, carefully confining the surprises to the occasional seldom-heard oldie ('The Baby Screams', 'Torture', 'Push') and the even more occasional cover version encore… 'Don't Believe A Word' again, and – tracking back equally far into Smith's rock lexicon, the Sensational Alex Harvey Band's 'Faith Healer'. Although it must be admitted, the sight of Smith teetering onstage, demanding 'let me put my hands on you…' was somewhat less awe-inspiring than watching Harvey do the same thing.

November then saw the group return to the road, this time for a trilogy of concerts, dedicated to a trilogy of albums – a concept whose realisation, Smith said, 'is one of the highlights of my time in the Cure. The albums *Pornography*, *Disintegration* and *Bloodflowers* are inextricably linked in so many ways…' – that it made sense to dedicate one entire concert to the three of them.

Smith was inspired to embark on the project after catching David Bowie's recent London shows, at which he unveiled track-by-track recreations of his albums *Low* and *Heathen*. It was, Smith said afterwards, 'the best I'd seen him on stage for years and years.' Days later, he was arranging for the Cure to undertake their own, similar concerts.

Three shows were organised, in Brussels on 7 November, and Berlin over 11-12 November (a fourth gig, in Hamburg on 9 November was not part of the sequence); it was important, Smith said, that the music be presented in a city whose own feel and imagery echoed that of the albums in question and, for a time, he toyed with the idea of staging shows in Moscow and Prague. From the travelling fans' point of view, the final venues were somewhat easier to get to… besides, both cities had their own special place in the group's iconography – Berlin, as a city that Smith had enjoyed playing 'right back to the early days,' and Brussels, as the last city to host a concert on the original *Pornography* tour.

Of the three albums that were recreated in their entirety across each show, it was *Pornography* that presented the greatest challenge, to the band and, following the release of the *Trilogy* DVD, to fans… 'old codgers like us,' as Gallup put it… who remembered the first time around.

As he geared himself up for the first rehearsal, in particular, Smith found himself recalling the sheer tension and abuse that had haunted that last tour; recalled, too, the absolute breakdown that had shattered his relationship with Gallup. What demons, he wondered, might be reawakened by the invocation of those haunted, hateful, emotions? And how much more hateful might they have grown in the intervening years? In the end, it was Gallup who calmed his fears, by pointing out that 'you have to realise you're only playing a song, you're not living the lifestyle.'

The problem… the weakness… that resulted from that realisation, of course, was that it was the lifestyle that gave *Pornography* so much of its emotion and its resonance. 'If we had tried to create [that],' Smith later pointed out, 'we wouldn't have come back on stage for *Disintegration*.' But by *not* recreating that, *Pornography* was shorn of much of the potency that rendered it so poignant in the first place.

Like Iggy Pop on the occasions he drags tracks from the *Metallic KO* live album into his modern set; like Bowie, when he tried recreating the best of *Ziggy Stardust*; like the Sex Pistols hauling out 'Anarchy In The UK', two decades past the last time it meant anything… they played the music, but they missed the point. The Cure of *Pornography* was less a band, more a state of mind, a state of being… a state of decay. And, without those particular states still surrounding the music, what are the eight songs that comprised the live show, but a faintly dreary, mildly depressing, and oddly one-dimensional gaggle of juvenile fancies, recreated in their sombre Sunday Best for a hastily convened convention of Mental Museum curators?

Individually, most of the songs were enjoyable – on the night, the brittle overtures of 'Siamese Twins' and 'The Figurehead' even brought tears to the eye. But they did so *not* for what the songs were saying, but for all that they once meant: to us, to the band, to a world that was hurtling past without a second glance at the funny little trio in black, playing their dismal little dirges to a couple of hundred social rejects. Or, in other words, fuck off Robert, those are my memories you're trampling on as well.

The remainder of the performance engenders less extremes of emotion, simply because – for all their much-vaunted 'similarities' – neither *Disintegration* nor *Bloodflowers* were as extreme or emotional as *Pornography* itself. Indeed, taking this particular opportunity to line the three albums up alongside one another, it is *Seventeen Seconds*, not *Pornography*, that most perfectly completes the trilogy – because it was with *Seventeen Seconds* that the Cure first deliberately set out to establish a definite mood with their music... just as *Disintegration* and *Bloodflowers* deliberately set to re-create it. *Pornography*, on the other hand, was not deliberate. It was desperate. And the only thing *Disintegration* and *Bloodflowers* truly have in common with it is, the erroneous assumption that the Cure stopped here.

Trilogy, too, was widely touted as the last 'new' release the Cure would ever put their name to, by Smith, at least. 'For me, that was the end of the Cure, because it summarized twenty-five years of our career, and about ten years with the same line-up. It pleased me, what we were doing, but I thought it was a good moment to leave it and pass to another thing.

'I spent a lot of time in my home studio to work on the material for the solo album. In an attempt to become free from the things I had done all these years, I worked together with a bunch of very different artists. I even booked some recording time in the studio. When we went to Berlin in 2002 for the Trilogy concerts, it was my intention to play the last Cure shows ever. The final ones. I really thought of those concerts as being the Cure terminus....'

Or so Smith said at the time. Unfortunately, once again, 'I didn't take into account how I'd feel about the band six months later. The DVD was 25 years after we formed, and it felt like a good full stop. [Then] I began to have ideas for a new album.'

Trilogy ranks among the most flawlessly performed, beautifully played and utterly enjoyable live DVDs yet released, with each of three sets packing more highlights than one would even want to try listing. The entire *Disintegration* set, in particular, is breathtaking in places, with the performances even outstripping those that dignify *Entreat* – itself one of the all-time great Cure live recordings.

Finally, the *Trilogy* DVD has a host of unexpected treats as follows: Split Screen – go to the Disintegration set (disc one) and select "Plainsong"; press LEFT; press ENTER. Lipstick Cam – go to the Disintegration set (disc one) and select "Same Deep Water As You"; press LEFT; press ENTER. Extra Interviews – go to the Interview menu (disc two) and select "End Of An Era?"; press LEFT; press ENTER.

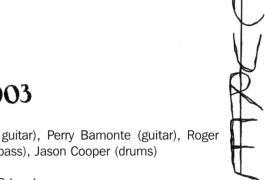

2003

LINE-UP #17 Robert Smith (vocals, guitar), Perry Bamonte (guitar), Roger O'Donnell (keyboards), Simon Gallup (bass), Jason Cooper (drums)

(TV) *This Is Dom Joly* (UK) 2 April 2003 London
UNR The Kiss
UNR Just Like Heaven

(TV) *The Late Late Show* (USA) 18 September 2003
UNR 10.15 Saturday Night
UNR Just Like Heaven
ORIGINAL RELEASE: unreleased
COMMENTS: A couple of isolated broadcasts, standing out in a year that saw the band play only two concerts – a K-ROQ festival a couple of days after the *Late Late Show*, and a Christmas benefit in Islington.

The Late Late Show was a gem regardless, as the manifold gremlins that can taunt live television rolled out in force to interrupt '10.15 Saturday Night' with a screech of feedback so piercing that the entire performance was brought to a halt and the song begun again.

(ALBUM) *ROBERT SMITH – BLINK 182: Blink 182*
0301 All Of This
ORIGINAL RELEASE: album *Blink 182*, Geffen 000133412, November 2003
COMMENTS: Blink 182's sixth album earned the band some raised eyebrows for what – within their own corner of punk music – was regarded as an ability for sonic experimentation. Smith's contributions are restricted to a semi-spoken backing vocal on a song whose apparent clumsiness is, in fact, one of its saving graces. It might not be enough to convert Cure fans to Blinkie buddies, of course, but it's an intriguing little diversion all the same.

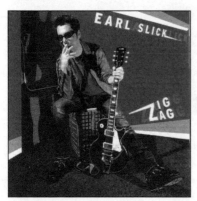

(ALBUM) ROBERT SMITH – EARL SLICK: *Zig Zag*
  0302 Believe
ORIGINAL RELEASE: Sanctuary 06076 84671, December 2003
COMMENTS: Ranked among rock's finest guitar-slingers since he first emerged, alongside David Bowie, back in the mid-1970s, Earl Slick has never really got the recognition he deserves in the Guitar Hero stakes, preferring to slink away from the limelight that has consumed other, infinitely less-gifted players – simply getting on with what he does best. But *Zig Zag*, the latest in a too-sporadic succession of Slick solo albums (the first appeared in 1976), could well have been the one that exploded his secrecy forever.

It's not simply the calibre of guest stars that makes it notable – Robert Smith's appearance, on the slow burning 'Believe', is accompanied by spots from Bowie, Def Leppard's Joe Elliott and the Motels' Martha Davis. From the opening slash of the near-instrumental 'Dancing With Eleanor', though to the closing purr of 'The Cat', *Zig Zag* merits comparison with the best of Jeff Beck's recent output – which means it, itself, is the best.

Never settling, never letting the listener's ears wander elsewhere for a moment, the ten tracks might conform to what one would expect from a "classic rock" veteran, but never lapse into laziness. Rather, Slick built his riffs and rhythms from the ground up, creating an almost organic maze of sound around the obvious technologies that percolate beneath. And, at its highest points, you can even forget who the guest stars are. Who needs heroes, when Slick is so slick?

(STUDIO) ROBERT SMITH – EARL SLICK
  0303 A Forest
ORIGINAL RELEASE: *Join The Dots*, 2004
COMMENTS: 'I did a track for his new album and, in return, he agreed to do something for us.' Thus Smith explained away the Cure's decision to rerecord 'A Forest' during 2003, and then hand the tape to Slick and producer Mark Plati to remix as 'a drum and bass thing with wild, groovy guitar. It's [a] very weird rework.'

It was. But it was not the only one.

2004

LINE-UP #17 Robert Smith (vocals, guitar), Perry Bamonte (guitar), Roger O'Donnell (keyboards), Simon Gallup (bass), Jason Cooper (drums)

(SINGLE) ROBERT SMITH – JUNIOR JACK – Da Hype
    0401 Da Hype (vocal mix)
    0401a Da Hype (vocal single mix)
    0401b Da Hype (Warren Clack Vocal Dub Mix)
    0401c Da Hype (Extended Vocal Mix)
ORIGINAL RELEASE: Defected, February 2004
COMMENTS: The wealth of remixes spreads not only across the various single formats, but also a compilation album, *Prime Cuts Dance*, and a full Junior Jack album, *Trust It*. Jack himself was riding high on one of 2003's biggest club hits, 'e-samba', and a string of dance-related awards; with Smith's vocals riding hard on the samples and beats, 'Da Hype' (wryly titled, of course, for his own recent pre-eminence), proved how much he deserved them.

(EP) ROBERT SMITH – BLANK AND JONES: *A Forest*
    0402a A Forest (Short Cut)
    0402 A Forest (Original Mix)
    0402b A Forest (Vegas Cossmo Remix)
    0402c A Forest (Tripeller Remix)
ORIGINAL RELEASE: Water Music Dance 302 060 404, February 2004
COMMENTS: Blank and Jones – Piet Blank and Jaspa Jones – transform 'A Forest' into a genuinely ear-catching rave, all throbbing electro and tricky beats… retro enough to entertain the oldsters among us, but furious enough that it became a hot club hit in early 04.

Smith agreed to join the stripy-suit clad duo after they sent him 'a load of CDs. I knew who [they] were,' he laughed; 'it might surprise some people to know that I listen to quite a lot of dance music. I just sit there and listen to it, and wish I could dance…. [And] I thought it was intriguing, doing such a well-known song as "A Forest".'

He had already devoted himself, that summer of 2003, to involving himself in 'different things, that'd make me sing in different ways, and thinking about music in different ways…' his partnerships with Blink 182 and Junior Jack were similarly designed to stretch his perceptions as he prepared to return to the studio with the Cure.

Similarly, his attempts to add a vocal to the backing track that the duo mailed him forced him to take drastic measures. 'I tried to do it in a studio and it sounded so contrived.' So he took the tape back to his home studio, where he had hitherto undertaken nothing more demanding than his own demos, and it 'worked straight away. I plugged it in and did it in two takes.'

The CD single also featured a DVD of the accompanying video and an entertaining interview between Blank, Smith and Jones.

(ALBUM) *One Perfect Day* original soundtrack
0403 Pictures Of You (Paul Mac Remix)
ORIGINAL RELEASE: Universal, February 2004
COMMENTS: An unreleased solo version of the *Disintegration* stand-out track, remixed for the sprawling soundtrack to the acclaimed Australian movie. Worth hearing, but not, perhaps, if you have to pay the imported 2CD price for it.

(ALBUM) ROBERT SMITH – JUNKIE XL: *Radio JXL – A Broadcast From The Computer Hell Cabin*
0404 Perfect Blue Sky
ORIGINAL RELEASE: (Koch), February 2004
COMMENTS: An army of special guests that ranged from Saffron and David Gahan, to Gary Numan and Solomon Burke, turned out to support Junkie XL, with Smith offering up one of his more understated, but characteristically sad, vocals on a bumpy little ballad.

(SINGLE) The End Of The World
0405 The End Of The World
0406 This Morning
0407 Fake
ORIGINAL RELEASE: Geffen B0003066-22, June 2004

(TV) *Tonight Show with Jay Leno* (USA) 30 April 2004
UNR The End Of The World
ORIGINAL RELEASE: unreleased
COMMENTS: Asked, during an Internet fan forum, which song he would play for the end of the world, Smith suggested 'Faith'. Good. For 'The End of the World' simply wouldn't work.

As breezy as the new album would get, 'The End Of The World' rumbles so good-naturedly along, that you're into at least the second chorus before you realize the song doesn't actually have a tune, or even a hook. But there's a playful keyboard warble, a catchy 'ooooh-ooooh' refrain, and a Smith vocal that sounds like it's halfway to Paradise already.

The two b-sides were more in keeping with the remainder of the album... fittingly, as both were included on the double-LP vinyl version. The seven minute plod of 'This Morning' would, in fact, reveal itself among the full length attraction's best numbers, with the 'years go by' section almost conjuring visions of an older, rougher, rawer sounding *Faith*. 'Fake', meanwhile, would

itself have made a great second single.

(ALBUM) *The Cure*
   0408 Lost
   0409 Labyrinth
   0410 Before Three
   0405 The End Of The World
   0411 Anniversary
   0412 Us Or Them
   0413 alt.end
   0414 (I Don't Know What's Going) On
   0415 Taking Off
   0416 Never
   0417 The Promise
UK vinyl bonus tracks
   0407 Fake
   0418 Going Nowhere
   0406 This Morning
   0419 Truth Goodness & Beauty
ORIGINAL RELEASE: Geffen B0002870, June 2004
COMMENTS: Demos for 'the new Cure album' existed as far back as 2001, and the routine of promotional activities tied in around *Greatest Hits*. The key to the band's continuance, however, was a meeting with Ross Robinson, the American producer whose career-so-far had seen him create a musical genre... if not force of nature... that had become as omnipresent as the Cure's own reputation: the so-called Nu-Metal explosion of Korn, Coal Chamber, Slipknot and so forth. And, just as nobody would ever have guessed that Robert Smith was a Korn fan, neither would they have suspected that Robinson loved the Cure. But he did.

Smith explained: 'A few years ago, I heard that Ross liked us, so I searched out what else he had done. I thought At the Drive-In was great. And I've always liked Korn – they're pioneers of that sound. A lot of the stuff I was kind of ambivalent towards, like Slipknot, but my younger nephews swear by those bands. What I found that held it all together was the intensity. Everything Ross did had a real sense of urgency about it.'

A meeting was arranged and all Smith's plans for the death of the Cure were thrown asunder. 'It's true. I met Ross and everything changed. Since the beginning, he insisted, "we must do another Cure album, we must do an album together... ". And it happened that eighteen months later, after calling me constantly by telephone, and writing piles of letters to me, he came to see me again. We spoke of the amount of new groups that quoted us as their influence in the interviews, of how some of them sounded... I noticed that a lot of new bands were talking about us: the Deftones, the Rapture, Hot Hot Heat and some others. Probably it has to do with the fact that those musicians grew up with *Disintegration* in their CD player. It's like a new generation is discovering what we have done back then. However, there seems to be some kind of revival. He told me, "you cannot leave it, you must do a new album"... and here I am.

Not quite. Smith's original intention was that Robinson would produce his solo album. Robinson, however, refused. 'He insisted the next album should be a Cure album. He said: "The time is right for a new Cure album. I have a gut feeling." So it put me to the difficult choice of sticking to my solo career plans or working together with a producer who seems to understand the Cure and who has a connection with a younger generation of artists and fans. Ultimately I chose the last option, thinking: "there's a chance I'm going to regret this." But I also felt that we hadn't met without a reason. So, when the *Trilogy* concerts were finished, I decided to put the solo album on hold and I totally went for The Cure. And, fortunately, this album is a lot better than the one that I would have created on my own.'

Robinson suggested Smith take a new approach to his songwriting, as well. 'We made an agreement: if the songs would have been comparable to what I love most of the Cure, I would have collected them under our name. The approach was to imagine that it took 25 years to reach this point and not to have 25 years of albums behind to overcome.'

A month after Smith agreed to go along with Robinson's ambition, the band were demoing; by the time the sessions were over, no less than 37 songs were 'almost ready.' Weeks later, the party moved to London, 'played through the 37 songs and we ended with 20... I wrote all the lyrics, made them to fit the music...'; and, while the rest of the world was absorbing *Join The Dots* in February, the Cure and Robinson were kicking off the six weeks of recording that would result in the finished album.

'Ross grew up with the Cure. On the first day of recording, he let us play for an hour, and then he just went absolutely mental. He kept saying, "Don't you know who you are? You're the Cure! What the fuck are you doing?" Everyone in the room thought, "Oh my God, he's saying really obvious things!" This is a band that is never usually confronted – it's usually just me saying to them, "Try to pull something out." Suddenly, we had this bloke kicking things over, going "Do you realize who you are?" I was almost crying with happiness. I knew at that moment that it was going to work.'

Released through Robinson's own I Am label, via Geffen Records, *The Cure*, in many ways, represented a new beginning for the band... another new beginning.

'We recorded it live, in a very narrow space. We were close one to the other and I felt the drums in my stomach. I had to tear my throat apart to hear myself. I was always competing with the drums, that's why I scream as I never did in the previous albums. For Ross, it was fundamental that I sang. He said that if I made the songs explode from the inside I would have provoked emotions in him. The rest didn't count. Partially this loaded me with responsibility, but it was also a great encouragement. He's been always following us, and he claims he realised every fan's dream: to tell me what to do.' *The Cure* wound up being completed in faster time than any Cure record in two decades, a mere six weeks. Plus, 'and I know all bands say this, but it was the most fun we've ever had in the studio. Was I worried it was going too easily? You're bloody joking, I'm making the most of it!'

The sense of freshness that dominated the proceedings was to communicate itself across the project, beginning with the cover art, a splash of touching simplicity conceived after Smith turned to his nieces and nephews, 'and asked them to do a drawing of a bad or good dream. The drawings were all over our studio. I thought "why bother with designers? These are perfect".

'When kids draw, there's no concept of cool, or that they're making art. I try to get that immediacy in our music. Oddly, the figure who cropped up most in their drawings was Lol Tolhurst, my brother-in-law (Tolhurst had married Smith's sister). I don't quite know what to make of that.'

That most pointedly unhelpful of album titles, too, was designed to dispense with preconceptions. Smith explained, 'if you haven't heard a Cure album before, I wanted this to be the one you could start with. It's got the poppier songs, it's got intensity, it's the ideal introduction to what we do. It represents everything what we have done to date.' And so it transpired, in many ways.

'Us Or Them' conjured the spirit of 'Shake Dog Shake'; 'Anniversary' and 'Labyrinthe' toyed with the so-slow-burning menace of the *Pornography* era... 'Hanging Garden', maybe, or even, 'Forever'; 'Before Three' fell in between stools, if not days; and so on. 'I think of this disc as if it was *Kiss Me, Kiss Me, Kiss Me*, a work that gathered different ideas from everything we had been during the 1980s....

'With *Bloodflowers*, the intention was to do an album that lasted one hour and that maintained one same feeling, that was an experience from the beginning until the end. But this album looks for other things, tries to be more accessible and more varied, even when it might be the album with a greater emotional load than [anything we've ever] done.'

That emotion can, it must be said, become a little wearing (at least one long-time Cure fan cast one ear to the album and dismissed it as 'shrill,') when song after song seems to find Smith in the middle of a petulant fit. He even swears his way through a few lyrics. Meanwhile, 'Lost' could have been a grunge-era Hole song, the overall sense of rage does hark back to some of Robinson's own past triumphs.

When the tantrums cease, however, *The Cure* sparkles, and concludes with what is certainly one of Smith's finest songs of the last decade or so, 'The Promise'. A ten minute epic built around a pulverized guitar that echoes so many early 70s British metal albums that you cannot simply pick on one (Sabbath's 'War Pigs' is in there, but so is the first Iggy & The Stooges LP). The lyric screams with a desertion and betrayal that Smith has not unleashed in a *very* long time.

The album was launched, of course, with a new tour – the inaugural Curiousa Festival outing, with Smith handpicking such support acts as the Rapture, Interpol, Thursday and Cursive. 'It would have been particularly stupid for me to put together a lineup of bands I wouldn't want to see myself,' he told *Rolling Stone*. 'I always place myself as the archetypal Cure fan. I'm the wrong age, but I still think that if I like anything particularly, our fans will.'

(RADIO) AOL Session (UK) 7 June 2004
   UNR Lost
   UNR Before Three
   UNR The End Of The World
   UNR Lovesong
   UNR Just Like Heaven
   UNR From The Edge Of The Deep Green Sea
   UNR One Hundred Years

(TV) *Friday Night With Jonathan Ross* (UK) 10 June 2004
   UNR In Between Days
   UNR The End Of The World

(TV) *Top Of The Pops* (Germany) 24 June 2004
   UNR The End Of The World

(TV) *TV Total* (Germany) 24 June 2004
   UNR The End Of The World

(TV) *J Kimmel Live* (USA) 26 August 2004
   UNR alt.end
   UNR Why Can't I Be You?
   UNR Lovesong
   UNR In Between Days
   UNR Just Like Heaven
   UNR Boys Don't Cry

(RADIO) *Music: Response* (UK) 29 September 2004
   UNR Three Imaginary Boys
   UNR Us Or Them
   UNR alt.end
   UNR Taking Off
   UNR 10:15 Saturday Night

(RADIO) *BBC Five Live* session (UK) 30 September 2004
   UNR Boys Don't Cry

(RADIO) *Zane Lowe Show* (UK) 05 October 2004
   UNR The End Of The World
   UNR Taking Off
   UNR Boys Don't Cry

(TV) *Canal+ 20th Anniversary* (France) 14 October 2004
UNR Taking Off

(RADIO) *Black Session* (France) 15 October 2004
UNR Plainsong
UNR High
UNR A Night Like This
UNR The End of the World
UNR Charlotte Sometimes
UNR Lovesong
UNR Taking Off
UNR Primary
UNR Jupiter Crash
UNR Us or Them
UNR Closedown
UNR Before Three
UNR From the Edge of the Deep Green Sea
UNR A Strange Day
UNR alt.end
UNR Disintegration
UNR If Only Tonight We Could Sleep
UNR The Kiss

(RADIO) XFM Session 19 October 2004
UNR alt.end
UNR Us Or Them
UNR Taking Off

(TV) *Later with Jools Holland* (UK) 22 October 2004 (rec 19 Oct)
UNR Taking Off
UNR Boys Don't Cry
UNR alt.end

(TV) *Tim Lovejoy Show* (UK) 27 October 2004
UNR Never
ORIGINAL RELEASE: unreleased
COMMENTS: A string of appearances tying into the release of *The Cure*. The Canal+ show is of especial interest, marking the birthday of France's first privately-owned TV station. The Cure were joined onstage by Placebo for a terrific version of 'If Only Tonight We Could Sleep'.

(ALBUM) ROBERT SMITH – TWEAKER: *2am Wake-Up Call*
  0420 Truth Is
ORIGINAL RELEASE: Imusic IM 01097, October 2004
COMMENTS: Former Nine Inch Nails programmer Chris Vrenna had led a less-than-high profile career since departing that band, but his one-man Tweaker nevertheless proved he had lost none of the intensity that he once shared with Trent Reznor, with *2am Wake-Up Call*, Tweaker's second album, actually proving a lot more listenable (and, accordingly, less precocious) than anything Reznor had since concocted.

Awash with guest stars, the album paired Vrenna with Psychotica's Clint Walsh, David Sylvian, Will Oldham, Johnny Marr and, for one track, Smith – whose lyric, Vrenna said, was required only to link in some way to the insomniac dreams and nightmares theme that the album itself adhered to. Vrenna explained, 'my wife was suffering a long bout of insomnia, where she would bolt awake every night, strangely, at exactly the same time: 2 a.m. It led to me sharing her insomnia, and I wound up staying up with her and discovered that when the world-at-large was fast asleep, I had unearthed a wealth of creative energy in myself. These were the hours when most of the work on *2 a.m. Wakeup call* occurred. It's a night-time record about things that keep us up at night.'

Smith's contribution is one of the most nightmarish of all, a wired, edgy vocal imposed – and imposing itself – over a somnambulistic rhythm; the song doesn't really do anything over the course of its four minute lifespan, but once it's over, the uneasiness lingers.

(SINGLE) Taking Off (UK)/alt.end (US)
0415 Taking Off
0421 Why Can't I Be Me?
0422 Your God Is Fear
0413 alt.end

ORIGINAL RELEASE: (UK) Geffen 9864491, (US) Geffen 0003650-32, October 2004

COMMENTS: Selecting the second single from *The Cure* was never going to be an easy task… in terms of being catchy, the Americans probably made the better choice, as dot.music's review of the UK release made clear. 'It's poppy, and it's romantic, but it's no "Friday I'm In Love." It's not even one of the latest album's… standout tracks, so it's hard to see what purpose this crow's-footed, jangle-by-numbers single fulfills other than a contractual obligation.' All of which is probably true.

Of the b-sides, 'Why Can't I Be Me?' certainly attracted the most attention, if only because its title – and, as it turned out, the feel of the song itself – so closely echoed a past Cure classic, albeit shot through with considerably less unself-consciousness than its near-namesake.

'Your God Is Fear', on the other hand, seemed to have an eye for reviving that ancient feud with New Order, as Gallup drops in a repeating bass line straight out of the Peter Hook school. Elsewhere, the backing track echoes *Disintegration*, before the lyric fastens on a catchphrase and takes it through hell and high water.

(ALBUM) various artists: *99X Live X9 Joyride*
0423 Taking Off

ORIGINAL RELEASE: 99XFM (Atlanta) radio CD, November 2004

COMMENTS: A new solo Smith version, recorded exclusively for the promo. Auf Der Mauer, Queens of the Stone Age and the Strokes also featured on the CD.

(ALBUM) ROBERT SMITH – BILLY CORGAN: *The Future Embrace*

ORIGINAL RELEASE: Martha's Music/Reprise 48712, June 2005

165

COMMENTS: The former Smashed Pumpkin played most of his pre-release cards close to his chest, but the one snippet he did give away was that a song on his forthcoming solo debut was co-written with Smith, and co-sung as well. In fact, the ensuing album revealed their collaboration to be a little less dramatic, as they linked instead to sing an utterly melancholic minor-key revision of the Bee Gees' oldie 'To Love Somebody.'

Corgan explained, 'I called Robert up and asked "will you sing on my record?" He said "sure, whatever you want." I said "it's a Bee Gees song." Over the Transatlantic line, I hear Robert Smith going "the Bee Gees?" I said "trust me, just do your thing and it will be fine. He did and it was great."'

Interviewed by the *Ottawa Citizen* in late October 2004, incidentally, Corgan confessed that he drew a lot of solace from the continuing existence of the Cure. 'The Cure, look at what's going on with the Cure now. The Cure have been so good for so long that, at some point, people go, "OK, you're great." And all those years of Robert (Smith) being made fun of in interviews, it's all going away now. It's all done. So it's all adding up, and for me it's kind of the same thing. The work at some point surpasses the wild Billy, pain-in-the-ass-caricature that, at some point, I turned into.'

THE FUTURE

"I want to finish my solo album. I started it in 1998. I wanted to be free to use or not use any instruments – if I don't have any bass on a song, Simon will be very bored in the studio. It might be totally instrumental. It started out as fairly regular songs, but now I think they sound better without any words. And, yes, I know my voice is my trademark. I'd like it to be instrumental, but to have a lyric sheet so fans can sing along anyway!" – Robert Smith, October 2004.

APPENDIX ONE
COMPILATION AND ARCHIVE RELEASES

(ALBUM) *Boys Don't Cry*
  7918 Boys Don't Cry
  7919 Plastic Passion
  7820 10.15 Saturday Night
  7908 Accuracy
  7910 Object
  7925 Jumping Someone Else's Train
  7911 Subway Song
  7819 Killing An Arab
  7914 Fire In Cairo
  7909 Another Day
  7901 Grinding Halt
  7812 World War
  7916 Three Imaginary Boys

ORIGINAL RELEASE: PVC 7916 (USA), February 1980; UK issue Fiction SPELP 26, September 1983.

COMMENTS: Unhappy with the UK track listing for the Cure's debut album, the North American PVC label compiled their own version, comprising eight tracks from *Three Imaginary Boys*, plus the three UK singles and one out-take ('World War') – to assemble an album that is, in many ways, superior even to *Three Imaginary Boys* itself. Certainly it offers a more representative snapshot of where the Cure stood throughout 1979.

Readily available as a not-too-expensive import in UK stores, *Boys Don't Cry* was finally given a full British release in September 1983, and appeared on CD three years later. However, only the earliest pressings of the latter feature the full, original album; reflecting Smith's own dissatisfaction with the release, subsequent pressings omitted 'World War' and replaced 'Object' with 'So What'.

(EP) *Japanese Whispers*
   8213 Let's Go To Bed
   8302 The Dream
   8214 Just One Kiss
   8303 The Upstairs Room
   8301 The Walk
   8306 Speak My Language
   8304 Lament
   8305 The Lovecats
ORIGINAL RELEASE. Fiction FIX 8, December 1983
COMMENTS: Originally intended for German and Japanese release only, this mini-album length compilation of the three fantasy singles and attendant b-sides was granted a hurried UK release just in time for Christmas, at the same time as Smith warned everybody, 'if *Pornography* took you to the edge of the cliff, the next one will plunge you over it.'

Of course it wouldn't; indeed, it couldn't – as Smith himself admitted a decade-plus later. 'When we first started, we weren't selling records, we were only playing to a few people, and we had to shout, because it was the only way to be noticed. Now we don't, because it's gone on so long that I know people do notice. There's enough people I've met who do understand.' And, with that understanding, there came calm.

(ALBUM) *Curiosity – Live 1977-1984*
   7704 Heroin Face
   7805 Boys Don't Cry
   7920 Subway Song
   8016 At Night
   8001 In Your House
   8111 The Drowning Man
   8113 The Funeral Party
   8211 All Mine
   8427 Forever
ORIGINAL RELEASE: Fiction FIX 10, October 1984
COMMENTS: Issued only on cassette, as part of that format's *Concert* release, *Curiosity* was, for many years, the ultimate gathering of the Cure's oddest odds and ends. Opening with a low-fi highlight from an Easy Cure concert, travelling on through an early demo version of 'Boys Don't Cry' and a clutch of apparently random live cuts, the set culminates with two previously unissued songs, live versions of the *Pornography*-era 'All Mine', and the longtime concert closer 'Forever'.

Smith drew the recordings from his own collection – from the earliest days, he had been recording shows 'so I could see how we were going and, if anyone was making mistakes, I'd go and visit them in their rooms in my Gestapo outfit and sort them out. There were certain things I thought would be fun for people to hear – I thought I'd pick out the best bits, put them onto one cassette and give the rest away – which I have done. It's interesting if you like the Cure, but, if you don't, you'll be bored by it. Very bored.'

(ALBUM) *Standing On A Beach*
 7819 Killing An Arab
 7918 Boys Don't Cry (original version)
 7925 Jumping Someone Else's Train
 8005 A Forest
 8101 Primary
 8113 Charlotte Sometimes
 8203 The Hanging Garden
 8213 Let's Go To Bed
 8301 The Walk
 8305 The Lovecats
 8401 The Caterpillar
 8501 In Between Days
 8509a Close To Me

Staring At The Sea: **CD bonus tracks**
 7820 10.15 Saturday Night
 8008 Play For Today
 8104 Other Voices
 8510 A Night Like This

ORIGINAL RELEASE: Fiction FIX 11, August 1986

COMMENTS: The Cure's tenth anniversary was rapidly approaching; but, even more crucially, their U.S. record label, Elektra, was agitating for some kind of bite-sized digest of the band's convoluted past, a "greatest hits" collection from a band, Smith joked, who had barely scored enough hits to fill an EP. Nevertheless, he bowed to their demands, pulling together a no-holds barred survey of the story-so-far, exclusively from the point of view of the band's singles output, 13 tracks stretching from 'Killing An Arab' to 'Close To Me'.

Such choices were a portrait of the band in every state of its being, from the speeding grime of 'Primary' to the simple-minded glee of 'Lovecats', from the knowing naïvety of 'Killing An Arab' to the in-built claustrophobia of 'Close To Me'. The CD's inclusion of four non-45 bonus tracks, again arranged chronologically within the running order, only heightens the experience, by the way – a rare occasion when 'more' really does offer the listener more.

Smith explained: 'The whole point of *Standing On A Beach* was saying to people, "you wouldn't buy a Cure album, but this is what we've done and you might like it," and it worked for a lot of people. It was the first Cure album they bought, and they thought "I quite like this", and a lot of people who bought that, bought Cure albums after that and found they liked them as well.

"That album was aimed at people who wouldn't normally buy a Cure album. It was like an old garage, you look around, "ah, I recognize that, ah 'Lovecats', I liked that, I'll get it to play in the car." They're not really buying a Cure album, they're buying songs they know. You're not really gonna expect that person to then buy *Faith*, and sit back and say, "ah, my life's changed."

At the time, too, Smith was extraordinarily proud of the collection. 'The most amazing thing for me… is, there is nothing in what we've done that I would do differently. I would do it differently if I did it all now, but there's nothing I would change from when it was done at the time.'

(VHS) *Staring At The Sea*
    7701 untitled
    7819 Killing An Arab
    7820 10.15 Saturday Night
    7918a Boys Don't Cry (new version)
    7920 It's Not You
    7925 Jumping Someone Else's Train
    8005 A Forest
    8008 Play For Today
    8101 Primary
    8104 Other Voices
    8113 Charlotte Sometimes
    8203 The Hanging Garden
    8213 Let's Go To Bed
    8301 The Walk
    8305a The Lovecats
    8401 The Caterpillar
    8501 In Between Days
    8509a Close To Me
    8510 A Night Like This
ORIGINAL RELEASE: Fiction, April 1986
COMMENTS: The *Staring At The Sea* video collection takes the same journey as the *Standing On A Beach* vinyl package, but to even greater effect. Although a handful of cuts had seen release just a year earlier, on the Japanese *Tea Party*

VHS release, this was their first appearance elsewhere, and Smith rejoiced, 'the first videos we did were hilarious. We thought we were apart from image building, so we stood in front of the camera, looking like very bored people, which we were. Now we're well known for videos, thanks to Tim Pope. He translates our ideas well.'

The earliest songs included ('Boys Don't Cry', 'Killing An Arab' and 'Jumping Someone Else's Train') were accompanied with specially shot new videos. The remainder, including the seldom-seen promos for 'Charlotte Sometimes' and 'The Hanging Garden', prompted *Smash Hits* to muse, 'in the space of one hour, Robert Smith changes from a fresh-faced, clean-cut youth, into the shambling figure of today.'

(ALBUM) *Unavailable B-Sides*
   7926 I'm Cold
   8006 Another Journey By Train
   8102 Descent
   8114 Splintered In Her Head
   8307 Mr Pink Eyes
   8402 Happy The Man
   8403 Throw Your Foot
   8502 The Exploding Boy
   8503 A Few Hours After This
   8513 A Man Inside My Mouth
   8514 Stop Dead
   8404 New Day
ORIGINAL RELEASE: Fiction FIXHC 11, August 1985
COMMENTS: Following on from *Faith* and *Concert*'s bonus inclusion of extra music on the cassette version, the tape of *Standing On A Beach* was issued with a round-up of the 12 Cure b-sides that had not hitherto appeared on some other collection – *Boys Don't Cry* and *Japanese Whispers* rounded up the remainder.

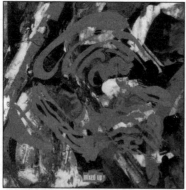

(ALBUM) *Mixed Up*
   8901b Lullaby (extended remix)

8904b Fascination Street (extended remix)

8908b Lovesong (extended remix)

8906b Pictures Of You (extended dub mix)

8712b Hot Hot Hot!!! (extended remix – 1988 original remix by Francois Kervorkian)

9005a Never Enough (big mix)

8509d Close To Me (Closer mix by Paul Oakenfold, June 1990)

9007 The Walk (Everything mix – rerecorded June 1990)

9008 A Forest (Tree mix – rerecorded June 1990)

8501a In Between Days (Shiver mix – by William Orbit, June 1990)

8401a The Caterpillar (Flicker mix – by Brian 'Chuck' New, May 1990)

ORIGINAL RELEASE: Fiction FIX 18, November 1990

COMMENTS: 1990's *Mixed Up* album was an ironic offering, in that Roger O'Donnell had been very keen on the band involving itself in dance music, but had already departed the group (to be replaced by Perry Bamonte) before they got round to trying it.

The original plan for *Mixed Up* was to compile together all of the band's original 12-inch remixes, only for Smith to realise, when he sat down to listen to them, that 'they were awful, really dull. So it seemed pointless to just bring it out as a kind of archive thing, and I thought we should use the opportunity to do something no-one's done before.' In other words, remix a significant slice of the band's back catalogue specifically for a release that still hangs oddly in the no-man's-land between a new album, and a grotesque hall-of-mirrors.

In fact, he did dip back into the past on occasion, as all four extended remixes from *Disintegration* were included in their original form, alongside Francois Kervorkian and Ron St Germain's 1988 remix of 'Hot Hot Hot!!!'

Against that, however, can be balanced the need to rerecord two tracks, 'A Forest' and 'The Walk', after the original master-tapes disappeared – the sessions, in June 1990, took place alongside the bulk of the remixing. But still *Mixed Up* was neither an easy, nor a particularly successful project, as too many songs seemed to have been molested for the sake of it, rather than because there was actually anything new to do with them.

Certainly nothing exceeded the joys that the last couple of singles... the 'Big Mix' of 'Never Enough', and the 'Close To You' b-sides... had already offered up, and the versions of 'The Walk' and 'The Caterpillar' remain, in fact, among the most execrable things ever to be found masquerading as Cure album tracks. (Worse remixes, of course, would soon be appearing.)

Smith himself had very little to do with the album, beyond selecting the tracks and the remixers and he was quick to confess that not every revision worked.

Still, he has proved a faithful defendant of the set. 'Everyone should listen to it at least once. The only reason we've ever released anything is because it's musically very good. A small nucleus of fans feels that certain old songs shouldn't be tampered with, but we're not that precious about it.

'We got savaged for it, but I still think it's a great album. When you get someone in that's good, and is sympathetic, like Paul Oakenfold, it really works. When remixes are done well, I think they're fantastic. But when they're done badly, they're the worst possible insult.'

(ALBUM) *Galore*
   8701 Why Can't I Be You?
   8704 Catch
   8710 Just Like Heaven
   8712 Hot Hot Hot!!!
   8901a Lullaby
   8904a Fascination Street
   8908a Lovesong
   8906a Pictures Of You
   9005 Never Enough
   8509c Close To Me (Closest Mix)
   9201 High
   9209 Friday I'm In Love
   9211 A Letter To Elise
   9607 The 13th
   9606 Mint Car
   9611 Strange Attraction
   9613 Gone!
   9701 Wrong Number

ORIGINAL RELEASE: Fiction FIX 30, October 1997 (CD), Fiction (VHS)

COMMENTS: 1997 marked the Cure's twentieth anniversary and, although Smith was already adamant that he was going to treat it no differently to any other year, still there was a sense of occasion welling up around the fan base, regardless of how long they'd actually been fans. And they were rewarded with *Galore*, a collection that even Smith – never a man to overstate the obvious, if understatement sounds just as good – admitted was 'kind of weird. The record company wanted a greatest hits album, a career compilation, but it's really just the last ten years of singles, the companion piece to *Standing On A Beach*, which was the first ten years.'

Ten years. Seventeen hits, and an eighteenth that would soon be joining them: 'Wrong Number', recorded with Bowie guitarist Reeves Gabrels, rounded off the album in mighty fine fettle, a fitting companion to those we have already loved: 'Hot Hot Hot!!!', 'Never Enough', 'Friday I'm In Love', 'The 13th'....

But, while the accompanying VHS offered a cornucopia of visual treats for all, this was not an album for Cure fans. Or it was, but it wasn't an album for Cure fans alone. Just as *Standing On A Beach* served as a shop window for wares which most normal folk had passed by so *Galore* cobbled ten years more for everyone who'd lived this long without *Disintegration*, but thought 'Love Song' was a groovy little toe-tapper, and vaguely remembered 'Mint Car' as well.

On the surface, it was conventional as hell. Drawn from five of the Cure's last eight albums (three live sets spawned no singles), *Galore* ignored the fan-club-only EPs, and had no time for bonus b-sides. But still it followed an uncompromising path, from the freak-ridden 'Why Can't I Be You?' to the loop-droning 'Wrong Number', via some of the most unpromising singles in anyone's catalogue: 'Catch', 'Gone!', 'Fascination Street'... and how many other top pop bands have had a hit with a song about being eaten alive by spiders?

Single by single, if not song-by-song, *Galore* outdid its predecessor in terms of audacity, and courageousness too. The Cure that issued 'Primary' never dreamed of a hit. The one that unleashed 'The 13th' was one of the biggest bands in the world. And the one that conceived *Galore* was one of the greatest there has ever been.

Smith continued, 'it's terrifying, listening back to it, it's ten years condensed into 75 minutes; it seems weird. But I think it's better than *Staring At The Sea*; there were some songs on there that weren't good singles, things like "Primary" and "Hanging Garden." They were poor singles, and they weren't written as singles. But they were the least obscure tracks on their respective albums. Whereas I think every song on *Galore*, apart from "Letter To Elise," was a really strong single.

'Going through it, things like "Just Like Heaven," they mean a lot to me, on an emotional level, so it does make a more worthwhile collection that the last one. I don't think it'll do as well as that; I think it should do better, but because of where we are now, compared to where we were then, I think *Staring At The Sea* will still be the biggest selling Cure album. And I know some people are going to think *Sea* is better, but I think that's purely because of what it means to them, and what it represents, a golden age or something. But taken purely on face value, what you'd actually like to listen to, I'd much rather listen to *Galore* than *Sea*'... so much so that, when both Elektra and Polydor made their suggestion that the Cure turn in a straightforward greatest hits album, drawing in tracks from the earlier compilation as well, Smith was forced to fight back.

'I resisted that... then I had to fight them on the release date, because they thought if it wasn't a straight greatest hits, it couldn't come out before Christmas because it wouldn't be able to compete, blah blah blah. So once again I resisted, and said it had to come out now because I wanted to get on with the new album, not have *Galore* hanging over me for the next six months.'

All of which left time for just one final question.

Why does the Cure's greatest hits collection have the same title as Kirsty MacColl's?

'For the same reason George Michael released an album called *Faith*.'

(ALBUM) *Greatest Hits*
   7918 Boys Don't Cry
   8005 A Forest
   8213 Let's Go To Bed
   8301 The Walk
   8305 The Lovecats
   8501 In Between Days
   8509 Close To Me
   8701 Why Can't I Be You?
   8710 Just Like Heaven
   8901a Lullaby
   8908a Lovesong
   9005 Never Enough
   9201 High
   9209 Friday, I'm In Love
   9606 Mint Car
   9701a Wrong Number (Single Mix)
   0101 Cut Here
   0121 Just Say Yes
ORIGINAL RELEASE: Polydor 5894342, November 2001
COMMENTS: With the Cure's demise (and Robert Smith's perennial unreleased solo album) still shrouded in uncertainty, *Greatest Hits* arrived to remind us of all that went before – and what they're doing now. 16 past classics, from 'Boys Don't Cry' to 'Wrong Number' hit the expected highpoints; while the crunchy 'Cut Here' and the exuberant 'Just Say Yes' spun off from sessions earlier in the year and sounded, of course, exactly like you'd hope they would.

There were, of course, sound business reasons for the release of an album that Smith had resisted for so long; reasons, as he explained to *Record Collector*, that were born when Chris Parry sold Fiction Records to Universal, without forewarning Smith. 'It feels strange to feel… duped, really. For about a day, it destroyed me – knowing someone that long and being sold out in that way. It wasn't as though he didn't make any money out of us when we were partners.'

The sale launched Smith on what would become an 18-month mission to regain the control over his own material that he'd hitherto taken for granted, a quest that would see him forced to make concessions that he personally despised – including the appearance, in 2004, of 'In Between Days' in a TV commercial. 'It's left me with a very sour taste in my mouth. I've fought so long to retain control over what we do, because I hate music being used to sell products. I feel that what we do should mean more than that, and it does, to a lot of people.'

The *Greatest Hits* CD was accompanied by a similarly titled DVD package (Fiction 40229-2), featuring the same main set, plus a bonus half-dozen cuts from the *Acoustic Hits* set. In addition, the DVD also featured three additional hidden videos accessible as follows: 'The Caterpillar': Go to the Song Select menu; Move the star icon to '*The Walk*'; Press down, right, right. 'Close To Me (remix)': Go to the Song Select menu; Move the star icon to 'Close To Me'; Press up, up, up. 'Pictures of You' – Go to the Song Select' menu; Move the star icon to 'Friday I'm In Love'; Press down, down, down.

(ALBUM) *Join The Dots: B-Sides & Rarities, The Fiction Years*
 7820 10.15 Saturday Night
 7919 Plastic Passion
 7813 Pillbox Tales
 7814 Do the Hansa
 7926 I'm Cold
 8006 Another Journey by Train
 8102 Descent
 8114 Splintered in Her Head
 8212 Lament (Flexipop Version)
 8214 Just One Kiss
 8302 The Dream
 8303 The Upstairs Room
 8304 Lament
 8306 Speak My Language
 8307 Mr Pink Eyes
 8402 Happy the Man
 8403 Throw Your Foot
 8404 New Day
 8502 The Exploding Boy
 8503 A Few Hours After This...
 8513 A Man Inside My Mouth
 8514 Stop Dead
 8702 A Japanese Dream
 8721 Breathe
 8722 A Chain of Flowers
 8723 Snow in Summer
 8724 Sugar Girl
 8715 Icing Sugar
 8709a Hey You!!!!!! (Kevorkian 12" Remix)
 8707a How Beautiful You Are (Bob Clearmountain 7" Remix)
 8720 To the Sky
 8902 Babble

8903 Out of Mind
8923 2 Late
8924 Fear of Ghosts
9004 Hello I Love You (Psychedelic Version)
9002 Hello I Love You
9003 Hello I Love You (A Short Return)
9006 Harold and Joe
8710a Just Like Heaven ('Chuck' Remix)
9202 This Twilight Garden
9203 Play
9219 Halo
9220 Scared as You
9256 The Big Hand
9257 A Foolish Arrangement
9208a Doing the Unstuck (Saunders 12" Remix)
9303 Purple Haze (Virgin Radio Version)
9303a Purple Haze
9401 Burn
9502 Young Americans
9501 Dredd Song
9608 It Used to Be Me
9609 Ocean
9610 Adonais
9619 Home
9620 Waiting
9621 A Pink Dream
9602b This Is a Lie (Ambient Remix)
9701e Wrong Number (P2P Remix)
9801 More Than This
9802 World in My Eyes
0011 Possession
0001b Out of This World (Oakenfold Remix)
0004d Maybe Someday (acoustic Remix)
0010 Coming Up
0103 Signal to Noise (Acoustic Version)
0102 Signal to Noise
0122a Just Say Yes (Curve Remix)
0303 A Forest (Plati/Slick Version)

ORIGINAL RELEASE: Rhino R2 78043, March 2004

COMMENTS: Planning for a career-consuming Cure b-sides collection began in 1996, with Smith musing, 'it'll probably just be fan based, stuff that's been missing. We did a tape in 1986, the cassette of *Standing On A Beach* had a b-side of b-sides, but that was it, just the tape.

'It's nice... no, it's not nice in some ways, because people will pay a lot of money to get it, but a lot of stuff in the past was released with the idea of it being just a one-off, just of the moment, disposable. If you make everything available for posterity, it's bit precious, really. There are some things that are best left obscure. But since the mid-1980s, it's been impossible for us to do something and believe that it was going to remain obscure. But before that, there were a lot of things, odd b-sides... no-one bought the a-sides, no-one bought the albums, we weren't trying to be obscure, it's like we were lucky to sell 50,000 world-wide of the album!'

O'Donnell continued, 'the thing now is, if you don't do something about the rare stuff, someone else will, and they won't do it as well as we would. Do it very cheap. A bootleg of Cure b-sides would cost 25 quid.'

'So we could put it out for 30,' Smith sniggered. 'But it smacks of 20th Anniversary Retrospective. Seeing other groups that have done it, iconic 80s groups who get towards the end of their career, so they package everything up together and make it very saleable. Maybe we should wait until we've stopped. Do a three-CD box, put it in a box and bury it.'

In fact, by the time the collection finally came to fruition, it had been transformed into a four-CD box, and the band had not yet stopped. Intended as a curtain-raiser to the impending, wholesale reissue of the Cure's back catalogue (with bonus tracks a-go-go), *Join The Dots* did indeed concentrate – 50 of its 70 tracks – on the b-sides, with Smith continuing, 'we are the sort of group that people do look to the b-sides. We have a tradition. I remember what I really liked about Siouxsie and the Banshees: they were one of the first groups where I'd buy all their singles because the b-sides were usually better than the a-sides. 'Love In A Void', that was great. In those days, I'd buy a single and I used to play the b-side first, because if that was good, you'd bought a good single. But it's a lost art now, because people just bung out... they use mixes, inane mixes, as an excuse for not doing anything different.'

That said, *Join The Dots* did boast its fair share of inane mixes, although it mercifully omitted the vast majority of the horrors perpetrated on fans during the 1990s; in their stead, sundry soundtrack and compilation appearances were joined by a smattering of (latter day) unreleased pieces, and a voluminous booklet via which Smith reiterated his own thoughts and opinions on the songs.

'I've proof read the artwork four times,' he told *Record Collector*. 'People ask does it really matter, but we've waited so long, it should be done right. Despite all that, there's still fucking mutterings on the internet about what I've left off... What people haven't understood is that the extras discs with the re-releases of the studio albums are going to contain the more esoteric stuff.

'I did the booklet with Simon [Gallup, Cure bassist since '79], so it will be the definitive version of events and some myths will be exploded. Simon's contributions were mostly unprintable, libellous anecdotes, but I thought at least if I did it in tandem with him, it would give me less incentive to elaborate. But then he started looking at me funny anyway – I think that was the beer...'

APPENDIX TWO
NON CURE AND RELATED RECORDINGS

(SINGLE) SIMON GALLUP/LOCKJAW: *Radio Call Sign*
   Radio Call Sign
   The Young Ones
ORIGINAL RELEASE: Raw 8, 1977
COMMENTS: Simon Gallup was the first member of any 'classic' Cure line-up to get on vinyl, after Lockjaw 'sent a tape to record company called Raw Records and they thought we were this really good suburban punk band but we were actually shit. They signed us and put out this record. If I see around today, I BREAK THEM.'

(SINGLE) THE OBTAINERS/ SIMON GALLUP – THE MAGSPIES
   Yeh Yeh Yeh
   Pussy Wussy
   Lifeblood
   Bombs
ORIGINAL RELEASE: Dance Fools Dance GLITCH 1, November 1979
COMMENTS: The Dance Fools Dance label was launched by Smith and Simon Gallup's brother Ric in late 1979, but issued just two singles during its three year lifetime – the second, by Animation, was released in 1982.

   The Obtainers were a pair of kids… 11 year old Robin Banks and 12 year old Nick Loot… whom Smith discovered; they played Tupperware and kitchen implements, and cut their two songs, 'Yeh Yeh Yeh' and 'Pussy Wussy', at Morgan Studios at the same session that produced the Cult Heroes 45. Smith produced. The two songs on the b-side, meanwhile, featured the Magspies, Simon Gallup and Matthieu Hartley's pre-Cure combo.

(ALBUM) ROBERT SMITH – THE ASSOCIATES: *The Affectionate Punch*
   The Affectionate Punch
   Amused As Always
   Logan Time
   Paper House
   Transport To Central
   A Matter Of Gender
   Even Dogs In The Wild
   Would I… Bounce Back?

Deeply Concerned

'A'

ORIGINAL RELEASE: Fiction, August 1980

COMMENTS: You wouldn't want to hazard a guess which songs he appears on, but Smith is noted among the backing vocalists on this album.

(TV) ROBERT SMITH – SIOUXSIE & THE BANSHEES: *Oxford Road Show* (UK) 3 December 1982

Melt!

Overground

ORIGINAL RELEASE: unreleased

COMMENTS: Robert Smith's TV debut with the Banshees served up one golden oldie ('Overground' from *The Scream*), alongside their most recent 45.

(ALBUM) ROBERT SMITH – THE GLOVE: *Blue Sunshine*

Like An Animal

Looking Glass Girl

Sex-Eye-Make-Up

Mr Alphabet Says

A Blues In Drag

Punish Me With Kisses

This Green City

Orgy

Perfect Murder

Relax

1990 CD bonus tracks

Mouth To Mouth

The Tightrope

Like An Animal (Club Mix)

ORIGINAL RELEASE: Wonderland SHELP 2, August 1983

(SINGLE) ROBERT SMITH – THE GLOVE: Like An Animal

Like An Animal

Mouth To Mouth

Like An Animal (Club Mix)

ORIGINAL RELEASE: Wonderland SHE 3, August 1983

COMMENTS: Superstar side projects have always rattled around the music scene, one-off outings conceived for any reason you like – to scratch a creative itch, to fulfil a personal vanity, or simply just to confuse and confound an audience that has been growing far too complacent.

You run out of toes trying to count the entrants into each of those categories – from the intriguing sidelines that ricocheted out of Roxy Music during the mid-1970s, through the syrupy superstar creations of the 80s, and onto such murky tangles as David Bowie's Tin Machine, great swathes of Mick Jagger's solo career and anything by the Travelin' Wilburys, there is a weighty encyclopedia... or, at least, an interminable term paper... to be compiled around the peculiar notion that, just because a couple of pop stars are friends, they should also, fleetingly, become bandmates.

Occasionally, of course, it works. The art-rock underground still thrills to the memory of the nights that Nick Cave, Marc Almond, Lydia Lunch and Jim Foetus came together as the Immaculate Consumptives, back in 1983; and the Gothic crowd still tremble at the memory of the Glove, the similarly shortlived, but superbly styled union of the Cure's Robert Smith and Siouxsie and the Banshees' Steve Severin.

Conceived by the duo back in 1981, the Glove was named after a character in the Beatles' *Yellow Submarine* movie, and that should tell the uninitiated a lot of what they might need to understand the group's *modus operandi*. Built around Smith and Severin's shared obsession with late 1960s psychedelia, in all its musical, cinematic and cultural guises, the Glove was to explode all the pasty-faced frauds who were then trying to initiate a "psychedelic revival" in the UK, by demonstrating once and for all that it was not all about whimsical ditties, Beardsley prints and smoked banana skins. There was a dark and sinister undercurrent to the era as well, and that was where the Glove looked for inspiration.

With the "group" completed by vocalist/dancer Jeanette Landray (at that time, Banshee's drummer Budgie's girlfriend), the duo's original idea was to cut a one-off single only. Their writing sessions, however, knew no such boundaries. Days turned to weeks, which transformed, in turn, to months. Smith later boasted, 'when we went into the studio, we ended up with 15 songs after three days. And we put them on a record. An odd record.'

In fact, the entire project consumed close to three months, but Smith was right about one thing. It was an odd record. More scattershot than either Smith or Severin could get away with via their day-jobs, the ensuing *Blue Sunshine* has variously been described as a psilocybic mess, or a fitting successor to the acid-drenched B-movie soundtracks that were their sole external stimuli as the record came together.

'We must have watched about 600 videos,' Smith marveled, 'and there'd be... all these after-images of the films we'd watched, cropping up in the songs.' *Inferno & Tenebrae*, *Driller Killer* and *Ms45 – Angel Of Vengeance* have all been acknowledged as influences on the proceedings; '[they] permeated our dreams,' Severin shuddered, 'and we brought them to bear on the record.'

The sessions were chaotic. According to Budgie, he and Siouxsie 'looked in on a couple of sessions, and couldn't believe what was going on... a situation obviously fuelled by parties and various substances.' Severin, however, later joked that the album's protracted birth was a deliberate manoeuvre on Smith's part. 'He'd got himself a dodgy perm. It was a complete disaster, so he needed those three months in hiding, so that he could grow his hair back.'

'We didn't want it to sound like a self-indulgent album made by two aging hippies,' Smith assured *International Musician*, but still *Blue Sunshine* is difficult to take in heavy doses, with Landray, perhaps surprisingly, best emerging from the proceedings with dignity intact.

According to Smith, 'she'd never really sung before... some of it she sings really well, but in other bits... she didn't have enough time to work on the songs.' More likely, she was simply reacting to Smith and Severin's own chaotic approach to the recordings; two years later, helming her own band, Kiss That, Landray revealed herself a fine (if infuriatingly unsung) vocalist. That said, *Sounds'* album review had nothing nice to say about her... or about the Glove in general.

'The Glove project reminds me of Yes solo splinters of days gone past, particularly those of Steve Howe and Chris Squire. At least *they* had the good sense not to include lyrics on their awful solo outpourings – they just rambled on. The Glove ramble on, but they also have an anonymous girl vocalist, one Landray, screaming away on top. What she screams are presumably young Smith's words, and they are pretty dreadful. Smith has either lost his mind, is having a privileged joke at his fans' expense, or drug abuse of the headier kind really has come into mode again.'

In fact, by the time the Glove album was actually released, that late summer of 1983, anybody attempting to seriously unearth the cryptic meanings behind the album's battery of gibberish was already at a grotesque disadvantage, as both the Banshees and the Cure stirred back into life – both were enjoying their biggest hit singles yet (the Banshees' cover of the Beatles' "Dear Prudence," the Cure's knockabout "The Lovecats"), both were preparing to record new albums (*Hyaena* and *The Top*); both were appearing on British television on an almost weekly basis. The Glove was simply buried beneath the weight of its peers.

Finally, though it is co-credited only to Severin, Marc Almond's 'Torment', from his 1983 album *Torment & Toreros* was originally conceived during the Glove period, after Severin and Smith together offered to write a song for the project.

(SINGLE) ROBERT SMITH – SIOUXSIE & THE BANSHEES: Dear Prudence
    Dear Prudence
    Tattoo
    There's A Planet In My Kitchen
ORIGINAL RELEASE: Wonderland SHE 4, September 1983
COMMENTS: Smith's studio debut with the Banshees saw the band cutting their next single. Having already decided to draw a song from their beloved Beatles' *White Album*, the band was split between 'Glass Onion' and 'Dear Prudence' – the latter won out, according to Budgie, because 'it was the only song that Robert was familiar with. He wasn't a *White Album* aficionado like the rest of us.'

Recorded in Stockholm in July 1983, and completed in Islington (where Smith's sister Janet joined in on the harpsichord break), 'Dear Prudence' became the band's biggest hit yet, rising to #3.

(LIVE) ROBERT SMITH – SIOUXSIE & THE BANSHEES: Royal Albert Hall, London, 30 September/1 October 1983
    intro
    Israel
    Dear Prudence

Paradise Place
Melt!
Cascade
Pulled To Bits
Night Shift
Sin In My Heart
Slowdive
Painted Bird
Happy House
Switch
Spellbound
Helter Skelter
Eve White Eve Black
Voodoo Dolly

ORIGINAL RELEASE: *Nocturne*, Wonderland SHAH 1, November 1983
COMMENTS: The Banshees' first live album was a double offering, recorded over two nights at the Albert Hall (an accompanying live video was also released). An enjoyably representative performance, riddled with the band's customary penchant for hauling out a few obscure b-sides just to keep the casual fans guessing, *Nocturne*'s greatest flaw is that it was not recorded earlier in the band's career.

Scratchy and unformed though it often was, the 1977-79 line-up of the group remains one of the most powerful concert memories any punk-era observer can retain; while the subsequent John McGeogh era unquestionably marked the all-time peak of the band. Smith's contributions to the show, though adequate, rarely stepped out into the realms of true *involvement* that his predecessors were prone to, reducing many of the tracks here to simple live facsimiles of their studios selves – a failing from which no other incarnation of the Banshees ever suffered.

(TV) ROBERT SMITH – THE GLOVE: *Riverside* (UK) 24 October 1983
Punish Me With Kisses
Orgy
ORIGINAL RELEASE: unreleased

(SINGLE) ROBERT SMITH – THE GLOVE: Punish Me With Kisses
Punish Me With Kisses
The Tightrope
ORIGINAL RELEASE: Wonderland SHE 5, October 1983
COMMENTS: Augmented by Paul Thompson and Andy Anderson, the Glove made an unexpected return to action, to promote their forthcoming second single, although Smith admitted that plans for a second album, an all-instrumental *Music For Dreams*, had still to graduate beyond the drunkenly conspiratorial stage.

(SINGLE) LOL TOLHURST – AND ALSO THE TREES: Shantell
    Shantell
    Wallpaper Dying
ORIGINAL RELEASE: Reflex FS 9, November 1983
COMMENTS: Inkberrow, Worcs, based And Also The Trees had been around since 1979, entering the Cure's orbit when the quartet – Simon Huw Jones (vocals), Jo-Justin Jones (guitar), Steve Burrows (bass) and Nick Hakas (drums) – responded to the call for unknown bands to mail in their demos, to fill support slots on the 1982 tour. Tolhurst recalls, "they were one who sent us something and we really liked it; they came on tour and, in the process of the tour became close buddies with all of us."

The tour over, Tolhurst stayed in touch and, when the time came for the Trees to cut their debut single, he was invited to produce. The result, firmly cut from a Cure-esque cloth as it is, was an excellent curtain raiser for what would prove a lengthy (decade-plus) and generally enjoyable career.

(TV) ROBERT SMITH/SIOUXSIE & THE BANSEES: *Top Of The Pops* (UK) 25 December 1983
    Dear Prudence
    The Lovecats (the Cure)
ORIGINAL RELEASE: unreleased
COMMENTS: Back in the days when both *Top Of The Pops* and Christmas still mattered, the show's annual Xmas Day bash was an opportunity for all of the year's biggest hitmakers to gather for one long, mad, celebration of their success. But whoever would have expected Robert Smith to turn up twice, with the Cure and the Banshees?

(TV) ROBERT SMITH – THE GLOVE, SIOUXSIE & THE BANSHEES: *Play At Home* (UK) 4 March 1984
    Blues In Drag
    Circle
ORIGINAL RELEASE: unreleased
COMMENTS: A short-lived series of Channel 4 rock-mock documentaries essentially allowed the lunatics to take over the asylum, and present whatever they wanted to the watching millions. For other spotlighted guests, this was the opportunity to get on with some earnest chest beating – the Angelic Upstarts chose to cover a Jarrow Workers' march, Level 42 offered up a musicians' workshop.

The Banshees, on the other hand, dressed up as characters from *Alice In Wonderland* to relate peculiar stories. A clutch of musical interludes included performances by the Banshees ('Circle'), Siouxsie and Budgie's Creatures ('Weathercade') and the Glove ('A Blues In Drag'), together with a full half hour of live footage, shot at the Royal Albert Hall in September.

The Banshees' performance did change the tide of the series; by August, and New Order's turn to come before the cameras, oddness was the order of the day: Peter Hook rode a motor bike, Stephen Morris played photographer and Gillian Gilbert sat in the bath with Factory label head Tony Wilson.

(TV) ROBERT SMITH – SIOUXSIE & THE BANSHEES: *Top Of The Pops* (UK) 29 March 1984
Swimming Horses

(SINGLE) ROBERT SMITH – SIOUXSIE & THE BANSHEES: Swimming Horses
Swimming Horses
Let Go
The Humming Wires
ORIGINAL RELEASE: Wonderland SHE 6, March 1984
COMMENTS: Not the strongest follow-up the band might have mustered for the all-conquering 'Dear Prudence', but a pleasant enough effort that certainly deserved more than its low Top 30 chart placing.

The song was based, Siouxsie explained, 'on a programme I saw about a female version of Amnesty, called *Les Sentinelle*. They rescue women who are trapped in certain religious climates in the Middle East, religions that view any kind of pre-marital sexual aspersions as punishable by death. There was this instance of a woman whose daughter had developed a tumour, and, of course, gossip abounded that she was pregnant. The doctor who removed the tumour allowed her to take it back to the village to prove that, no, it wasn't a baby – but they wouldn't believe her. The woman knew her daughter would have to be stoned to death so she poisoned her, out of kindness, to save her from a worse fate....'

(SINGLE) LOL TOLHURST – BAROQUE BORDELLO: Today
Today
From Your Eyes
Les Algues
ORIGINAL RELEASE: Alg Records (France) 1984
COMMENTS: A Lol Tolhurst production; Baroque Bordello were a French band, but the single was recorded in London, around the same time (and with the same synthesizer set-up) as 'The Walk'.

(ALBUM) LOL TOLHURST – AND ALSO THE TREES: *And Also The Trees*
So This Is Silence
Talk Without Words
Midnight Garden
The Tease The Tear
Impulse Of Man
Shrine
Twilight Pool
Out Of The Moving Life Of Circles
ORIGINAL RELEASE: Reflex LEX 1, March 1984

(SINGLE) LOL TOLHURST – AND ALSO THE TREES: The Secret Sea
The Secret Sea
Secrecy
There Were No Bounds
The Tease The Tear
Midnight Garden
Wallpaper Dying
ORIGINAL RELEASE: Reflex RE 3, April 1984
COMMENTS: Reconvening with And Also The Trees in November 1983, following the release of 'Shantell', Tolhurst remains modest about his latest taste of outside production. 'It was interesting because, if I look back on it now, I'm not sure how much production I actually did. I turned up and brought a load of electronic bits and pieces and made various noises all over it for them. I think more than anything it was just the fact they had somebody other than themselves there, which is always useful; that's really the role I had there. We had a pretty good engineer and that always helps, in the same way as most of the early Cure records were made, we generally found ourselves a sympathetic engineer and kind of did it with them. And it was the same with the Trees.'

Still, the album and its accompanying 12-inch single both confirmed the promise of the 'Shantell' 45; indeed, for any Cure fans feeling distanced by their heroes' own smart swerve away from the pastures of Faith and Pornography, And Also The Trees made a fine substitute... an attribute that won them few friends in the music press, but assured a strong cult following.

(SINGLE) ROBERT SMITH – SIOUXSIE & THE BANSHEES: Dazzle
Dazzle
Dazzle (remix)
I Promise
Throw Them To The Lions
ORIGINAL RELEASE: Wonderland SHE 7, May 1984
COMMENTS: With *Sounds* commending the single as 'a lustrous jostling of strings swarming forward, before dying slowly to reveal Siouxsie's rich, textured voice,' 'Dazzle' started life, said Smith, sounding 'like the Glitter Band or the Sweet or something, really raw. And then they got in the orchestra.' The strings were, in fact, originally composed by Siouxsie on a toy piano. 'The sentiment behind [the song] is of lying on the gutter but still looking up at the stars. I'd seen *Marathon Man*, and I was really intrigued by the guy swallowing diamonds to keep them, and then realising it was like swallowing glass, that they would pass through his system and tear him apart. So that's the line, "swallowing diamonds, cutting throats".'

(ALBUM) ROBERT SMITH – SIOUXSIE & THE BANSHEES: *Hyaena*
Dazzle
We Hunger

Take Me Back
Belladonna
Swimming Horses
Bring Me The Head Of The Preacher Man
Running Town
Pointing Bone
Blow The House Down

ORIGINAL RELEASE: Wonderland SHEH 1, June 1984

COMMENTS: Twenty years later, Banshees drummer Budgie would tell biographer Mark Paytress, 'I was unaware that Robert was doing two shifts. We never spoke about stuff.' Throughout the recording of his first album with the Banshees, *Hyaena*, Smith was also working towards his fifth with the Cure, *The Top*… add the Glove project to the workload and it is small wonder that Smith now insists, 'I don't remember making any of them.'

Recording of the album was, in fact, delayed by Smith's Cure commitments. Severin told *Sounds*, 'we always knew he'd be taking December and maybe January off to record *The Top*, but we'd started recording stuff for the Banshees album as long ago as last June; so, at the start, it seemed such a long way off that it wasn't really important. But we had to start speeding things up towards the end and, even then, it meant we had to mix the album without Robert, which is a pity because he's really good in studios, and it's always useful to have an extra pair of ears.'

In fact, *Hyaena* itself scarcely ranks among the Banshees' most memorable albums. Siouxsie has confessed that the success of 'Dear Prudence' completely threw the band; the pressure for a follow-up was the most intense they'd ever experienced, and they went into the studio with less ideas than had accompanied them for any previous record. 'It was a relief to see the back of it.'

'We wrote everything in the studio,' Severin continued, 'and that's the first time we've ever done something like that, and it wasn't ideal. Before, we'd either gone in with most of it written, or, as with *Dreamhouse*, had two or three songs to be getting on with. But this time we had nothing, only the constant thought that we had to come up with an album of songs, and we don't wake up every morning *wanting* to write a song.'

Smith, too, was unimpressed by the finished item. 'After the Glove, and playing about with the psychedelia thing, it was time the Banshees got raw again, and I thought that was the way it would go. It shouldn't have been *Kiss In The Dreamhouse* part two.' In fact, many of the ideas that he and Severin took to the sessions were 'really rough and very powerful. But then the production smoothed it all out.'

The album did have its magical moments. Beyond the singles, 'Bring Me The Head Of The Preacher Man' and 'Point The Bone' both followed in the footsteps of the *Juju*-era band, proof that, even in a holding pattern, the Banshees were worth more than many of their contemporaries.

Plans for the group to tour in the wake of the album, however, were shattered when Smith announced that he was physically and emotionally incapable of lifting a finger – and even produced a note from his doctor to prove it. 'I had a kind of breakdown. I was physically exhausted. It was like the vengeance of God; I had all these boils and my skin started to fall off. It was like my body saying, "if you refuse to stop, I will stop you".'

The Banshees replaced him with Clock DVA's John Carruthers, but Siouxsie remained unforgiving. She told Mark Paytress, 'I never trusted Robert. I always thought he had another agenda, that he was using the situation. When he left, it felt a bit like "thanks for the ride, I'm off." All that bollocks about a sick note. That wounded sparrow act doesn't wash with me.'

(ALBUM) SIMON GALLUP – FOOL'S DANCE: *Fool's Dance*
   The Priest Hole/Happy Families
   Waiting (At The Sky Lab Landing Bay)
   I'm So Many (Talk Talk)
   Ba'Ha
   The Doh Diddy Song
   Synergy Music
ORIGINAL RELEASE: Lambs To The Slaughter LTS 18

(SINGLE) SIMON GALLUP – FOOL'S DANCE: They'll Never Know
   They'll Never Know
   The Collector
   The Empty Hours
   The Ring
ORIGINAL RELEASE: Lambs To The Slaughter LTS 22, 1984
COMMENTS: Metamorphosing out of the earlier Cry, with Gallup and former Cure roadie Gary Biddles now joined by guitarist Stuart Curran, Fool's Dance emerged a powerful, yet distinctly under-achieving outfit, best distinguished for most critics by the "ex-Cure" stickers that bedecked the LP sleeve, and the guest presence of Strangler Jean Jacques. Not that the band really stuck around long enough to notice, of course....

(ALBUM) LOL TOLHURST – THE BONAPARTES: *Welcome To The Isle Of Dogs*
   Winter
   Voodoo Revenge
   Welcome To The Isle Of Dogs
   Hymn
   Pushing Too Hard
   Girls
   6054 Stars
   Christian's Life
   Mr Webster
ORIGINAL RELEASE: Principe Logique (France) A4: 86, 1985
COMMENTS: A Lol Tolhurst production, dating back to sessions undertaken in

1982, during the Cure's post-*Pornography* lay-off. 'We recorded in Paris,' Tolhurst recalled. 'It was pretty intense, because we ended up recording them on the roof of the studio in the middle of the night.'

(SINGLE) LOL TOLHURST – PRESENCE: In Wonder
   In Wonder
   Soft
   In Wonder (2 mixes)
ORIGINAL RELEASE: Reality LOL 1, 1991

(SINGLE) LOL TOLHURST – PRESENCE: All I See
   All I See
   Distortion
   Amazed
   All I See (Butler-Walsh mix)
ORIGINAL RELEASE: Reality LOL 2, 1991
COMMENTS:

(SINGLE) LOL TOLHURST – PRESENCE: Act Of Faith
   Act Of Faith
   Earthquake
   Soft
   Tomorrow
ORIGINAL RELEASE: Reality LOL 3, January 1992

(SINGLE) LOL TOLHURST – PRESENCE: Never
   Never
   Act Of Faith
ORIGINAL RELEASE: Smash PRCD 264, March 1992

(ALBUM) LOL TOLHURST – PRESENCE: *Inside*
   Never
   Fragments

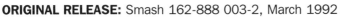

Act Of Faith
On Ocean Hill
Revolve
Highest Peak
Pause
Raindown
Missing
In Wonder
All I See
Inside

ORIGINAL RELEASE: Smash 162-888 003-2, March 1992

COMMENTS: Reuniting with one time Cure roadie/Fool's Dance vocalist Gary Biddles, Tolhurst began piecing together a new band within months of his departure from the Cure. Ex-Then Jericho keyboardist Chris Youdell, drummer Alan Burgess and Shelleyann Orphan bassist Roberto Suave completed the team, and it was pointless denying it, but the soothsayers were right.

Presence *did* sound like the Cure and, while the Cure certainly didn't have the monopoly on that, still it struck many folk as just a little cheeky when their old mates start playing the same game. Especially, as *Alternative Press*, put it, 'when the old mate in question is Lol Tolhurst, and *Inside*, his first post-Cure outing, kicks off with a scream straight out of "Why Can't I Be You?". Or was it "Subway Song"? Or does it even matter, because he and Smith co-wrote a lot of songs to begin with, and who's to say who came up with the trademarks in the first place?'

Besides (and this was the important bit), Presence sounded like the Cure if Smith *hadn't* seized control after *Kiss Me*, and hung on ever since. Or, we'd heard Robert's side of the Creative Differences battleground; now it was Tolhurst's turn.

The deliciously twee 'Act Of Faith', and the 'Pictures'-esque 'On Ocean Hill' both echoed the Cure's music. Elsewhere, however, the raw-splintered 'Never', the melancholy 'Pause' and the haunted/haunting title track kicked with a genuine passion, unheard from other quarters since *The Head On The Door* days. And, for anybody still reeling from the horrors of the Cure's own most recent release, if *Wish* was the cure, then *Inside* was the plague with the built-in immunity.

Warmly received by the critics (*AP* rated it higher than *Wish*), *Inside* suffered instead from poor promotion, a scenario that Presence themselves accelerated by only ever undertaking one tour, of the UK. Tolhurst shrugged. 'I don't really know why – just one of those strange things…'

'Presence did a second album, you know,' he reflected a decade later. 'But Island declined to release it. It was more of the same, but a little more evolved really – we did it [in LA] with John Porter, but there were other things going on with Island, so it just got shelved.' With Tolhurst's own enthusiasm for the project taking its own savage beating from this unexpected turn of events, no attempt was ever made to find an alternative home for the tapes and, today,

Tolhurst doesn't even own a copy of them.

'I enjoyed doing the first album, because we did most of it at my house, ourselves. But by the time we came to the second album, I think it had become far too democratic. We spent an inordinate amount of time recording it, going over everything, figuring out what songs we were going to do – and I was left at the end of it thinking, "I don't know, but I'm not sure that's really what I want for the second album." I spent the next few months trying to figure out what to do with it, and then Island told me they weren't going to put it out, and that was it.'

Presence broke up soon after.

(ALBUM) LOL TOLHURST – GLENN HUGHES: *The Return Of Crystal Karma*
　　The State I'm In
　　Midnight Meditated
　　It's Alright
　　Switch The Mojo
　　Gone!
　　The Other Side Of Me
　　Angela
　　Owed To J
　　This Life
　　Days Of Avalon
ORIGINAL RELEASE: SPV 085-21812 DCD, June 2000
COMMENTS: Years after the teenage Cure gathered around the stereo to listen to Deep Purple records ('we were all fans'), Tolhurst teamed up with former Purple bassist Hughes, on the metal superstar's highly praised (and remarkably forward looking) *Crystal Karma* album. 'I did some remixes for him, added some various electronica… that was a bizarre change for me, but a good change.'

(EP) LOL TOLHURST – LEVINHURST: *Levinhurst*
　　Hope
　　Sorrow
　　Despair
ORIGINAL RELEASE: Full Contact (no cat) 2004

(ALBUM) LOL TOLHURST – LEVINHURST: *Perfect Life*

Vinti
Let's Go
Sorrow
Sadman
Lost
Insomniac
Despair
Hope
Behind Me
Perfect Life
More/Mad

ORIGINAL RELEASE: Full Contact 001, April 2004

COMMENTS: Lol Tolhurst's return from a decade in obscurity… or, a regular life in LA, watching his son grow up… and a magnificent album that was both all you could hope it might be, and a lot that you never expected. 'People ask me what's *Perfect Life* is about,' Tolhurst says. 'Well, it's not a pun; it kind of looks like it might be, but it isn't. To horribly misquote Shakespeare, "nothing's good or bad except thinking makes it so".'

Tolhurst's partnership with Cindy Levinson and Dayton Borders began stirring in mid 2003, although Tolhurst himself dates his return to action to some three years earlier, following the Glenn Hughes sessions. "I had a false start back then… we called ourselves Orpheus, and I went on the road for about three weeks, a crazed vacation around California and Oregon. I went around to all these towns and said hello to people I'd not seen in 15, 20 years, maybe played a couple of songs, DJ-ed a little bit, and it was good fun. But it was an awful name… I think it had more to do with my manager of the time… so I stopped it and I didn't seriously do anything else until I met Jay Frank, our [current] manager, in 2002, and we started fermenting the idea of it all.'

It was Frank who prevailed on the band to excerpt their still in-progress recording sessions for a limited edition three track sampler for distribution to press and media, as a means of testing the waters some months before the album's release. Tolhurst agreed – much of the record was now completed. 'But I didn't have any song titles at the time, so I reached back into my Cure dictionary and pulled some from there – "Hope," "Sorrow" and "Despair." It's a little tongue in cheek, but it's also the reality of what had happened over the past ten years. And that's why I kept a lot of the lyrical things very short and concise.

'I wanted them to percolate through peoples' brains, not be too flowery, I wanted them to be very precise in what they're saying and that worked. I met someone in Chicago on the first Levinhurst tour, and they started saying to me the same thing about these songs that people used to say to us about Cure lyrics, so that's good.

'People come to see us, and I think they're quite surprised that, though some of the themes are quite dark, the overall feel of the show is very up. There were two things I wanted to do... I was very excited by a lot of the electronic music that was coming up, it was kind of like punk, I thought, people doing things for themselves; and I read a quote by John McLaughlin, saying "nowadays, I don't listen to my contemporaries, because they're all trying to recreate the 60s." He's 60 years old and he listens to Trip Hop and Acid Jazz, things that are not necessarily very musical, but which have all the exciting ideas.

'And that was what excited me about the electronic stuff. There were some things that were astounding to me and I thought, "I want to have some of that in there, because I enjoy it and it moves me." But I didn't want to do it too much, because then I'd be like the oldest teenager in town. I'm 45 years old, I can't go out and pretend to be younger. So I had that thought, but I also knew there was very little point in me disguising my past, because I'm still very proud of what we did, I still enjoy the way we put things across. So, there has to be an element of that.'

APPENDIX THREE
TRIBUTE ALBUMS

'There have been a couple of Cure tribute albums in the past 3 or 4 years. One came from Scandinavia and one came out of America, but they were both very low key, I mean not really comparable, I shouldn't dismiss them because they were done by bands who like The Cure and wanted to um, it's kinda more of a thank you I think. There were bits that I liked about it, it's sort of strange, I mean, I don't know how [other people] feel about a tribute album, it's kind of… it's almost like an end of career thing. It's like "this is your legacy." But I listened to them, and I wrote to the groups involved thanking them for their efforts. It was alright, I dunno, it's a difficult subject actually' – Robert Smith, 1998.

(SINGLE) Terry Edwards, Remembers The Cure
    Friday I'm In Love
    In Between days
    Killing An Arab
    Show Me A Sane Man And I Will Cure Him For You.
ORIGINAL RELEASE: 12-inch single Stim 006, 1994).
COMMENTS: This was the projected fourth in a series of tribute 12-inchers featuring saxophonist Edwards, Mark Bedford and others. Earlier releases celebrating the works of the Fall, the Jesus and Mary Chain and Miles Davis, released during 1991-92, were ultimately compiled onto the album *Plays, Salutes And Executes*; the Cure project, however, travelled no further than a handful of white label promos.
    The final track on the disc, incidentally, is an Edwards original.

(ALBUM) *Fictional: A Tribute To The Cure*
    Automatic – Friday I'm in love
    Sombre View – Lullaby
    Kiethevez – Lovesong
    Vision System – The walk
    Blipp ! – The Caterpillar
    Esrange – Faith
    Laura Effect – In Between Days
    Sombre View – The Same Deep Water As You
    Children Within – A Forest
    Kiethevez – A Foolish Arrangement

Close To Nature – The Hanging Garden.

ORIGINAL RELEASE: October OCT 1 (Sweden) 1995

COMMENTS: The first ever Cure tribute album is, unfortunately, something of a mixed blessing. It's nice to know that so many Swedish bands love the group, but a shame that none of them are actually especially good at conveying that love in their music. Pedestrian revamps vie with pointless reappraisals, and the entire package can be left for dead without a second thought.

(ALBUM) *Give Me The Cure*

Shudder To Think – Shake Dog Shake
The Ropers – Jumping Someone Else's Train
Chisel – Six Different Ways
Eggs – Catch
DJ Bootious Maximus – The Lovecats
Candy Machine – 10.15 Saturday Night
Glo-Worm – Friday I'm In Love
Cinnamon Toast – Piggy In The Mirror
Frodus – Killing An Arab
Peter Hayes – A Night Like This
Tuscadero – Boys Don't Cry
Edsel – Plastic Passion
Mud- The Blood
Rollercoaster – All Cats Are Grey
My Life In Rain – Pictures Of You
Dismemberment Plan – Close To Me
Jawbox – Meathook
Trampoline – Charlotte Sometimes.

ORIGINAL RELEASE: Radiopaque 792487900125 (USA) 1995

COMMENTS: A collection of Washington DC-and-area bands brought together to raise funds for AIDS research, and running the gamut of musical styles to conjure a remarkably varied, and enjoyable romp through an often surprising array of selections. DJ Bootious offers perhaps the most startling revision, although Shudder To Think and Mud (not the 1970s British hitmakers) are also in the business of dropping eye-opening revisions.

(ALBUM) *100 Tears*

Nosferatu – One Hundred Years
The Electric Hellfire Club – Killing An Arab
Laeather Strip – Lullaby
Kill Switch... Klick – Jumping Someone Else's Train
The Shroud – Sinking
Fahrenheit 451 – The Blood
Crocodile Shop – Let's Go To Bed
Ex-Voto – Shake Dog Shake
Wreckage – Pornography

Razed In Black – Disintegration
Test Infection – A Night Like This
Death Lies Bleeding – A Forest
Bell Book & Candle – Primary

ORIGINAL RELEASE: Cleopatra CLP 0001-2 (USA) 1997

COMMENTS: With Cleopatra long established as the USA's leading Gothic-electro label, and one of the most active of all labels working in the tributes field, a Cure effort was more or less inevitable. Thankfully, it was also worth waiting for, as the label hauled out most of its heaviest hitters for the occasion, to deliver some defiantly un-Cure like covers, almost all of which rank among the finest the band has yet been subjected to – Electric Hellfire Club, the Shroud and Razed In Black offer especially atmospheric moods amid their modern affectations and, while the overall mood of the album does get a little wearing after time, still *100 Tears* can hold its head high.

(ALBUM) *Here's The Real Cure*
Sleepers – Give Me It
Six Pack – Seventeen Seconds
Near Death Experience – A Forest
Foggy Bottom – In Your House
Belly Button – Killing An Arab
Seven Hate – In Between Days
Prime Time Victim Show – Fascination Street
Junior Cony – A Strange Day
Mektoub – The Hanging Garden / Siamese twins
Nothing More – Boys Don't Cry
Y Front – Charlotte Sometimes
Lt. No – One Hundred Years.

ORIGINAL RELEASE: Diabolik DIA009 (France) 1998

COMMENTS: A limited edition release, dominated by both trad and hardcore punk bands.

(ALBUM) *Porque No Puedo Ser Tu*
Don Pepe – Why Can't I Be You? (Porque No Puedo Ser Tu?)
Si-Se – Just Like Heaven (Como el Cielo)
El Manjar De Los Dioses – If Only Tonight We Could Sleep (Si Solamente Pudiesemos Dormir Esta Noche)
Man Ray – In Between Days (Entre Dias)
Volumen Cero – Lovesong (Canción de Amor)
Maria Fatal – 10.15 Saturday Night (10.15 Sabado a la Noche)
Dolores Delirio – M
Acida – Apart (Separado)
Cromafactor/Janice – The Lovecats (Gatos de Amor)
Fulano De Tal – The Blood (La Sangre)
Icaro Azul – Friday I'm In Love (Viernes Voy Por Ti)

Estados Alterados – A Forest (El Bosque)
Si-Se – Cure Megamix).
ORIGINAL RELEASE: WEA Latina 28265-2 (South America) 1999
COMMENTS: Further evidence of the Cure's massive popularity in Latin lands, a tribute sung entirely in Spanish.

(ALBUM) *15 Imaginary Songs*
   One – A Forest
   Whispers In The Shadow – Cold
   Artwork – Fascination Street
   This Vale Of Tears – Killing An Arab
   XIII – Lullaby
   Puppetland – Lovesong
   Wintermute – Pornography
   Stahlinorgel – The Walk
   The Escape – The Figurehead
   Morbid Poetry – Push
   The Caves – Just Like Heaven
   Dichroic Mirror – Jumping Someone Else's Train
   Stone 588 – The Hanging Garden
   Sofia Run – Untitled
   Decadence – Disintegration.
ORIGINAL RELEASE: Equinoxe 003 (Germany) 1999
COMMENTS: It had to happen… and it did. A tribute album that dives straight to the seething black heart of the Cure's most-hackneyed reputation, to reposition the repertoire to the place it would have laid if the band really did deserve that tag. Screaming maidens, creaking doors, flapping bats, rattling chains and Bela Lugosi's dad are all present and correct, and the entire thing is either the funniest album you'll find in this book; or a colossal waste of electricity.

(ALBUM) *Disintegrated*
   Cave In – Plainsong
   Chimaira – Fascination Street
   Compression – Prayers For Rain
   Another Nothing – The Same Deep Water As You
   Neck – Last Dance
   Converge – Disintegration
   Bad Luck Thirteen Riot Extravaganza – Pictures Of You
   Home Thirty Three – Homesick
   Together We Fall – Untitled
   Voice Of Reason – Lullaby
   When Fear And Weapons Meet – Closedown.
ORIGINAL RELEASE: Too Damn Hype Recording TDH38, United States, 2000,
COMMENTS: A pleasingly varied attempt to recreate *Disintegration* through

eyes that range from the speed-punk Voice of Reason, the hardcore Together We Fall and the electro Converge. There's also an opportunity to catch a glimpse of Chimaira, before they were 'famous'.

(ALBUM) *One Thousand Screaming Children*
    Daryl – Boys Don't Cry
    Wiseguy – Jumping Someone Else's Train
    Parker Barrow – Fire In Cairo
    Destination Venus – Seventeen Seconds
    The Standards – The Blood
    Lust Murder Box – The Baby Screams
    The Lollipop Guild – Six Different Ways
    Sunfactor – In Between Days
    The End Of Julia – Just Like Heaven
    Level – Lovesong
    Uncredited bonus track – I'm A Cult Hero.
ORIGINAL RELEASE: . Ballyhoo Withdrawall Bally005 (US) 2000
COMMENTS: Texas plays the Cure.

(ALBUM) *Pink Pig – The Whole Cure In A Mirror*
    Skip Kent – See The Children
    Pimmel – I Just Need Myself
    The Waterhouse – I Want To Be Old
    Filthy Vagrants – Faded Smiles
    Gavin Rhodes – Heroin Face
    Lumpy Froth – Killing An Arab
    Silence The Eyes – 10:15 Saturday Night
    The Isolated – Accuracy
    Mix – Grinding Halt
    LA One Way – Another Day
    Orso – Object
    Spaccshccp – Subway Song
    Home For The Def – Meathook
    Sugar Bureau – So What
    Adam Lane – Fire In Cairo
    Binge – It's Not You
    Cult Of Saints And Ferkle – Three Imaginary Boys
    Martin Esteban – The Weedy Burton
    Garden Of Dreams – Boys Don't Cry
    Fallopia – Jumping Someone Else's Train
    Whende & Stephen Martin – World War
    Orangabelle – A Reflection
    Inovercy – Play For Today
    Triple A#1 – Secrets
    Millepede – In Your House

Gauri Nanda – Three
El Chancho Flaco – The Final Sound
Ludise – A Forest
Jeff Boortz – M
Midnight – At Night
Anton – Seventeen Seconds
Clear – The Holy Hour
Jewel & Beaux – Primary
John Forester – Other Voices
Phonica – All Cats Are Grey
Kalte Sterne – The Funeral Party
Narcan – Doubt
The Baron – The Drowning Man
Pornography – Faith
Mark Palmer – Charlotte Sometimes
Christmas Island – One Hundred Years
COiN – A Short Term Effect
Arkham – The Hanging Garden
Wish 54 – Siamese Twins
Fourteen Explicit Moments – The Figurehead
Augustus M – A Strange Day
Uwe/Michael/Annett – Cold
Monkey Torture – Pornography
Pablo Dog – Let's Go To Bed
Alex Arrowsmith – The Dream
Tea Of June – Just One Kiss
This Violet Skies – The Upstairs Room
Elemental – The Walk
Absinthe Tuna – Speak My Language
Lydia – Lament
Danny Bearl & Allan Mitchell – The Lovecats
The Lust Grenades – I'm A Cult Hero
Sharp Pain – I Dig You
ThouShaltNot – Pillbox Tales
The Rand Ecliptic – Do The Hansa
Sad Parade – Plastic Passion
Helga – I'm Cold
No:id – Another Journey By Train
Requiem – Ariel
Uyea – Carnage Visors
Tiger 2 – Descent
Red Shift – Splintered In Her Head
Dead City Rodent – All Mine
The Palpatines – Forever
Dan Smith – Mr. Pink Eyes

Alven – Mr. Alphabet Says
Exit – Perfect Murder
Half-Sick Of Shadows – Relax
Vecinos De Jesus – Shake Dog Shake
Matthew Clines – Birdmad Girl
Radiostatic – Wailing Wall
The Living Daylights – Give Me It
A.K.A. Zero – Dressing Up
Instituto Del Quemado – The Caterpillar
Fish Panning Method – Piggy In The Mirror
Tantalus – The Empty World
Five Year Crush – Bananafishbones
Ultramar – The Top
Make-Believe – Happy The Man
In My Head – Throw Your Foot
Fictile Noize – In Between Days
Theorythirteen – Kyoto Song
LRI – The Blood
The Deep Green Eye – Six Different Ways
Robinson/Arnston – Push
NOC – The Baby Screams
Birdmad Girl Featuring Arantxa – Close To Me
Fluoresce – A Night Like This
Sunflower – Screw
Haokus – Sinking
For Esmé – The Exploding Boy
Lucho Giesso – A Few Hours After This
Damon Boyce – A Man Inside My Mouth
Kalliope – New Day
Squireofgougou – Stop Dead
The Glove Featuring Belladone – Eyemou
Rachounc – The Kiss
Wash – Catch
Brian Stillman – Torture
J.D. Arbelaez – If Only Tonight We Could Sleep
E. Koven – Why Can't I Be You?
Dreams Of Creamson – How Beautiful You Are...
Jaime Sin Tierra – The Snakepit
Co/Dev. Space – Hey You!!!
Entranced – Just Like Heaven
Manicure – All I Want
Paul Fiction – Hot Hot Hot!!!
Fornever – One More Time
Puppeteer – Like Cockatoos
The Boot – Icing Sugar

Supermika – The Perfect Girl
Tom LoMacchio – A Thousand Hours
Olivier Vanderkelen – Shiver And Shake
Freddy And Tormod – Fight
Dji – A Japanese Dream
Pierre And Wendy – Breathe
Venus – A Chain Of Flowers
Adrift – Snow In Summer
Marc Lavenant – Sugar Girl
Work In Progress – To The Sky.
C. Kiefer And J.S. Long – Plainsong
Jenner – Pictures Of You
Greene Project – Closedown
For The Perfect Girl – Lovesong
Timothée And Thierry – Last Dance
The Remedy – Lullaby
Dishwasher – Fascination Street
Phaedra – Prayers For Rain
Morangos Mofados – The Same Deep Water As You
Voodoo Smile – Disintegration
Jack Campbell – Homesick
Tita & The Squid – Untitled.
The Black Fez – Never Enough
Spider – Tape
Pain And Its Relief – Open
Relative – High
Explodingboy – Apart
L. Grodoski – From The Edge Of The Deep Green Sea
Hemp With The Exploding Boy – Wendy Time
Benjamin Weiner – Doing The Unstuck
The Bazoches – Friday I'm In Love
The Medics – Trust
Forever – A Letter To Elise
Greg And Mellisa Callaway – Cut
Belladone – To Wish Impossible Things
Patrick "Shatner" Reinartz – End
Sugar Addict – Uyea Sound
Las Caritas – Cloudberry
Wake Up Sleepyhead – Off To Sleep...
Charlie Fernandes – The Three Sisters
Voluptuous – Babble
Dark Wish – Out Of Mind
Vertigo – 2 Late
Her Lying Head – Fear Of Ghosts
Satélite M.V.R. – Harold And Joe

Hypee And The Faithfuls – This Twilight Garden
Pauls/Canziani – Play
Holding Mercury – Halo
Soliamos Ser – Scared As You
Stephen Martin – The Big Hand
Daniel – A Foolish Arrangement.
Lamentia – Want
Miss – Club America
Julieann Thilmany – This Is A Lie
Pedro Boyd – The 13th
Anillaco – Strange Attraction
Erik Pischel – Mint Car
Orient Ambulance – Jupiter Crash
Spleen – Round And Round And Round
Michaela Kubikova – Gone !
Insect Lounge – Numb
Fractured Atlas – Return
Corazones De Lego – Trap
Thomas Moynahan – Treasure
The Krauts – Bare.
Joshua Heinrich – Burn
Dean Reid – Dredd Song
Sleeping Children – It Used To Be Me
LizEmo – Ocean
Freddy And Tormod – Adonais
Homeboy – Home
I a Nada – Waiting
Paul & Jerome – A Pink Dream
Alter Ego – Wrong Number
G & A – More Than This
Nacho Dimari – A Sign From God.
The Ghost Of Manhattan Ruiz – Out Of This World
Bluecrescentmoon – Watching Me Fall
Brian Soto – Where The Birds Always Sing
Philippe Hoang – Maybe Someday
Fractured – Coming Up
St. Eve – The Last Day Of Summer
Grant Small – There Is No If...
Alex Can't Sleep – The Loudest Sound
Blame – 39
Nothing – Bloodflowers
La Isla Del Bicho – Spilt Milk
Entranced – Just Say Yes
J. Greevers – You're So Happy (you Could Kill Me !).
ORIGINAL RELEASE: Pink Pig MMBCD2000, Argentina, 2000

COMMENTS: The most legendary tribute of all, as no less than 204 different performers and bands come together to record versions of *every* Cure song issued up until that point... a task that ultimately consumed two years and no less than 14 CDs.

Soliciting contributions from the band's fan base was not, of course, any way to guarantee quality; indeed, such considerations went right out of the window in favour of making sure there was not a single song left behind... and, from the earliest demos, to the newly released and hastily added *Bloodflowers*, none is, as the band's regular catalogue was complemented by rarities, obscurities, bootlegs... the one radio broadcast-only 'Ariel' is here, so is 'Carnage Visors', so is 'Heroin Face'. And, if the discerning listener will find even one disc difficult to sit through, as a handful of genuinely competent performers are joined by a plethora of japesters, jack-asses and star-for-a-day hopefuls, still there is solace to be taken from the knowledge that no other band on earth has inspired the inauguration *and* completion of a similar project.

(ALBUM) *Prayers For Disintegration*
   Tres Hombres – The Holy Hour
   Michelle – Pictures Of You
   God's Bow – Plainsong
   Thule – Lullaby
   Le Fleur – Want
   La Faucheuse – Burn
   EM – To Wish Impossible Things
   Piotr Piekos – Apart
   T.H.O.R.N. – Lovesong
   PCM – Fascination Street
   Lorien – Fight
   Ania Zachar i Dave Blomberg – Charlotte Sometimes
   Usta Bilizowane – The Lovecats
   Eva – Plastic Passion
   Common Dream – Bloodflowers.
ORIGINAL RELEASE: Black Flames Records BFCD 007 (Poland) 2001
COMMENTS: The Polish alternative scene turns out....

(ALBUM) *A Night Like...*
   Escape With Romeo – In Your House
   Behind The Scene – Killing An Arab
   In Mitra Medusa Inri – Just Like Heaven
   Close Encounters – Lullaby
   Cat Fud – The Baby Screams
   Convent – M
   Sophya – The Figurehead
   Passion Plastique – The Funeral Party
   Pilori – If Only Tonight We Could Sleep

Whispers In The Shadow – Seventeen Seconds
The Crack Of Doom – A Night Like This
Yendri – The Lovecats
Another Tale – Boys Don't Cry
Sonic Boom vs. Psyche – Charlotte Sometimes
Battery – All Cats Are Grey.

ORIGINAL RELEASE: SPV CD 085-81192 (Germany) 2001

COMMENTS: Battery's gorgeous cover of 'All Cats Are Grey', first heard on their own *Aftermath* CD, might be the best track here, but it is by no means the sole highlight on an electro-industrial gathering that matches the Cleopatra *100 Tears* package in terms of intensity and fun. There are a few clinkers, of course, but the madcap version of 'The Lovecats' is irresistible, while 'Charlotte Sometimes' will either raise eyebrows or hackles.

(ALBUM)...*Imaginary songs*
Curtis Newton – A Night Like This
M – Close To Me
Lt.No – Seventeen Seconds
Polagirl – Just Like Heaven
Apple Jelly – Lullaby
Tara King TH – Cold
The Little Rabbits – Killing An Arab
Mickey 3D – Three Imaginary Boys
ELM – Apart
Dominic Sonic – Give Me It
Yell – Charlotte Sometimes
Dionysos – A Forest
(Tulip) – The Top
Migala – Plainsong.

ORIGINAL RELEASE: Mudah Peach Records 589 481-2 (France) 2002

COMMENTS: Another French effort, but generally regarded as darkly inferior to its predecessor, and that despite the reappearance of the apparently legendary Lt.No.

(ALBUM) *Whisper – The String Quartet Tribute To The Cure*
Lullaby
Pictures Of You
Boys Don't Cry
Lovesong
Hot Hot Hot!!!
The Lovecats
Bloodflowers
Maybe Someday
Just Like Heaven
Zazen

ORIGINAL RELEASE: Vitamin, 2002

COMMENTS: One more release in a series that, if not unstoppable, is at at least unrepentantly incorrigible. The formula is simple – pick a band, *any* band; then rearrange a clutch of their best-loved songs for, indeed, a string quartet. Ideal for aging post-punkers' cocktail parties, and doubtless extraordinarily worthy. But one cannot help but feel that albums like this (and there are dozens of them now) exist for precisely the same reason as sundry international orchestras are likewise persuaded to give a classical once-over to pop records. The money.

One original track (the closing 'Zazen') is put over as the Quartet's own tribute to the Cure's influence. But you probably won't listen that far.

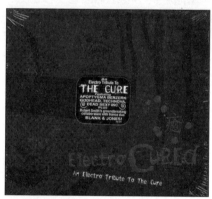

(ALBUM) *Electro-Cured: An Electro Tribute to the Cure*
  Apoptygma Berzerk – A Strange Day
  Godhead – Fascination Street
  Razed In Black – Disintegration
  Ganymede – A Forest
  Bellatronica – The Walk
  Dead Sexy Inc – Let's Go To Bed
  Inertia – Hot Hot Hot!!!
  Joy Electric – Pictures Of You
  Technova – Hanging Garden
  Laeather Strip – Lullaby
  Kill… Switch Klick – Jumping Someone Else's Train
  The Shroud – Sinking
  Blank & Jones featuring Robert Smith – A Forest

ORIGINAL RELEASE: Cleopatra CLP 13372, 2004

COMMENTS: Reprising a handful of cuts from the earlier *100 Tears* compilation (and, the Shroud aside, not necessarily the best ones), another throbbing thrust through the back pages of Curedom, reprogrammed (it says here) into 'digitally realized, vein throbbing auralgasms.' In fact, there no real surprises on board, although the 'special bonus track' inclusion of Blank & Jones' 'A Forest' does raise this set above most of the others. So long as you don't have the single, of course.

APPENDIX FOUR
NINETEEN IMAGINARY BOYS
A BRIEF DIRECTORY OF CURE MEN PAST AND PRESENT

Clifford 'Andy' Anderson (drums): ex-Brilliant, took over on drums from Tolhurst in 1984, as the latter switched to keyboards only. Sacked due to a drinking problem in October, 1984 whilst touring Japan, and later joined Jeffrey Lee Pierce.

Perry Bamonte (keyboards): Long-time Cure crew member replaced O'Donnell in 1991, while claiming he'd never played keyboards in his life. Switched to guitar when O'Donnell returned for the *Wild Mood Swings* sessions.

Jason Cooper (drums): Former member of My Life Story and Strangler Jean Jacques Burnel's solo band, Cooper answered a *Melody Maker* ad and replaced Boris Williams in the Cure in 1993.

Michael Dempsey (bass): Founder member quit in November, 1979, after the first album, to join The Associates. Replaced by Simon Gallup. He returned briefly to shoot the 'Boys Don't Cry' video in 1986.

Vince Ely (drums): The ex-Psychedelic Fur who replaced Anderson for 11 live shows in the US in October/November, 1984.

Simon Gallup (bass) Since replacing Michael Dempsey in November 1979, the former Magspies bassist has been the closest thing to an ever-present that Robert Smith has ever known. Notwithstanding a hiatus between June 1982 and early 1985 (during which time he reunited with Matthieu Hartley in the Cry/Fool's Dance), Gallup has remained on board ever since.

Steve Goulding (drums): ex-Wreckless Eric's band, Goulding joined Tolhurst and Smith to record 'Let's Go To Bed' in 1982.

Matthieu Hartley (keyboards): Joined alongside Magspies bandmate Gallup in late 1979, in time to make *Seventeen Seconds*; quit following the 1980 Australian tour. When the Cure split in 1982, Gallup briefly joined him in a new band, Cry, which, in turn became Fool's Dance... which, in turn, broke up.

Norman Fisher Jones (bass): Stood in for Thornally on a February 1984 BBC session.

Martin (keyboards) Lol Tolhurst's flatmate stood in for Williams on French TV in April 1986.

Roger O'Donnell (keyboards): An auxiliary Psychedelic Fur who joined in 1988 to supplement Lol Tolhurst's keyboards. Quit following *Disintegration*, then returned once *Wish* was out of the way. Sensible chap.

Peter O'Toole (vocals): Ariola-Hansa era vocalist, seen in the few moments of footage that opens the *Staring At The Sea* VHS, but otherwise apparently unrecorded.

Steve Severin (bass): Banshee Severin joined a lone Robert Smith to record 'Lament' in the summer of 1982. He also made a BBC TV appearance alongside Smith and Tolhurst in March, 1983. He was never a member of the Cure, but he was not never a member either. Still a Banshee, though.

Robert Smith (vocals, guitar): Without whom…

Derek Thompson (bass): SPK member drafted in for a few moments in 1983, to help promote 'The Walk' single.

Porl Thompson (guitar, keyboards): A member of the pre-Cure Easy Cure, in 1977, returned for a *Top Of The Pops* performance in July, 1983, then joined full time in spring, 1984. Departed in 1993, to join Robert Plant and Jimmy Page's reconvened union, to whom he gifted a surprisingly effective version of 'Lullaby'.

Phil Thornally (bass): The engineer on *Pornography* joined up in mid-1983; but quit in February, 1985, to be replaced by the returning Gallup.

Lawrence Tolhurst (drums, keyboards): Founder member sacked loudly, and litigiously, in March, 1989. Launched his own shortlived band Presence in 1991, splitting following completion of an unreleased second album. A lawsuit launched against the Cure, arguing over the definition of his role in the band was defeated in September, 1993, and Tolhurst remained largely out of sight until 2003, when he resurfaced with Levinhurst.

Boris Williams (drums): ex-Thompson Twins, replaced Ely in November, 1984. Quit following the *Wish* tour in 1992, to be replaced by Jason Cooper.

ACKNOWLEDGEMENTS

Thanks to everyone whose ideas, thoughts, theories, memories and, most of all, record collections helped to make this book what it is: Amy Hanson, Jo-Ann Greene, Mike Scharman, Ella and Sprocket for filling in some details; and *Singles Going Steady* (Seattle's greatest record store) for filling in some gaps.

To Robert Smith, Lol Tolhurst, Simon Gallup, Roger O'Donnell, Jason Cooper and Perry Bamonte for the interviews that form the foundation of this book, and to the library's worth of old magazines that helped confirm my suspicions.

To Sean Body and all at Helter Skelter; and to everybody else who now walks around with 'A Night Like This' stuck in their heads… Snarleyyowl the Cat Fiend, K-Mart (not the store), Dave Makin, Gaye and Tim, Karin and Bob, Rita, Eric, Sam and Jacob, Anchorite Man, the Bat family (and Crab), Blind Pew, Barb East, Gef the Talking Mongoose, the Gremlins who live in the furnace, Geoff Monmouth, Nutkin, Squirrels, a lot of Thompsons, Turkish Magic Monkey, Neville Viking and the Walrus Ball.

BIBLIOGRAPHY

Various issues of: *New Musical Express, Sounds, Melody Maker, Record Collector, Q, Mojo, Goldmine, Alternative Press, Smash Hits, Flexipop*

For obvious reasons, my principle references included my own past writings on the Cure. However, a number of additional volumes also served well....

The Cure by Jo-Ann Greene (Bobcat Books 1985)

The Cure: 10 Imaginary Years by Barbarian, Steve Sutherland, Robert Smith (Zomba Books 1988)

The Cure, A Visual Documentary by Dave Thompson & Jo-Ann Greene (Omnibus Press 1989)

The Cure on Record by Daren Butler (Omnibus Press 1995)

The Cure: Faith by Dave Bowler and Bryan Dray (Sidgwick & Jackson 1995)

The Cure: The Making of Disintegration by Dave Thompson (CGP 1996)

In The Reptile House: The Dark Reign of Gothic Rock by Dave Thompson (Helter Skelter 2003)

Numerous other volumes detail different aspects of the Cure's career. Those referred to most frequently while writing this book include: *Rock Family Trees* by Pete Frame (Omnibus Books, various editions); *The Great Rock...* and *Alternative/Indie Discography* by Martin Strong (Canongate Books, various editions); *Guinness Book Of British Hit Singles... Albums* (Guiness World Records, various editions); *Top Pop Singles... Albums* by Joel Whitburn (Record Research, various editions); *In Session Tonight* by Ken Garner (BBC Books, 1992); *The Top 20 Book* by Tony Jasper (Blandford Books, various editions).

Other Titles available from Helter Skelter

Coming Soon

Belle and Sebastian: Just A Modern Rock Story
By Paul Whitelaw

Formed in 1996, this enigmatic Glasgow band have risen to become one of Britain's most respected bands.

For years, Belle and Sebastian were shrouded in mystery – the 23-piece ensemble led by singer-songwriter Stuart Murdoch refused interviews and the band scarcely ever toured. Their early singles though built them a strong and committed cult following. Their debut mail-order only album *Tigermilk* sold out within a month of its release. The follow-up, *If You're Feeling Sinister*, with its Nick Drake-influenced melodies and dark, quirky lyrics, found favour in alternative circles as far afield as San Francisco, Japan, South America, and especially France where a 1996 poll by influential magazine *Les Inrockuptiles* placed them above Oasis. The 1998 album, *The Boy With the Arab Strap* entered the UK LP charts at 12. Their latest Trevor Horn-produced album *Dear Catastrophe Waitress* is their highest profile release to date.

This is not only the first biography ever written on the band, but the most official that might ever hit the market. The band have agreed to participate in the project and to give the author extended interviews, paraphernalia and both personal and publicity still photos. Stuart Murdoch himself has agreed to design artwork for the cover.

Paul Whitelaw is an arts writer from Glasgow who has met and interviewed Belle and Sebastian on several occasions and he was the first journalist to champion the band in print.

Paperback   ISBN 1-900924-98-6   234 X 156mm   16pp b/w photos
UK £14.99

Kicking Against The Pricks: An Armchair Guide to Nick Cave
By Amy Hanson

Nick Cave is the only artist to emerge from the post–punk era whose music and career can truly be compared with legends such as Bob Dylan or Van Morrison, with a string of acclaimed albums including *Junkyard (Birthday Party)*, *Tender Prey* and *Abattoir Blues/The Lyre of Orphcus*.

Cave left Australia to become part of a maelstrom unleashed to awestruck London audiences in the late seventies: the Birthday Party. Miraculously, Cave survived that band's excesses and formed the Bad Seeds, challenging his audience and the Godfather-of-Goth tag: as a bluesman with a gun in one hand, a Bible in the other; a vamp-ish torch singer with echoes of Vegas-era Elvis and a sensitive writer of love songs.

Kicking Against The Pricks chronicles in depth these diverse personalities and the musical landscapes that Cave has inhabited, with a penetrating commentary on all his themes and influences. Cave's memorable collaborations and forays into other media are covered too: duets with Kylie Minogue, PJ Harvey and Shane MacGowan, the acclaimed novel *And The Ass Saw The Angel*, film appearances such as Wim Wenders' *Wings of Desire*, and his stint as Meltdown 2000 curator. Ultimately, it reveals Cave as the compelling and always-relevant musical force he is.

Paperback   ISBN 1-900924-96-X   234 X 156mm   16pp b/w photos
UK £14.99   US $19.95

Save What You Can: The Day of The Triffids and the Long Night of David McComb
By Bleddyn Butcher

Finely crafted biography of cult Australian group and their ill-fated front man who was simply the greatest lyricist of his generation.

Charismatic front man McComb's finely crafted tales of misfits and troubled outsiders and lost souls, merged Dylan with Carver and a Perth sensibility to brilliant effect, while his sprawling melodies set against 'Evil' Graham Lee's slide guitar created an achingly beautiful sound best exemplified by critics' favourites, *Born Sandy Devotional* and *Calenture*. In spite of rave critical plaudits, the Triffids' sales were mediocre and in 1990 the band split and returned to Australia. McComb put out one excellent solo album in 1994 before the sense of ominous foreboding that lurked throughout his music was proved prescient when he collapsed and was rushed to hospital to undergo a full heart transplant. Months later he was back in hospital with even more agonising intestinal surgery. McComb made a partial recovery, but the medication he was taking kept him in a permanent state of drowsiness. On Saturday, January 30th, 1999, he fell asleep at the wheel of his car. Though McComb survived the crash and discharged himself from hospital, he died suddenly three days later.

Paperback	ISBN 1-900924-21-8	234 X 156mm	16pp b/w photos
UK £14.99	US $19.95		

Rush: The Definitive Biography
By Jon Collins

Acclaimed Marillion biographer Collins draws on hundreds of hours of new interviews to tell the full in-depth story of the enduring Canadian trio who are one of the most successful cult groups in the world. From early days in Canada to platinum albums, stadium shows and the world's stage, taking in tragedy, triumphs and a wealth of great music, this is the definitive study of one of rock's great enigmas.

Paperback	ISBN 1-900924-85-4	234 X 156mm	16pp b/w photos
UK £14.99	US $19.95		

David Bowie: The Shirts He Wears
By Jonathan Richards

A Bowie book with a difference, this is a study of Bowie as a cultural icon that draws together his music, artworks and fashion to paint a fascinating portrait of one of rock's most important figures.

Paperback	ISBN 1-900924-25-0	234 X 156mm	16pp b/w photos
UK £14.99	US $19.95		

John Martyn
By Chris Nickson

First ever biography of the pioneering guitarist best-known for his still-revered 70s album *Solid Air*. Draws on interviews with many friends and associates.

Paperback	ISBN 1-900924-86-2	234 X 156mm	16pp b/w photos
UK £14.99	US $19.95		

Action Time Vision: The Story of Sniffin' Glue, Alternative TV and Punk Rock
By Mark Perry

The legendary founder-editor of *Sniffin' Glue* – the definitive punk fanzine – gives his own account of the punk years. An eyewitness account of the key gigs; an insider's history of the bands and personalities; the full story of the hugely influential fanzine and the ups and downs of Perry's own recording career with Alternative TV.

Paperback	ISBN 1-900924-89-7	234 X 156mm	16pp b/w photos
UK £14.99	US $21.95		

The Who By Numbers
By Alan Parker and Steve Grantley

Detailed album-by-album, song-by-song commentary on the songs of one of rock's most important and enduring acts, by Sid Vicious biographer and Lennon expert Parker, teamed with Stiff Little Fingers' drummer, Grantley.

Paperback	ISBN 1-900924-91-9	234 X 156mm	16pp b/w photos
UK £14.99	US $19.95		

John Lydon's Metal Box: The Story of Public Image Ltd
By Phil Strongman
In between fronting rock's most iconoclastic group, the Sex Pistols, and re-emerging in the 21st century as a reality TV hero on *I'm A Celebrity*, Lydon led the post-punk pioneers Public Image Ltd who tore up the rulebook and merged disco funk and industrial punk to create coruscating soundscapes with catchy tunes – from *Death Disco* and *Flowers of Romance* to *Rise* and *This Is Not A Love Song* – and caused riots at their gigs. An essential chapter in the growth of post-punk music and one that reveals Lydon as always forward-thinking and always compelling.
Paperback   ISBN 1-900924-66-8   234 X 156mm   16pp b/w photos
UK £14.99   US $19.95

Music in Dreamland: The Story of Be Bop Deluxe and Bill Nelson By
Paul Sutton-Reeves
Draws on hours of new interviews with Bill Nelson and other members of the band, as well as admirers such as David Sylvian, Stone Roses' producer John Leckie, Steve Harley and Reeves Gabrel. Cover artwork especially designed by Bill Nelson himself.
Paperback   ISBN 1-900924-08-8   234 X 156mm   16pp b/w photos
UK £14.99   US $19.95

'77 – The Year of Punk and New Wave
By Henry Bech Poulsen
As 1967 was to the Haight-Ashbury scene, so 1977 was to punk: a year in which classic singles and albums by all the key bands made it the only musical movement that counted, and before its energy and potential was diluted and dampened by the forces of conservatism and commercialism. '77 tells the story of what every punk and new wave band achieved in that heady year – from The Pistols, Clash and Damned to The Lurkers, The Adverts and The Rezillos, and everyone in between.
Paperback   ISBN 1-900924-92-7   512pp 245 X 174mm   Illustrated throughout
UK £20.00   US $25.00

Linda Ronstadt: A Musical Life
By Peter Lewry
Ronstadt's early backing band became The Eagles and she has had success with songs by Neil Young, Jackson Browne and Hank Williams. After a US number 1 single and Grammy winning country rock albums in the 1970s, she has continued to challenge preconceptions with albums of Nelson Riddle-produced standards, a record of mariachi songs and a collaboration with Dolly Parton and Emmylou Harris. This is her first ever biography.
Paperback   ISBN 1-900924-50-1   256pp 234 X 156mm   16pp b/w photos
UK £12.99   US $25.00

Suede: An Armchair Guide
By Dave Thompson
The first biography of one of the most important British Rock Groups of the 90s who paved the way for Blur, Oasis *et al*. Mixing glam and post-punk influences, fronted by androgynous Bret Anderson, Suede thrust indie-rock into the charts with a string of classic singles, in the process catalysing the Brit-pop revolution. Suede's first album was the then fastest selling debut of all time and they remain one of THE live draws on the UK rock circuit, retaining a fiercely loyal cult following.
Paperback   ISBN 1-900924-60-9   234mm X 156mm   256pp 8pp b/w photos
UK £14.00   US $19.95

Currently Available from Helter Skelter Publishing

True Faith: An Armchair Guide to New Order
By Dave Thompson

Formed from the ashes of Joy Division after their ill fated singer Ian Curtis hung himself, few could have predicted that New Order would become one of the seminal groups of the 80s, making a series of albums that would compare well with anything Joy Division had produced, and embracing club culture a good ten years before most of their contemporaries.

From the bestselling 12 inch single 'Blue Monday' to later hits like 'Bizarre Love Triangle' [featured in the movie *Trainspotting*] and their spectacular world cup song 'World In Motion' the band have continued making innovative, critically revered records that have also enjoyed massive commercial success.

This book is the first to treat New Order's musical career as a separate achievement, rather than a postscript to Joy Division's and the first to analyse in depth what makes their music so great.

Paperback   ISBN 1-900924-94-3 8   234mm X 156mm   256pp 8pp b/w photos
UK £12.99   US $19.95

Wheels Out of Gear: Two Tone, The Specials and a World on Fire
By Dave Thompson

When the punks embraced reggae it led to a late 1970s Ska revival that began in Coventry with Jerry Dammers' Two Tone record label and his band, The Specials. Original 60s rude boy fashions – mohair suits, dark glasses and the ubiquitous pork pie hats – along with Dammer's black & white themed logo were the emblems for a hugely popular scene that also comprised hit-making groups such as Madness, The Beat and The Selecter.

Paperback   ISBN 1-900924-84-6   234 X 156mm   256pp, 16pp b/w photos
UK £12.99   US $19.95

Electric Pioneer: An Armchair Guide to Gary Numan
By Paul Goodwin

From selling 10 million records in 2 years, both with Tubeway Army and solo, to more low key and idiosyncratic releases through subsequent decades, Gary Numan has built up an impressive body of work and retained a hugely devoted cult following. *Electric Pioneer* is the first ever guide to his recorded output, documenting every single and album and featuring sections on his live shows, memorabilia and DVD releases.

Paperback   ISBN 1-900924-95-1   234 X 156mm   256pp, 16pp b/w photos
UK £14.99   US $19.95

Al Stewart: Lights, Camera, Action – A Life in Pictures
By Neville Judd

Best known for his 70s classic 'The Year of The Cat', Al Stewart continues to record and tour and retains a large and loyal international fan base. This is a unique collection of rare and unpublished photographs, documenting Al's public and private life from early days in 1950s Scotland, through to his success in Hollywood and beyond.

Luxury Paperback ISBN 1-900924-90-0   310 X 227mm   192pp
All pages photos, 16pp of colour
UK £25.00   US $35.00

Sex Pistols: Only Anarchists are Pretty
By Mick O'Shea

Drawing both on years of research and on creative conjecture, this book, written as a novel, portrays the early years of the Sex Pistols. Giving a fictionalised fly-on-the-wall account of the arguments, in-jokes, gigs, pub sessions and creative tension, it documents the day-to-day life of the ultimate punk band before the Bill Grundy incident and Malcolm Mclaren-orchestrated tabloid outrage turned their lives into a media circus.

Paperback   ISBN 1-900924-93-5   234mm X 156mm   256pp 8pp b/w photos
UK £12.99   US $19.95

Bob Dylan: Like The Night (Revisited)
By CP Lee

Fully revised and updated edition of the hugely acclaimed document of Dylan's pivotal 1966 show at the Manchester Free Trade Hall where fans called him Judas for turning his back on folk music in favour of rock 'n' roll. The album of the concert was released in the same year as the book's first outing and has since become a definitive source.

'A terrific tome that gets up close to its subject and breathes new life into it... For any fan of Dylan this is quite simply essential.' *Time Out*

'Putting it all vividly in the context of the time, he writes expertly about that one electrifying, widely-bootlegged night.' *Mojo*

'CP Lee's book flushed 'Judas' out into the open.' *The Independent*

'An atmospheric and enjoyable account.' *Uncut* (Top 10 of the year)

Paperback   ISBN 1-900924-33-1   198mm X 129mm   224pp 16pp b/w photos
UK £9.99   US $17.05

Everybody Dance
Chic and the Politics of Disco
By Daryl Easlea

Everybody Dance puts the rise and fall of Bernard Edwards and Nile Rodgers, the emblematic disco duo behind era-defining records 'Le Freak', 'Good Times' and 'Lost In Music', at the heart of a changing landscape, taking in socio-political and cultural events such as the Civil Rights struggle, the Black Panthers and the US oil crisis. There are drugs, bankruptcy, up-tight artists, fights, and Muppets but, most importantly an in-depth appraisal of a group whose legacy remains hugely underrated.

Paperback   ISBN 1-900924-56-0   234mm X 156mm   256pp 8pp b/w photos
UK £14.00   US $19.95

This Is a Modern Life
Compiled by Enamel Verguren

Lavishly illustrated guide to the mod revival that was sparked by the 1979 release of *Quadrophenia*. *This Is a Modern Life* concentrates on the 1980s, but takes in 20 years of a mod life in London and throughout the world, from 1979 to 1999, with interviews of people directly involved, loads of flyers and posters and a considerable amount of great photos.

'Good stuff ... A nice nostalgic book full of flyers, pics and colourful stories.' *Loaded*

Paperback   ISBN 1-900924-77-3   264mm X 180mm   224pp photos throughout
UK £14.99   US $19.95

Smashing Pumpkins: Tales of A Scorched Earth
By Amy Hanson

Initially contemporaries of Nirvana, Billy Corgan's Smashing Pumpkins outgrew and outlived the grunge scene with hugely acclaimed commercial triumphs like *Siamese Dream* and *Mellon Collie and The Infinite Sadness*. Though drugs and other problems led to the band's final demise, Corgan's recent return with Zwan is a reminder of how awesome the Pumpkins were in their prime. Seattle-based Hanson has followed the band for years and this is the first in-depth biography of their rise and fall.

'Extremely well-written ... A thrilling and captivating read.' *Classic Rock*

'Sex, bust-ups, heavy metal, heroin death and a quadruple-platinum dream-pop double album... The first ever 'serious' Pumpkins biography.' *NME*

'A fascinating story ... Hanson has done her research.' *Q*

Paperback   ISBN 1-900924-68-4   234mm X 156mm   256pp 8pp b/w photos
UK £12.99   US $18.95

Be Glad: An Incredible String Band Compendium
Edited by Adrian Whittaker

The ISB pioneered 'world music' on '60s albums like *The Hangman's Beautiful Daughter* – Paul McCartney's favourite album of 1967! – experimented with theatre, film and lifestyle and inspired Led Zeppelin. *Be Glad* features interviews with all the ISB key players, as well as a wealth of background information, reminiscence, critical evaluations and arcane trivia, this is a book that will delight any reader with more than a passing interest in the ISB.

Paperback   ISBN 1-900924-64-1   234mm X 156mm   288pp,   b/w   photos throughout
UK £14.99   US $22.95

ISIS: A Bob Dylan Anthology
Edited by Derek Barker

ISIS is the best-selling, longest lasting, most highly acclaimed Dylan fanzine. This ultimate Dylan anthology draws on unpublished interviews and research by the *ISIS* team together with the best articles culled from the pages of the definitive Bob magazine. From Bob's earliest days in New York City to the more recent legs of the Never Ending Tour, the *ISIS* archive has exclusive interview material – often rare or previously unpublished – with many of the key players in Dylan's career: friends, musicians and other collaborators, such as playwright Jacques Levy and folk hero Martin Carthy.

Fully revised and expanded edition features additional previously unpublished articles and further rare photos;

'Astounding … Fascinating… If you're more than mildly interested in Bob Dylan then this is an essential purchase.' *Record Collector*

'This book is worth any Dylan specialist's money.' Ian MacDonald – **** *Uncut*

Paperback   ISBN 1-900924-82-X   198mm X 129mm   352pp, 16pp b/w photos
UK £9.99   US $17.95

Waiting for the Man: The Story of Drugs and Popular Music
By Harry Shapiro

From marijuana and jazz, through acid-rock and speed-fuelled punk, to crack-driven rap and ecstasy and the dance generation, this is the definitive history of drugs and pop. It also features in-depth portraits of music's most famous drug addicts: from Charlie Parker to Sid Vicious and from Jim Morrison to Kurt Cobain.

Chosen by the BBC as one of the Top Twenty Music Books of All Time.

'Wise and witty.' *The Guardian*

Paperback   ISBN 1-900924-58-7   198mm X 129mm   320pp
UK £10.99   US $17.95

Jefferson Airplane: Got a Revolution
By Jeff Tamarkin

With smash hits 'Somebody to Love' and 'White Rabbit' and albums like *Surrealistic Pillow*, Jefferson Airplane, the most successful and influential rock band to emerge from San Francisco during the 60s, created the sound of a generation. To the public they were free-loving, good-time hippies, but to their inner circle, Airplane were a paradoxical bunch – constantly at odds with each other. Jefferson Airplane members were each brilliant, individualistic artists who became the living embodiment of the ups and downs of the sex, drugs and rock 'n' roll lifestyle.

Tamarkin has interviewed the former band members, friends, lovers, crew members and fellow musicians to come up with the definitive full-length history of the group.

"A compelling account of a remarkable band." *Record Collector*

"A superb chunk of writing that documents every twist and turn in the ever-evolving life of a great American band." *Record Collector*

Paperback   ISBN 1-900924-78-1   234mm X 156mm   408pp , 16pp b/w photos
UK £14.99   US No rights

216

Surf's Up: The Beach Boys on Record 1961-1981
By Brad Elliott

The ultimate reference work on the recording sessions of one of the most influential and collectable groups.

'factually unimpeachable ... an exhausting, exhilarating 500 pages of discographical and session information about everything anybody connected with the group ever put down or attempted to put down on vinyl.' *Goldmine*

Paperback   ISBN 1-900924-79-X   234mm X 156mm   512pp, 16pp b/w photos
UK £25.00   US No rights

Get Back: The Beatles' Let It Be Disaster
By Doug Suply and Ray Shweighardt

Reissued to coincide with the release of *Let It Be ... Naked*, this is a singularly candid look at the greatest band in history at their ultimate moment of crisis. It puts the reader in the studio as John cedes power to Yoko; Paul struggles to keep things afloat, Ringo shrugs and George quits the band. 'One of the most poignant Beatles' books ever.' *Mojo*

Paperback   ISBN 1-900924-83-8   198mm X 129mm   352pp
UK £9.99   No US rights

The Clash: Return of the Last Gang in Town
By Marcus Gray

Exhaustively researched definitive biography of the last great rock band that traces their progress from pubs and punk clubs to US stadiums and the Top Ten. This edition is further updated to cover the band's induction into the Rock 'n' Roll Hall of Fame and the tragic death of iconic front man Joe Strummer.

'A must-have for Clash fans [and] a valuable document for anyone interested in the punk era.' *Billboard*

'It's important you read this book.' *Record Collector*

Paperback   ISBN 1-900924-62-5   234mm X 156mm   512pp, 8pp b/w photos
UK £14.99   US No rights

Steve Marriott: All Too Beautiful
by Paolo Hewitt and John Hellier

Marriott was the prime mover behind 60s chart-toppers The Small Faces. Longing to be treated as a serious musician he formed Humble Pie with Peter Frampton, where his blistering rock 'n' blues guitar playing soon saw him take centre stage in the US live favourites. After years in seclusion, Marriott's plans for a comeback in 1991 were tragically cut short when he died in a house fire. He continues to be a key influence for generations of musicians from Paul Weller to Oasis and Blur.

'One of the best books I've read about the backwaters of rock music.' *Daily Mail*

'A riveting account of the singer's life, crammed with entertaining stories of rebellion and debauchery and insightful historical background... Compulsive reading.' *The Express*

'Revealing... sympathetic, long overdue.' ****Uncut*

'We won't see the like of him again and *All Too Beautiful* captures him perfectly. A right riveting read as they say.' Gary Crowley, BBC London.

'Hewitt's portrayal makes compelling reading.'**** Mojo

Hardback   ISBN 1-900924-44-7   234mm X 156mm   352pp 32pp b/w photos
UK £20   US $29.95

Love: Behind The Scenes
By Michael Stuart-Ware

LOVE were one of the legendary bands of the late 60s US West Coast scene. Their masterpiece Forever Changes still regularly appears in critics' polls of top albums, while a new-line up of the band has recently toured to mass acclaim. Michael Stuart-Ware was LOVE's drummer during their heyday and shares his inside perspective on the band's recording and performing career and tells how drugs

and egos thwarted the potential of one of the great groups of the burgeoning psychedelic era.
Paperback   ISBN 1-900924-59-5   234mm X 156mm   256pp
UK £14.00   US $19.95

A Secret Liverpool: In Search of the La's
By MW Macefield

With timeless single 'There She Goes', Lee Mavers' La's overtook The Stone Roses and paved the way for Britpop. However, since 1991, The La's have been silent, while rumours of studio-perfectionism, madness and drug addiction have abounded. The author sets out to discover the truth behind Mavers' lost decade and eventually gains a revelatory audience with Mavers himself.
Paperback   ISBN 1-900924-63-3   234mm X 156mm   192pp
UK £11.00   US $17.95

The Fall: A User's Guide
By Dave Thompson

A melodic, cacophonic and magnificent, The Fall remain the most enduring and prolific of the late-70s punk and post-punk iconoclasts. *A User's Guide* chronicles the historical and musical background to more than 70 different LPs (plus reissues) and as many singles. The band's history is also documented year-by-year, filling in the gaps between the record releases.
Paperback   ISBN 1-900924-57-9   234mm X 156mm   256pp, 8pp b/w photos
UK £12.99   US $19.95

Pink Floyd: A Saucerful of Secrets
By Nicholas Schaffner

Long overdue reissue of the authoritative and detailed account of one of the most important and popular bands in rock history. From the psychedelic explorations of the Syd Barrett-era to 70s superstardom with *Dark Side of the Moon*, and on to triumph of *The Wall*, before internecine strife tore the group apart. Schaffner's definitive history also covers the improbable return of Pink Floyd without Roger Waters, and the hugely successful *Momentary Lapse of Reason* album and tour.
Paperback   ISBN 1-900924-52-8   234mm X 156mm   256pp, 8pp b/w photos
UK £14.99   No rights

The Big Wheel
By Bruce Thomas

Thomas was bassist with Elvis Costello at the height of his success. Though names are never named, *The Big Wheel* paints a vivid and hilarious picture of life touring with Costello and co, sharing your life 24-7 with a moody egotistical singer, a crazed drummer and a host of hangers-on. Costello sacked Thomas on its initial publication.
'A top notch anecdotalist who can time a twist to make you laugh out loud.' *Q*
Paperback   ISBN 1-900924-53-6   234mm X 156mm   192pp
UK £10.99 $17.95

Hit Men: Powerbrokers and Fast Money Inside The Music Business
By Fredric Dannen £14.99

Hit Men exposes the seamy and sleazy dealings of America's glitziest record companies: payola, corruption, drugs, Mafia involvement, and excess.
'This is quite possibly the best book ever written about the business side of the music industry.' *Music Week*
'This is simply the greatest book about the business end of the music industry.' *Q******
'So heavily awash with cocaine, corruption and unethical behaviour that it makes the occasional examples of chart-rigging and play list tampering in Britain during the same period seem charmingly inept.' *The Guardian*.
Paperback   ISBN 1-900924-54-4   234mm X 156mm   512pp, 8pp b/w photos
UK £14.99   No rights

I'm With The Band: Confessions of A Groupie
By Pamela Des Barres
Frank and engaging memoir of affairs with Keith Moon, Noel Redding and Jim Morrison, travels with Led Zeppelin as Jimmy Page's girlfriend, and friendships with Robert Plant, Gram Parsons, and Frank Zappa.

'Long overdue reprint of a classic 60s memoir – one of the few music books to talk openly about sex.' *Mojo*

'One of the most likeable and sparky first hand accounts.' *Q****

'Miss Pamela, the most beautiful and famous of the groupies. Her memoir of her life with rock stars is funny, bittersweet, and tender-hearted.' Stephen Davis, author of *Hammer of the Gods*

| Paperback | ISBN 1-900924-55-2 | 234mm X 156mm | 256pp, 16pp b/w photos |
| UK £14.99 | $19.95 | | |

Psychedelic Furs: Beautiful Chaos
By Dave Thompson
Psychedelic Furs were the ultimate post-punk band – combining the chaos and vocal rasp of the Sex Pistols with a Bowie-esque glamour. The Furs hit the big time when John Hughes wrote a movie based on their early single 'Pretty in Pink'. Poised to join U2 and Simple Minds in the premier league, they withdrew behind their shades, remaining a cult act, but one with a hugely devoted following.

| Paperback | ISBN 1-900924-47-1 | 234mm X 156mm | 256pp, 16pp b/w photos |
| UK £14.99 | $19.95 | | |

Marillion: Separated Out
By Jon Collins
From the chart hit days of Fish and 'Kayleigh' to the Steve Hogarth incarnation, Marillion have continued to make groundbreaking rock music. Collins tells the full story, drawing on interviews with band members, associates, and the experiences of some of the band's most dedicated fans.

| Paperback | ISBN 1-900924-49-8 | 234mm X 156mm | 288pp, illustrated throughout |
| UK £14.99 | $19.95 | | |

Rainbow Rising
By Roy Davies
The full story of guitar legend Ritchie Blackmore's post-Purple progress with one of the great 70s rock bands. After quitting Deep Purple at the height of their success, Blackmore combined with Ronnie James Dio to make epic rock albums like *Rising* and *Long Live Rock 'n' Roll* before streamlining the sound and enjoying hit singles like 'Since You've Been Gone' and 'All Night Long'. Rainbow were less celebrated than Deep Purple, but they feature much of Blackmore's finest writing and playing, and were one of the best live acts of the era. They are much missed.

| Paperback | ISBN 1-900924-31-5 | 234mm X 156mm | 256pp, illustrated throughout |
| UK £14.99 | $19.95 | | |

Back to the Beach: A Brian Wilson and the Beach Boys Reader
REVISED EDITION
Edited by Kingsley Abbott
Revised and expanded edition of the Beach Boys compendium *Mojo* magazine deemed an "essential purchase." This collection includes all of the best articles, interviews and reviews from the Beach Boys' four decades of music, including definitive pieces by Timothy White, Nick Kent and David Leaf. New material reflects on the tragic death of Carl Wilson and documents the rejuvenated Brian's return to the boards. 'Rivetting!' **** *Q*

'An essential purchase.' *Mojo*

| Paperback | ISBN 1-900924-46-3 | 234mm X 156mm | 288pp |
| UK £14.99 | $19.95 | | |

Harmony in My Head
The Original Buzzcock Steve Diggle's Rock 'n' Roll Odyssey
By Steve Diggle and Terry Rawlings

First-hand account of the punk wars from guitarist and one half of the songwriting duo that gave the world three chord punk-pop classics like 'Ever Fallen In Love' and 'Promises'. Diggle dishes the dirt on punk contemporaries like The Sex Pistols, The Clash and The Jam, as well as sharing poignant memories of his friendship with Kurt Cobain, on whose last ever tour, The Buzzcocks were support act.

'Written with spark and verve, this rattling account of Diggle's time in the Buzzcocks will appeal to those with an interest in punk or just late-1970s Manchester.' *Music Week*

'This warts 'n' all monologue is a hoot...Diggle's account of the rise, fall and birth of the greatest Manchester band of the past 50 years is relayed with passion and candour...but it works best as a straightforward sex, drugs and rock 'n' roll memoir.' – *Uncut* ****

Paperback   ISBN 1-900924-37-4   234mm X 156mm   224pp, 8pp b/w photos
UK £14.99 $19.95

Serge Gainsbourg: A Fistful of Gitanes
By Sylvie Simmons

Rock press legend Simmons' hugely acclaimed biography of the French genius.

'I would recommend *A Fistful of Gitanes* [as summer reading] which is a highly entertaining biography of the French singer-songwriter and all-round scallywag' – JG Ballard

'A wonderful introduction to one of the most overlooked songwriters of the 20th century' (Number 3, Top music books of 2001) *The Times*

'The most intriguing music-biz biography of the year' *The Independent*

'Wonderful. Serge would have been so happy' – Jane Birkin

Paperback   ISBN 1-900924-   198mm X 129mm   288pp, 16pp b/w photos
UK £14.99 $19.95

Blues: The British Connection
By Bob Brunning

Former Fleetwood Mac member Bob Brunning's classic account of the impact of Blues in Britain, from its beginnings as the underground music of 50s teenagers like Mick Jagger, Keith Richards and Eric Clapton, to the explosion in the 60s, right through to the vibrant scene of the present day.

'An invaluable reference book and an engaging personal memoir' – Charles Shaar Murray

Paperback   ISBN 1-900924-41-2   234mm X 156mm   352pp, 24pp b/w photos
UK £14.99 $19.95

On The Road With Bob Dylan
By Larry Sloman

In 1975, as Bob Dylan emerged from 8 years of seclusion, he dreamed of putting together a travelling music show that would trek across the country like a psychedelic carnival. The dream became a reality, and *On The Road With Bob Dylan* is the ultimate behind-the-scenes look at what happened. When Dylan and the Rolling Thunder Revue took to the streets of America, Larry 'Ratso' Sloman was with them every step of the way.

'The War and Peace of Rock and Roll.' – Bob Dylan

Paperback   ISBN 1-900924-51-X   234mm X 156mm   448pp
UK £14.99 $19.95

Gram Parsons: God's Own Singer
By Jason Walker £12.99

Brand new biography of the man who pushed The Byrds into country-rock territory on *Sweethearts of The Rodeo*, and quit to form the Flying Burrito Brothers. Gram lived hard, drank hard, took every drug going and somehow invented country rock, paving the way for Crosby, Stills & Nash, The Eagles and Neil Young. Parsons' second solo LP, *Grievous Angel*, is a haunting masterpiece of country soul. By the time it was released, he had been dead for 4 months. He was 26 years old.

'Walker has done an admirable job in taking us as close to the heart and soul of Gram Parsons as any author could.' **** *Uncut* book of the month

Paperback   ISBN 1-900924-27-7   234mm X 156mm   256pp, 8pp b/w photos
UK £12.99 $18.95

Ashley Hutchings: The Guvnor and the Rise of Folk Rock – Fairport Convention, Steeleye Span and the Albion Band
By Geoff Wall and Brian Hinton £14.99

As founder of Fairport Convention and Steeleye Span, Ashley Hutchings is the pivotal figure in the history of folk rock. This book draws on hundreds of hours of interviews with Hutchings and other folk-rock artists and paints a vivid picture of the scene that also produced Sandy Denny, Richard Thompson, Nick Drake, John Martyn and Al Stewart.

Paperback   ISBN 1-900924-32-3   234mm X 156mm   288pp, photos throughout
UK £14.99 $19.95

The Beach Boys' *Pet Sounds*: The Greatest Album of the Twentieth Century
By Kingsley Abbott £11.95

Pet Sounds is the 1966 album that saw The Beach Boys graduate from lightweight pop like 'Surfin' USA', *et al*, into a vehicle for the mature compositional genius of Brian Wilson. The album was hugely influential, not least on The Beatles. This is the full story of the album's background, its composition and recording, its contemporary reception and its enduring legacy.

Paperback   ISBN 1-900924-30-7   234mm X 156mm   192pp
UK £11.95 $18.95

King Crimson: In The Court of King Crimson
By Sid Smith £14.99

King Crimson's 1969 masterpiece *In The Court Of The Crimson King*, was a huge US chart hit. The band followed it with 40 further albums of consistently challenging, distinctive and innovative music. Drawing on hours of new interviews, and encouraged by Crimson supremo Robert Fripp, the author traces the band's turbulent history year by year, track by track.

Paperback   ISBN 1 900924-26-9   234mm X 156mm   288pp, photos throughout
UK £14.99 $19.95

A Journey Through America with the Rolling Stones
By Robert Greenfield
Featuring a new foreword by Ian Rankin

This is the definitive account of The Stones' legendary '72 tour.

'Filled with finely-rendered detail … a fascinating tale of times we shall never see again' *Mojo*

'The Stones on tour in '72 twist and burn through their own myth: from debauched outsiders to the first hints of the corporate business – the lip-smacking chaos between the Stones' fan being stabbed by a Hell's Angel at Altamont and the fan owning a Stones' credit card.' – Paul Morley #2 essential holiday rock reading list, *The Observer*, July 04.

Paperback   ISBN 1-900924-24-2   198mm X 129mm   256pp
UK £9.99 $19.95

The Sharper Word: A Mod Reader
Edited by Paolo Hewitt

Hewitt's hugely readable collection documents the clothes, the music, the clubs, the drugs and the faces behind one of the most misunderstood and enduring cultural movements and includes hard to find pieces by Tom Wolfe, bestselling novelist Tony Parsons, poet laureate Andrew Motion, disgraced Tory grandee Jonathan Aitken, Nik Cohn, Colin MacInnes, Mary Quant, and Irish Jack.

'An unparalleled view of the world-conquering British youth cult.' *The Guardian*

'An excellent account of the sharpest-dressed subculture.' *Loaded*, Book of the Month
Paperback   ISBN 1-900924-34-X   198mm X 129mm   192pp
UK £9.99 $19.95

BACKLIST
The Nice: Hang On To A Dream By Martyn Hanson
1900924439   256pp   £13.99
Al Stewart: Adventures of a Folk Troubadour By Neville Judd
1900924366   320pp   £25.00
Marc Bolan and T Rex: A Chronology By Cliff McLenahan
1900924420   256pp   £13.99
Razor Edge: Bob Dylan and The Never-ending Tour By Andrew Muir
1900924137   256pp   £12.99
Calling Out Around the World: A Motown Reader Edited by Kingsley Abbott
1900924145   256pp   £13.99
I've Been Everywhere: A Johnny Cash Chronicle By Peter Lewry
1900924226   256pp   £14.99
Sandy Denny: No More Sad Refrains By Clinton Heylin
1900924358   288pp   £13.99
Animal Tracks: The Story of The Animals By Sean Egan
1900924188   256pp   £12.99
Like a Bullet of Light: The Films of Bob Dylan By CP Lee
1900924064   224pp   £12.99
Rock's Wild Things: The Troggs Files By Alan Clayson and J Ryan
1900924196   224pp   £12.99
Dylan's Daemon Lover By Clinton Heylin
1900924153   192pp   £12.00
XTC: Song Stories By XTC and Neville Farmer
190092403X   352pp   £12.99
Born in the USA: Bruce Springsteen By Jim Cullen
1900924056   320pp   £9.99
Bob Dylan By Anthony Scaduto
1900924234   320pp   £10.99

Firefly Publishing: An Association between Helter Skelter and SAF

The Nirvana Recording Sessions
By Rob Jovanovic £20.00
Drawing on years of research, and interviews with many who worked with the band, the author has documented details of every Nirvana recording, from early rehearsals, to the *In Utero* sessions. A fascinating account of the creative process of one of the great bands.

The Music of George Harrison: While My Guitar Gently Weeps
By Simon Leng £20.00
Often in Lennon and McCartney's shadow, Harrison's music can stand on its own merits. Santana biographer Leng takes a studied, track by track, look at both Harrison's contribution to The Beatles, and the solo work that started with the release in 1970 of his epic masterpiece All Things Must Pass. 'Here Comes The Sun', 'Something' – which Sinatra covered and saw as the perfect love song – 'All Things Must Pass' and 'While My Guitar Gently Weeps' are just a few of Harrison's classic songs.
　Originally planned as a celebration of Harrison's music, this is now sadly a commemoration.

The Pretty Things: Growing Old Disgracefully
By Alan Lakey £20
First biography of one of rock's most influential and enduring combos. Trashed hotel rooms, infighting, rip-offs, sex, drugs and some of the most remarkable rock 'n' roll, including landmark albums like the first rock opera, *SF Sorrow*, and Rolling Stone's album of the year, 1970's *Parachute*.
　'They invented everything, and were credited with nothing.' Arthur Brown, 'God of Hellfire'

The Sensational Alex Harvey
By John Neil Murno £20
Part rock band, part vaudeville, 100% commitment, the SAHB were one of the greatest live bands of the era. But behind his showman exterior, Harvey was increasingly beset by alcoholism and tragedy. He succumbed to a heart attack on the way home from a gig in 1982, but he is fondly remembered as a unique entertainer by friends, musicians and legions of fans.

U2: The Complete Encyclopedia By Mark Chatterton £14.99

Poison Heart: Surviving The Ramones By Dee Dee Ramone and
Veronica Kofman £9.99

Minstrels In The Gallery: A History Of Jethro Tull By David Rees
£12.99

DANCEMUSICSEXROMANCE: Prince – The First Decade By Per Nilsen
£12.99

To Hell and Back with Catatonia By Brian Wright £12.99

Soul Sacrifice: The Santana Story By Simon Leng £12.99

Opening The Musical Box: A Genesis Chronicle By Alan Hewitt £12.99

Blowin' Free: Thirty Years Of Wishbone Ash By Gary Carter and Mark
Chatterton £12.99

www.helterskelterbooks.com

All Helter Skelter, Firefly and SAF titles are available by mail order from www.helterskelterbooks.com
Or from our office:
Helter Skelter Publishing Limited
Southbank House
Black Prince Road
London SE1 7SJ
Telephone: +44 (0) 20 7463 2204 or Fax: +44 (0)20 7463 2295
Mail order office hours: Mon-Fri 10:00am – 1:30pm,
By post, enclose a cheque [must be drawn on a British bank], International Money Order, or credit card number and expiry date.
Postage prices per book worldwide are as follows:

UK & Channel Islands	£1.50
Europe & Eire (air)	£2.95
USA, Canada (air)	£7.50
Australasia, Far East (air)	£9.00

Email: info@helterskelterbooks.com